Makeup in the World of Beauty Vlogging

Makeup in the World of Beauty Vlogging

Community, Commerce, and Culture

Edited by Clare Douglass Little

LEXINGTON BOOKS
Lanham • Boulder • New York • London

Published by Lexington Books
An imprint of The Rowman & Littlefield Publishing Group, Inc.
4501 Forbes Boulevard, Suite 200, Lanham, Maryland 20706
www.rowman.com

6 Tinworth Street, London SE11 5AL, United Kingdom

British Library Cataloguing in Publication Information Available

Library of Congress Cataloging-in-Publication Data

Library of Congress Control Number: 2020942616
ISBN 978-1-4985-9245-1 (cloth : alk. paper)
ISBN 978-1-4985-9246-8 (electronic)

Contents

Acknowledgments vii

Introduction 1

Part I: Vlogging Celebrities and the Cult of Personality

1 When Makeup Gets Ugly: The Complicated Commerce of Marketing Image, Authenticity, and Social Awareness in the Online Makeup Tutorial 17
Clare Douglass Little

2 The Popularity of Fenty Beauty and How It Reflects the Online Beauty Community 37
April Wilson

3 Microcelebrity, Class, and Participatory Entitlement: The Cases of Jaclyn Hill and Jeffree Star 65
Anna Barritt

4 Subscribe to My Empire: Jeffree Star and Self-Branding on YouTube 85
Alexandra Hauke and Florian Zitzelsberger

Part II: Makeup (Vlogging) as Empowerment

5 The Ladies' Dressing Rooms: Cosmetic "Trickery" from Tertullian's Eve to Kandee Johnson's Barbie 103
Elizabeth Johnston Ambrose

6 The Pigments of Patriarchy and Femme Trans Exclusion in the History of the "All Natural" Makeup Movement 127
Laken Brooks

7 "What's the Point in Covering Them Up?": Visible Disability and the Invitation to Stare in YouTube Makeup Tutorials 143
Katherine Anderson Howell

Part III: Makeup and the Individual: Navigating Culture with Makeup

8 Not Just for the Boys: Some Aspects of the Grotesque in Men Selling and Wearing Makeup 161
Michael V. Perez

9 Hijabi Makeup?: The Muslim Female Face and the Practice of Exposure 185
Fatma Sagir

Conclusion 209

Index 213

About the Contributors 221

Acknowledgments

First, I want to thank my husband, Ryan, for his support and encouragement. He not only cheered me on in the writing and editing process and put up with my hours of watching makeup tutorials on YouTube (not always entirely for research purposes), he allowed me the free time to focus on writing and revising when I needed it. He makes me laugh, he makes me think, and I love him, today and always. I could not have completed the project without the endless joy and enthusiasm of my children, Lilly and Callum, who, perhaps without realizing it, helped me along the way as well, as did the unconditional love and support of my parents, Ann and Bill. I love you all! I certainly could not have completed the project without the feedback and editorial support of my friend and mentor Lynnette Porter, the best (not to mention most prolific) academic writer I know and a true friend who has helped me in countless ways over the years. Finally, this book would not be possible without the remarkable work of its tireless contributors or the thoughtful guidance of the Lexington editorial staff, specifically Nick Johns and Lindsey Falk, who initially saw the project's potential, and Judith Lakamper and Shelby Russell, who really guided this project to its completion, helping and guiding me (and answering countless emails) every step of the way. It has been an honor to work with such an incredible team. Love and thanks to you all!

Introduction

Beginning in the second half of the twentieth century, makeup and manipulation of or emphasis on outer appearance was viewed by many as promoting artifice, objectification, and a devaluing of the self. However, even more recently, largely with the rise of the makeup tutorial, there has been an effort to realize makeup as a means of personal empowerment, a way to re-create one's identity on a daily basis. Furthermore, through the popular medium of the online makeup tutorial, subscribers and followers of YouTube celebrities, with their tutorials, makeup-challenge tags, and advice, have shown that makeup can bring the individual into a larger virtual community. This project acknowledges the makeover makeup has received through the tutorial platform and explores the dramatic power of beauty vloggers and the use of the makeup tutorial genre specifically as a space where individual entrepreneurship and virtual communities come together. In a society defined by digital experiences, the makeup tutorial makes social influence, economic success, and even fame accessible to anyone with a computer and a cell phone or digital camera and reflects what Graeme Turner defines as the "demotic turn," "referring to the increasing visibility of the 'ordinary person' as they have turned themselves into media content through celebrity culture, reality TV, DIY web-sites, talk radio and the like,"[1] "the like" here applying to YouTube and the makeup tutorial more specifically. At the same time, it promotes what constitutes intimacy in our modern society via cross channel communication with other YouTubers and interactive on-screen dialogue with channel subscribers, who can gain further "intimacy" with these make-up gurus through additional outlets like Snapchat, Twitter, and Instagram. Following a range of YouTube celebrities, many of whom have taken their internet popularity into the realm of commerce by partnering with established makeup brands, and examining the social and economic impact of makeup and beauty vloggers, this project demonstrates the true "power of makeup" in crafting the complex culture surrounding the online makeup tutorial.

I can't even tell you exactly how I discovered the world of online makeup tutorials, and I'm sure my moment of "discovery" marked a rather late arrival to the already popular YouTube phenomenon. My experience, I imagine, was much like that of the millions of other subscribers who seek out makeup-application tips only to find themselves immediately swept into the personality-driven, visually stimulating world of these makeup mavens, who, crossing and blending gender and cultural divides, draw audiences in through their amazing artistry and seemingly accessible, certainly inspiring, transformations. Alison Hearn speaks to the particular appeal of the "transformation, or makeover" as a "narrative palliative for the psychological and physical precariousness of life in the West under the post-Fordist mode of production—a life made even more complex and volatile by increasing technologization, mediatization and globalization."[2] While Hearn's approach focuses on the medium of television, the appeal of such transformations certainly can be found in the medium of the internet and the makeup tutorial specifically, and the appeal of the genre only intensifies when experienced in the space of YouTube and other social media, where viewers communicate with beauty gurus with whom they feel a sense of personal connection. The support, even legitimizing power, of countless followers, allows these makeup influencers to make a case for self-empowerment and the fluidity of identity and gender, built on the premise that makeup actually has great power.

My initiation into the world of makeup tutorials began with the YouTube channel NikkieTutorials, run by Nikkie de Jager, a makeup enthusiast from the Netherlands who began demonstrating makeup techniques online in 2008 at the age of fourteen. This internet sensation now has over thirteen million subscribers to her YouTube channel (as of 2020), and her meteoric rise highlights the vast potential of this platform to bring great social and financial power to those who find an audience and navigate the medium and genre successfully. Nikkie struck a particularly powerful chord for her many viewers in her "Power of Makeup" tutorial (2015), in which she demonstrates the physical power of makeup to transform her appearance as she pushes back against the idea that makeup demeans women and represents merely an overvaluing of the superficial and a sign of feminine insecurity.[3] Counter to this idea, she presents makeup as an ideal outlet for self-expression and condemns makeup "haters." Her video served as a rallying call for all makeup lovers searching for validation of their supposedly "superficial" interests. Her own dramatic style, heavily influenced by drag aesthetics, further acts as a bold defense of this argument. In "Unpacking the Beauty Vlogger Phenomenon," Vera Hanson suggests that "the way [vloggers] continue to contribute to an industry pioneered by women plays a large role in explaining why beauty vlogging, at its core, can actually be quite feminist."[4] Along these same lines, Samara Anarbaeva points to the power of digital spaces to provide a voice and platform to women as well, focusing more specifically on the fact that "[w]omen of color are putting themselves on the map of cyberspace by demanding their right to be beautiful in their own way and not the way the media tells them."[5] The reality of this idea as it pertains to YouTube and the makeup tutorial is something explored in this project as well.

Nikkie returned to her point and defense of makeup explicitly in a 2017 video as a reaction to what she identifies as "makeup shaming" of a woman on Snapchat.[6] This episode of hurtful trolling, or cyber-bullying, in which a viewer commented that things had "gone too far" with over-the-top, exaggerated makeup, prompted Nikkie to defend the young woman and present her argument again. Her defense of this woman, and so all individuals, to wear makeup (or not wear makeup, as the case may be), serves the larger case for individuals' freedom to shape their own identities and the power of beauty vlogging to demonstrate this. Of course, Nikkie's investment in promoting dramatic makeup styles and her benefiting financially from these messages does, perhaps, complicate the moral stand she takes, yet another layer of this complex topic that will be explored further.

Even more recently, Nikkie demonstrated yet again how makeup and the makeup tutorial can function as mediums for self-expression, community building, and social commentary, this time in an explicitly personal way for Nikkie herself. In her January 13, 2020, video, titled "I'm Coming Out," Nikkie reveals, "When I was younger, I was born in the wrong body, which means that I am transgender."[7] She goes on to describe having fully "transitioned" by the age of nineteen, stating, "I transitioned while on YouTube." Despite likely coming as a surprise to many, her revelation received an overwhelmingly positive response, as reflected in the supportive comments of her viewers, and even led to an interview on Ellen DeGeneres's daytime talk show. What started as a personal outlet for a young girl became a powerful social platform for a strong, entrepreneurial woman and artist, one that, in the words of Nikkie herself, demonstrates "Not the power of makeup, but the power of me, the power of you."[8]

The makeup tutorial is not a new genre, but the modern tutorial is different, with the message of tutorials today emphasizing the power of makeup to promote creativity, self-expression, and identity shaping, as powerfully evident in Nikkie's revelation. While Hanson does highlight the potential for makeup influencers to promote feminist messages, she fails to acknowledge another characteristic of the modern makeup tutorial: the power of beauty vlogs to promote gender freedom more broadly. Nikkie, for example, is only one among many makeup influencers in a virtual world where men can have as big an impact as women and gender becomes all the more evident as a construct, a fact that points to the remarkable power of the platform to promote artistry and creativity while encouraging and supporting identify and gender fluidity. Manny MUA, for example, sporting his signature facial stubble, offers makeup demonstrations and product reviews, typically beginning his videos with the refrain, “As always, if you guys don’t like this video, if you guys don’t like me, please don’t fucking watch. You know the drill with that.”[9] Intriguingly, Manny preemptively shuts down critics, revealing a measure of vulnerability, perhaps belying past experiences, even as he boldly asserts the right of men to not only teach makeup but to wear it. Flexibility in identity and gender are further reinforced through shared vlogger communities, as channel crossovers frequently occur as well. For example, both Nikkie and Manny have made videos with the acerbic, in-your-face Jeffree Star (an influencer, with whom Manny has since had a dramatic falling out, discussed in multiple chapters here and whose videos are as rife with profanity and biting reviews as they are with insightful tips). On the other end of the spectrum is the more strait-laced, traditional KathleenLights, whose quirky humor and accessible demeanor and style allow her to use her channel not only to instruct but to share her personal struggles with anxiety and her parents’ divorce. In their own, very different, ways, these, and countless other YouTube personalities, appeal to viewers, often the same viewers, drawn to the artistry, the freedom, and the promise of what could be as well as the supposed accessibility and intimacy the internet fosters. Other channel hosts, like Nyma Tang, Jackie Aina, Alissa Ashley, and even Stephanie Nicole, among others, all of whom appear in this work, demonstrate the power of the makeup tutorial as a platform for increasing social, cultural, and racial awareness. In this way, we see not only the power of the tutorial to encourage and promote personal creativity and freedom but to offer a community, both for channel creators and for channel viewer-participants, who connect with the beauty vlogger and fellow viewers via the many comments and dialogues available on each page.

These moments of inspiration and community building, however, frequently occur in conjunction with product recommendations, giving popular YouTubers not only great social power but immense financial power, and this ability to influence often leads to the development of collaborations with established makeup brands or even the launch of an independent line, made possible by the already established cohort of viewer-buyers. Nikkie’s inspiring “Power of Makeup” video, for example, with its catchy and provocative tagline, perfect for marketing products, resulted in a collaboration between Nikkie and the established makeup brand Too Faced. All the excitement surrounding that initial video combined with the hype leading up to the product-line launch, a release of the promoted eye shadow palette bundled with a few other products, was doomed to be underwhelming, but the larger concern, perhaps, should be in regard to using a message of individuality and empowerment to make money.[10] It is an intriguing and complex dynamic: on the one hand, the idea of combining an important social message with selling product seems troubling, but, on the other hand, there is an appeal to supporting the message by acquiring a piece of it, to bring it home and physically introduce it into one's life. Furthermore, the product represents a way to more immediately access not only the message but the YouTube celebrities themselves, and, along with the help of additional platforms like Snapchat and Instagram, to create an even greater sense of intimacy and relationship between the makeup influencer and the captivated follower. In a society in which marking a feeling, an experience, or an event by the purchasing of a souvenir, a society in which whole communities are being built as spaces where living, shopping, and dining are integral to the community design, this blending of inspiring creativity and marketing product should really be no surprise. In fact, this situation, of a YouTuber amassing a sufficient number of fans for a makeup brand to take notice and offer collaboration, has become quite common, as countless beauty vloggers team up with established, if not always massive, makeup lines: for example, Manny MUA with Makeup Geek; KathleenLights with ColourPop; Jaclyn Hill, another YouTube sensation, with BECCA Cosmetics and Morphe; Kandee Johnson, with Sinful Colors Professional nail polishes; and KatheenLights, Manny MUA, and even Nikkie (of NikkieTutorials) with OFRA Cosmetics, just to name a few. At times, they even come together for these collaborations, as when KathleenLights, Manny MUA, and another YouTuber challenging gender expectations, PatrickStarrr, joined forces with Benefit Cosmetics to promote their Cheekathon Palette, a product and experience featured on Patrick's YouTube channel as his "Dreams Come True Vlog"[11] in 2016.

Of course, if makeup influencers reach a sufficient level of success, they may even launch an independent line. Jeffree Star, for instance, has his own line, known for its velour liquid lip color, highlighters, and bold eye shadow palettes. His line, in fact, became so comfortably established that he reached out to other makeup influencers such as Manny MUA, whose friendship and later feud with Star have been documented on YouTube, for collaborations, further cementing the idea that various levels of community building and marketing are at work. KathleenLights, too, launched her own line of nail polishes, KL Polish, which ultimately did not survive but led Kathleen to create a new line called Lights Lacquer. Manny MUA and Jaclyn Hill have also launched their own makeup lines, though not without controversy, particularly in the case of Jaclyn Hill and concerns about quality control in recent product launches.[12] Part of what draws viewers into watching these channels and following their hosts in the first place are the product reviews and application lessons, which always feature a list of the products mentioned or used below the video and, not infrequently, a discount code for viewers that provides a "kick-back" to the makeup influencer, so it should come as no surprise that these celebrities take things to the next level and benefit more formally from their knowledge and popularity. The particular medium of YouTube, with its built-in communities and channel subscribers, allows for such collaborations and product promotions to be incredibly successful and lucrative. Claire Hopwood, in "How YouTube Celebrities Are Transforming the Beauty Industry, and What Companies Can Learn from It," points specifically to the idea that "[c]onsumers seek a two-way dialogue"[13] and the potential for this via YouTube, where viewers not only post comments and make requests but makeup influencers actually respond and engage with their audiences. This dynamic may allow beauty vloggers to introduce marketing into their videos more readily without necessarily offending subscribers, as viewers feel they actually participate and influence the vlogger and product development in some way.

Clearly, a successful YouTube channel can be very lucrative, something explained by other channels and online resources that walk through the speculated monthly income (often tens of thousands of dollars) of these individuals, and, as long as these makeup influencers do not overstep the bounds of this complex promotion/inspiration dynamic, then viewers embrace the opportunity to take a piece of their favorite YouTube sensation and promised creative potential home, for a reasonable price.

If, however, one of these makeup celebrities oversteps accepted boundaries, viewers race to offer corrective, no-holds-barred criticism. YouTuber credibility and integrity represent key areas for followers. These makeup influencers have a sense of this, as they identify videos sponsored by particular brands up front and show great sensitivity and deference in peddling their discount codes for products, all to avoid alienating those audiences upon whom they depend. When viewers even get a whiff of insincerity or question a channel host's motives, they quickly call that host out, as evident in a demonstration of Jeffree Star's Androgyny eye shadow palette by Manny MUA.[14] As a protégé of Jeffree at one time, Manny's credibility in this circumstance was far from certain, as reflected in viewers' comments, posted and available below the video. Viewer Nataly Mendez commented, "Nothing against Manny because his make up is on point all the time but this eyeshadow was just blah! So patchy & not blended whatsoever . . . but it's obvious he is not gonna give bad reviews because he is friends with Jeffrey star [*sic*]."[15] Even more aggressively, another viewer, coconutanddvanilla, posted, "[D]ammmn those shadows look so shit and chalky. Clearly your head is sooooo far up Jeffrees ass to not notice how bad those shadows looked."[16] Of course, other fans immediately weighed in, rushing to Manny's defense, some even referring to his opening disclaimer to not watch the video if potential viewers don't like the host. In this way, the platform, as well as viewers' investment in the material, the medium, and the makeup influencers themselves, affords followers the opportunity to play prosecution and defense and so keep these public figures in line, accountable for their words and actions at the risk of losing the community that may provide some personal validation but certainly provides financial support.

Beyond the regular back and forth of followers, constantly evaluating each YouTuber's tutorials and product reviews, channels devoted entirely to policing and reporting on the content and behavior of these makeup influencers have appeared, some channels rivaling the YouTubers they police in number of followers. John Kuckian, the Brit who, at one time told viewers to get a cup of tea in preparation for the gossip and drama to unfold, and Sanders Kennedy, among many others, represent a significant contingent of YouTubers who devote their videos to tracking and weighing in on the latest scandals and developments of the more established makeup influencers. On occasion, these moderators themselves have felt the sting of a celebrity hitting back, as was the case when Jeffree Star lashed back at John Kuckian and his supposed conspiracy theories (as excerpted and discussed at one point on Kuckian's own channel).[17] While drama mongering certainly benefits these channel police, and, in that bad publicity is still publicity, probably benefits the makeup influencers as well, the idea that there is a sort of moral code which channel hosts must follow provocatively highlights the appealing role of viewers, who do, in fact, hold the power to make or break these beauty vloggers.

Of course, this begs the question, "who are these viewers that have the power to make or break a beauty vlogger, and what sort of digital communities are they forming?" Part of the appeal of both makeup videos and viewer communities is the ever-increasing diversity that can be found and experienced via these platforms, so to pigeonhole or stereotype viewers as one particular thing would not only be unfair it would be inaccurate. At a minimum, though, they share a fascination with the general content and standard fare of beauty-vlogging videos. The website *Statista*, which tracks statistics and trends in user-generated and social media content, shows a dramatic increase in the popularity of "beauty-related content on YouTube," with "beauty-related content generat[ing] more than 169 billion views on the video platform" in 2018.[18] Results of another 2018 *Statista* survey indicate that 57 percent of participants watch YouTube on a daily basis, while 23 percent view YouTube content two to three times per week.[19] Clearly, YouTube remains a regular feature of our digital lives, and the appeal of beauty vlogs and content only seems to be increasing, but other media platforms and social media sites, as well as the tastes and trends of viewers and consumers, will continue to shape beauty vlogging and the beauty industry as a whole, even as focus continues to expand beyond YouTube. In fact, signs of content and viewer interest evolving could account for an increase in more "lifestyle" type videos, in which channel hosts invite viewers into other aspects of their lives—what they eat, where they shop, their fitness routines, what an average day for them is like, and recommendations of products ranging from home goods and clothing to books. Of course, part of this evolution could reflect the desire of fans and viewers to feel even more connected to their favorite channel hosts, something that can also be experienced by following influencers on all of their various social platforms, from Instagram to Snapchat and beyond.

While one might assume the followers of most makeup tutorials are teens and young adults, these lifestyle videos, often representing aspects of adult, independent living, even parenting, suggest that the audience may be more broad than that. In fact, demographic statistics from the digital marketing agency Omnicore indicate that those in the age groups of thirty-five and older and fifty-five and older represent "the fastest growing YouTube demographics."[20] Further expanding that audience is the presence and popularity of beauty channels hosted by women, and men, in their forties (Risa Does Makeup), fifties (HotandFlashy), and sixties (Melissa55). While some of the content likely would be more relevant for viewers of a similar age, to suggest that age or gender is entirely indicative of who watches the channel, that viewers are only interested in hosts that look and act like them, would be overly reductive and inaccurate.

What draws an individual to YouTube, whether as a viewer, content creator, or both, represents an intriguingly complex topic—one that often involves seeking a voice and community through whatever those intangible connections might be. Judging from my own experience, I sought out beauty vloggers for instruction and then found myself drawn to their video personas and seeming accessibility. Lehua Ledbetter describes her journey to and on YouTube in her article "The Rhetorical Work of YouTube's Beauty Community: Relationship- and Identity-Building in User-Created Procedural Discourse."[21] Ledbetter identifies herself as being "of mixed (half second-generation Japanese American, half white) heritage and, as one of very few persons of mixed race at [her] institution, [she] often felt isolated."[22] She goes on to explain that she "sought instructional content and the sense of belonging that [she] often could not find in [her] physical environment."[23] From being a viewer of instructional content, Ledbetter went on to become a beauty-content creator, and, intriguingly, her description of what she gained from posting content mirrors my own (and presumably others) sense of what is gained through watching videos and connecting with vloggers and other viewers—"the purpose of the videos . . . was often twofold: content could be instructional in nature and also serve as a means for communication between community members and expression of identity."[24] The appeal on both sides, as creator or consumer, appears to be teaching/learning and connecting, with that connection and community building, perhaps, being paramount.

Surely, there are trends and variations among viewing audiences and video creators that deserve greater study, but the focus of this work will be less concerned with statistics than with the social and cultural significance of makeup, makeup tutorials, and the power of beauty vloggers and the communities with which they connect. These and many other topics are explored in the following chapters, as contributors analyze the complex world of YouTube makeup tutorials.

The nine chapters in this book, divided into three sections, encourage a better understanding of the makeup tutorial as a medium and cross section of social commentary, economic innovation, and virtual community building. In addition to providing a broad overview of the tutorial's social and commercial power, the chapters in this collection, each focusing on very particular aspects of the tutorial and its audiences, look beyond the surface of this trend to break down the impact of the medium on and for specific individuals and the group(s) with which they identify. Connecting these in-depth, micro studies within the larger macro narrative of the text as a whole distinguishes this work, which, in its entirety, covers a range of intersecting topics, from the dynamics of virtual communities to issues relating to identity, gender, and multi-cultural norms and expectations.

The book's sections reflect the chapters' subjects and methodologies. The first part, "Vlogging Celebrities and the Cult of Personality," includes four chapters that consider how beauty vloggers gain and exert social influence through marketing and community building. In chapter 1, "When Makeup Gets Ugly: The Complicated Commerce of Marketing Image, Authenticity, and Social Awareness in the Online Makeup Tutorial," the complex dynamic between beauty guru and follower is further explored by considering how these gurus rely on an image of authenticity to gain and maintain audiences (and so the financial success they bring). The chapter looks at how the commercial aspect of makeup tutorials and even individual actions outside the digital space of YouTube and its edited videos can undercut the channel host's perceived authenticity. Furthermore, the chapter looks at how another version of authenticity can be experienced when influencers use their tutorial platforms to heighten cultural awareness and so put social causes above personal financial gain.

Chapter 2, "The Popularity of Fenty Beauty and How It Reflects the Online Beauty Community," considers the narrow, homogenous audiences historically targeted by the beauty industry to situate Rihanna's makeup brand, Fenty Beauty, as a company revolutionary for its inclusivity as reflected in its extensive range of foundation shades. Furthermore, the chapter considers how Rihanna herself functions as an essential component of the brand and its social media presence.

Chapter 3, "Microcelebrity, Class, and Participatory Entitlement: The Cases of Jaclyn Hill and Jeffree Star," focuses on two beauty influencers in particular and applies the original concept of "participatory entitlement" to explain how and why audiences respond differently to influencers' often meteoric rise in economic status. This first chapter, and the one following, examine the dynamic between makeup tutorial audiences and creators and how beauty gurus carefully craft and maintain their online personas.

By returning to the popular but controversial figure of Jeffree Star, chapter 4, "Subscribe to My Empire: Jeffree Star and Self-Branding on YouTube," further complicates and examines the careful crafting and marketing of the YouTuber's image. Looking more specifically at how Star has developed his own successful business, the chapter emphasizes that much of this success lies in his creation of himself, his product, and his channel as a brand in which viewer-consumers can participate and to which they can belong.

Three chapters make up the second part, "Makeup (Vlogging) as Empowerment," which explores how makeup and vlogging can allow content creators to challenge and reframe expectations regarding gender, identity, and (dis)ability. Chapter 5, "The Ladies' Dressing Rooms: Cosmetic 'Trickery' from Tertullian's Eve to Kandee Johnson's Barbie," begins this second section and features yet another YouTube success story, Kandee Johnson, who first gained a large audience on YouTube in the platform's earlier years. By highlighting the reality that channels often implicitly value artifice while explicitly calling for viewers to be themselves, the chapter resists some views of the makeup tutorial as a wholly liberating genre. Spanning centuries, from Swift and his satires exposing the feminine deceits to the present makeup tutorial, this chapter demonstrates the true complexity of the makeup tutorial and why it should be approached with a critical eye.

The following chapter considers how gender boundaries and identity can be challenged and redefined through makeup. In chapter 6, "The Pigments of Patriarchy and Femme Trans Exclusion in the History of the 'All Natural' Makeup Movement," makeup is shown to be a way for men and transgender people in particular to shape identity and even create an external image that more accurately reflects their internal reality. In this way, makeup, and the makeup tutorial as a legitimizing and empowering platform, can be understood as more natural than the artificial idea promoted by the "all natural" movement often used to condemn both men and women who appear made-up.

Chapter 7, "'What's the Point in Covering Them Up?' Visible Disability and the Invitation to Stare in YouTube Makeup Tutorials," acknowledges that visible disability can resist the conventions and expectations associated with the makeup tutorial format. However, the chapter highlights that, in mediating and controlling the viewer's stare, these channel hosts experience personal empowerment while demonstrating another way to understand the value and function of makeup tutorials.

The final section, "Makeup and the Individual: Navigating Culture with Makeup," contains two chapters particularly distinctive for their methodology. Both chapters combine academic research with autoethnography to compellingly demonstrate makeup (and the online makeup tutorial) as a tool for identity creation and exploration, particularly powerful (and empowering) when confronted with the constraints of gender, culture, and religion. Chapter 8, "Not Just for the Boys: Some Aspects of the Grotesque in Men Selling and Wearing Makeup," begins the final section of the book with its autobiographical elements and introduces Flannery O'Connor's "Southern Grotesque" as a critical lens for understanding how the drag aesthetic and men in makeup tutorials can both appeal and repulse. The chapter recognizes a continuum of artistry and identity construction from the early days of drag to the popularization of drag on reality TV and in the accessible platform of the makeup tutorial, specifically, where the "extreme" has been, to an extent, normalized through imitation by both men and women in makeup.

Finally, chapter 9, "Hijabi Makeup? The Muslim Female Face and the Practice of Exposure," demonstrates the impact of the makeup tutorial on a global, cross-cultural scale. The chapter discusses personal experiences with culture and makeup as well as popular, Muslim beauty vloggers who show how the tutorial format not only allows for Muslim women to communicate with other Muslim women but how it can challenge limiting perceptions of what a Muslim woman can and should be. In this way, the chapter highlights how these influencers, at the forefront of the Modest Fashion movement, use elements of makeup and fashion to cross and redefine cultural barriers.

As in any situation in which ideology and the arts blend with concerns of business and commerce, viewers can find a complex, often mixed, message of inspiration, a model of self-expression, and a realization or model of economic success, one that may feel particularly accessible to viewers in this case. For me, a lover of makeup and, admittedly, at times an easy target for related marketing strategies, I see in this intriguing combination of inspirational community building and consumer-centered, product-peddling my conflicted self and our modern society as a whole. YouTube, vlogging, and the modern makeup tutorial demonstrate that our culture is one in which ideals, identity, community, and commerce are inextricably linked, that our power, at least in part, lies in our comments, our votes, our clicks, our purchases. In watching the makeup tutorial, we not only learn about applying highlighter, shaping eyebrows, and creating the perfect eyeliner wing; we also see the potential to remake, to "make up" ourselves, the potential to connect, and the power we share as both consumers AND creators. Perhaps, then, one of the most provocative things we see when we look at the faces of these tutorials is the mirror showing us ourselves and the reality of our power and responsibility in shaping our lives and culture.

NOTES

1. Graeme Turner, *Ordinary People and the Media: The Demotic Turn* (London: Sage Publications, 2009), 2.

2. Alison Hearn, "Insecure: Narratives and Economies of the Branded Self in Transformation Television," *Continuum* 22, no. 4 (2008): 495, DOI:10.1080/10304310802189972.

3. NikkieTutorials, "The Power of Makeup!," YouTube Video, 6:50, May 10, 2015, https://www.youtube.com/watch?v=a4Ov8qvZ2_w.

4. Vera Hanson, "Unpacking the Beauty Vlogger Phenomenon," *girls like giants*, December 3, 2014, https://girlslikegiants.wordpress.com/2014/12/03/unpacking-the-beauty-vlogger-phenomenon/.

5. Samara Anarbaeva, *YouTubing Difference: Performing Identity in Online Do-It-Yourself Communities*, Doctoral dissertation, (Graduate College of Bowling Green State University: Bowling Green, OH, 2011), 35, http://scholarworks.bgsu.edu/media_comm_diss/5.

6. NikkieTutorials, "Ending Makeup Shaming! -Go-To Ultra Glam Makeup Tutorial," YouTube Video, 10:18, March 5, 2017, https://www.youtube.com/watch?v=WU67VUUG3vM.

7. NikkieTutorials, "I'm Coming Out," YouTube Video, 17:13, January 13, 2020, https://www.youtube.com/watch?v=QOOw2E_qAsE.

8. Ibid.

9. Manny MUA, "Beauty Killer Eyeshadow Pallette Makeup Tutorial! | MannyMua," YouTube Video, 18:18, May 23, 2016, https://www.youtube.com/watch?v=Qdn3pMABJeI.

10. This particular commercial collaboration, however, proved most controversial for what is largely viewed as an abuse of a rising vlogger by an established makeup brand, as Too Faced paid Nikkie a lower flat fee rather than a more lucrative, and, to many, fair, percentage of the profits. The website *Insider* and numerous other sites and vloggers have discussed what they view as the injustice of this makeup deal. Kat Tenbarge, "Makeup YouTuber Nikkie Tutorials Explained Why She Took a Deal for Only $50k for Her Too Faced Collaboration after Jeffree Star Said She Took 'dirt,'" *Insider*, October 6, 2019, https://www.insider.com/nikkie-tutorials-50k-too-faced-contract-palette-dawson-jeffree-star-2019-10.

11. PatrickStarrr, "Drams Come True Vlog | PatrickStarr," YouTube Video, 10:28, May 4, 2016, https://www.youtube.com/watch?v=_WvINzTXpFE.

12. Numerous sources can be found discussing Hill's failed lipstick-line launch, dubbed "Lipstick Gate." Hannah Preston, "Jaclyn Cosmetics Scandal: Biochemist Refutes Claims of Lipstick Contamination, but Viewers Remain Skeptical," *Newsweek*, July 13, 2019, https://www.newsweek.com/jaclyn-cosmetics-biochemist-video-contamination-test-1447438.

13. Claire Hopwood, "How YouTube Celebrities Are Transforming the Beauty Industry, and What Companies Can Learn from It," *Visioncritical*, January 4, 2019, https://www.visioncritical.com/blog/beauty-influencers.

14. Manny MUA, "New Jeffree Star Androgyny Pallette Makeup Tutorial | Manny MUA," YouTube Video, 8:41, February 18, 2017, https://www.youtube.com/watch?v=wqUXE2jvPpI.

15. Ibid.

16. Ibid.

17. kucki tea, "Jeffree Star Disses John Kuckian Hard!!!," YouTube Video, 11:35, December 3, 2016, https://www.youtube.com/watch?v=K0pG_5UaqWo&t=52s.

18. J. Clement, "Annual Beauty-Related Content Views on YouTube from 2009 to 2018," *Statista*, December 4, 2019, https://www.statista.com/statistics/294655/youtube-monthly-beauty-content-views/.

19. Alexander Kunst, "How Often Do You Use YouTube?," *Statista*, January 6, 2020, https://www.statista.com/forecasts/1011631/frequency-of-using-youtube-in-the-us.

20. Salman Aslam, "YouTube by the Numbers: Stats, Demographics, and Fun Facts," *Omnicore*, Last updated February 10, 2020, https://www.omnicoreagency.com/youtube-statistics/.

21. Lehua Ledbetter, "The Rhetorical Work of YouTube's Beauty Community: Relationship- and Identity-Building in User-Created Procedural Discourse," *Technical Communication Quarterly*, 27:4, (2018): 287–299, DOI:10.1080/10572252.2018.1518950.

22. Ibid., 288.

23. Ibid.
24. Ibid.

BIBLIOGRAPHY

Anarbaeva, Samara. *YouTubing Difference: Performing Identity in Online Do-It-Yourself Communities*. Doctoral dissertation. Graduate College of Bowling Green State University, Bowling Green, OH, 2011. http://scholarworks.bgsu.edu/media_comm_diss/5.

Aslam, Salman. "YouTube by the Numbers: Stats, Demographics, and Fun Facts." *Omnicore*. Last updated February 10, 2020. https://www.omnicoreagency.com/youtube-statistics/.

Clement, J. "Annual Beauty-Related Content Views on YouTube from 2009 to 2018." *Statista*, Dec. 4, 2019. https://www.statista.com/statistics/294655/youtube-monthly-beauty-content-views/.

Hanson, Vera. "Unpacking the Beauty Vlogger Phenomenon." *girls like giants*, Dec. 3, 2014. https://girlslikegiants.wordpress.com/2014/12/03/unpacking-the-beauty-vlogger-phenomenon/.

Hearn, Alison. "Insecure: Narratives and Economies of the Branded Self in Transformation Television." *Continuum* 22, no. 4 (2008). 495–504, DOI:10.1080/10304310802189972.

Hopwood, Claire. "How YouTube Celebrities Are Transforming the Beauty Industry, and What Companies Can Learn from It." *Visioncritical*, January 4, 2019. https://www.visioncritical.com/blog/beauty-influencers.

kucki tea. "Jeffree Star Disses John Kuckian Hard!!!" YouTube Video, 11:35, Dec. 3, 2016. https://www.youtube.com/watch?v=K0pG_5UaqWo&t=52s.

Kunst, Alexander. "How Often Do You Use YouTube?" *Statista*, January 6, 2020. https://www.statista.com/forecasts/1011631/frequency-of-using-youtube-in-the-us.

Ledbetter, Lehua. "The Rhetorical Work of YouTube's Beauty Community: Relationship- and Identity-Building in User-Created Procedural Discourse." *Technical Communication Quarterly* 27:4 (2018): 287–299. DOI:10.1080/10572252.2018.1518950.

Manny MUA. "Beauty Killer Eyeshadow Pallette Makeup Tutorial! | MannyMua." YouTube Video, 18:18, May 23, 2016. https://www.youtube.com/watch?v=Qdn3pMABJeI.

———. "New Jeffree Star Androgyny Pallette Makeup Tutorial | Manny MUA." YouTube Video, 8:41, February 18, 2017. https://www.youtube.com/watch?v=wqUXE2jvPpI.

NikkieTutorials. "Ending Makeup Shaming! -Go-To Ultra Glam Makeup Tutorial." YouTube Video, 10:18, March 5, 2017. https://www.youtube.com/watch?v=WU67VUUG3vM.

———. "I'm Coming Out." YouTube Video, 17:13, January 13, 2020. https://www.youtube.com/watch?v=QOOw2E_qAsE.

———. "The Power of Makeup!" YouTube Video, 6:50, May 10, 2015. https://www.youtube.com/watch?v=a4Ov8qvZ2_w.

PatrickStarrr. "Dreams Come True Vlog | PatrickStarrr." YouTube Video, 10:28, May 4, 2016, https://www.youtube.com/watch?v=_WvINzTXpFE.

Preston, Hannah. "Jaclyn Cosmetics Scandal: Biochemist Refutes Claims of Lipstick Contamination, but Viewers Remain Skeptical." *Newsweek*. July 13, 2019, https://www.newsweek.com/jaclyn-cosmetics-biochemist-video-contamination-test-1447438.

Tenbarge, Kat. "Makeup YouTuber Nikkie Tutorials Explained Why She Took a Deal for Only $50k for Her Too Faced Collaboration after Jeffree Star Said She Took 'dirt.'" *Insider*, October 6, 2019. https://www.insider.com/nikkie-tutorials-50k-too-faced-contract-palette-dawson-jeffree-star-2019-10.

Turner, Graeme. *Ordinary People and the Media: The Demotic Turn*. London: Sage Publications, 2009.

Part I

Vlogging Celebrities and the Cult of Personality

Chapter One

When Makeup Gets Ugly

The Complicated Commerce of Marketing Image, Authenticity, and Social Awareness in the Online Makeup Tutorial

Clare Douglass Little

The last few years have seen an explosion in the popularity of makeup tutorials and beauty influencer[1] channels on YouTube, and with this popularity has come a remarkable opportunity for individual success and economic advancement. Within a matter of months, YouTubers can make ever-increasing sums of money based on the number of subscribers they have and the advertising, sponsorships, and brand collaborations that result from those growing audiences. In fact, this easy-to-track data reflected in the number of subscribers listed on each YouTuber's channel becomes so important, not only in legitimizing the channel host's content and virtual identity but in offering businesses a barometer of how profitable a partnership with that guru might be, that reaching certain benchmark numbers of subscribers, say one thousand or 500,000 or even one million, becomes a celebration shared with followers and formally recognized on the hosts' channels. Of course, in the virtual world of makeup tutorials, makeup influencers often compete for the same audiences, audiences essential for their professional and financial success not only on YouTube but in platforms like Snapchat, Instagram, and Twitter. Through the popular medium of the online makeup tutorial, subscribers and followers of YouTube celebrities, with their tutorials, makeup-challenge tags, and advice, have shown that makeup has immense power in bringing the individual into a larger virtual community, one that has the potential to be quite lucrative even as it positions the YouTuber as an agent of heightened cultural criticism and awareness.

Although leaders in such makeup communities often promote one another and participate in cross channel dialogues and challenge tags, they also engage in critiques of other YouTubers with whom they may not have formed such personal or professional associations. However, amassing and maintaining a high number of followers is a complicated process, one that relies on beauty gurus' fostering an image of honesty and transparency, even as they rely on companies paying them to review particular products, for, as Alex Abad-Santos points out in an article for *Vox*, "Beauty gurus themselves have become products" whose "authority is born out of a perception of authenticity."[2] Whether it is an accusation of dishonest product reviews because of suspected brand kickbacks or outright nastiness when attacking a fellow makeup influencer, cross-channel spats have become a common occurrence and even potentially part of the appeal for the more drama-hungry fans. Entire channels featuring the latest YouTube makeup-influencer fights and celebrity dramas have appeared, boasting their own ever-growing audiences.

However, not all commentaries center on such personal critiques and attacks. In fact, some channel hosts attempt to distinguish themselves from this sort of infighting, either by not engaging with such matters and avoiding negative commentary altogether or by attempting to use their influence to promote what they view as positive social (occasionally political) agendas through videos and reviews that might feature underrepresented, small, minority-owned makeup brands, for example. Comparing and contrasting various popular makeup influencers by analyzing a representative cross section of YouTube celebrities demonstrates how the tutorial landscape can be as socially progressive and unifying as it is divisive and malicious. Engaging with the social complexities of the makeup tutorial in this way allows for a richer understanding of it as a social phenomenon functioning as both a mirror and product of society. Ultimately, both drama mongering and fostering an image of honesty and authenticity and even social awareness can earn a YouTube celebrity devoted fans and the financial support they bring. Each approach, though, also raises questions about what it means to carefully craft and market one's image and identity in a world that both relies on and combats artifice. This chapter follows several YouTube influencers and explores the use of the makeup tutorial genre specifically as a space where individual entrepreneurship and virtual communities come together.

The success and popularity of YouTube makeup tutorials relies largely on a sense of trust and authenticity created by the channel host and subscribed to by the viewer. Beauty gurus often walk that line of being knowledgeable yet accessible, appealing but not "too perfect"; their entrepreneurship inspires viewers, even as the success of the channel relies on the hosts' not seeming too concerned with the money they make because of brand sponsorships and those same viewers' support. The very format of YouTube, with its space for supposedly candid conversations between viewers and hosts in the comment section and videos in which their creators very openly refer to the filming/editing process and even the type and quality of their equipment, promotes this notion of intimacy and sincerity. Andrew Tolson highlights that "the authenticity of vlogging, if it is to be perceived as such, is located in its excessive direct address, in its transparent amateurishness and in the sheer volume and immediacy of 'conversational' responses."[3] If that trust and sense of authenticity are to be maintained, however, viewers cannot feel that the channel hosts puts their own financial interests or those of beauty companies ahead of their obligation to the subscribers who support them in YouTube and other social media platforms. The reality that established beauty influencers receive free products from makeup companies expecting their items to be reviewed on these hosts' channels makes walking that line of trust all the more challenging for the beauty influencer. Viewers embrace these influencers, at least in part, for their sense of accessibility and honesty, but this image of candor can be rather precarious, for, as Tolson goes on to point out, "because it is contingent and relative, this authenticity effect always seems vulnerable to critique."[4]

Two examples of intense beauty-community drama from 2018 highlight the complex dynamic that occurs when community and commerce occupy the same virtual space. The first incident began when Marlena Stell, a YouTube veteran and head of her own independent makeup company, Makeup Geek, posted a video on YouTube titled "My Truth Regarding the Beauty Community."[5] In this video, Stell candidly speaks to the viewer about the reality, her "truth," concerning the money beauty influencers make for reviewing products on their channels. She mentions the shocking rate of $60,000 as a price some influencers charge companies for such reviews and cites this exorbitant amount as one reason audiences might not have seen Makeup Geek featured on many channels in the past year: in other words, Stell, as head of a relatively small company, cannot afford to buy that kind of public relations boon. Naturally, this revelation, one viewers already knew or suspected to be the reality of the beauty business, reinforced concerns about influencers' honesty and transparency. While some viewers dismissed the video as a desperate effort to blame waning brand popularity on materialism in the beauty community, others viewed the video as exposing a disturbing reality, even if the specific rate provided was exaggerated. In response to Stell's post, beauty influencers flocked to their channels to post videos challenging Stell's claims by pointing out that not all influencers make that kind of money from sponsorships and by breaking down the business of YouTube and the beauty community. Some channel hosts very candidly presented their own "truths," sharing that creating and editing content for their viewers is their job, how they support themselves, and that a massive company paying an influencer a small percentage of what a large-scale commercial campaign would cost is not unreasonable. A common belief shared by Stell and these other beauty gurus, one that allows them to distance themselves from those "other" deceitful, money-grubbing members of the beauty community, is that when an influencer is paid to review a product, that sponsorship should be revealed at the start of the video in which the brand's products are being discussed.[6] The fact that this simple admission could protect an influencer's legitimacy and so retain audiences highlights the fragile nature of that community-commerce dynamic.

In the world of the YouTube makeup tutorial, in which beauty gurus, to a large extent, create and sell a version of themselves—one that, again, must be characterized by a sense of authenticity—they must carefully craft and protect their own sort of brand, an idea that could best be understood in light of Alice Hearn's explanation of "branding":

> Branding is a distinct form of marketing practice intended to link products and services with resonant cultural meanings through the use of narratives and images. . . . While the material form of the brand as an image, logo, or trademark was initially intended to guarantee quality, it has now become the sign of a definite type of social identity, which then summons consumers into relationship with it.[7]

If the YouTuber's brand functions as a "social identity" with which viewer-consumers connect, anything that threatens that influencer's brand can result in a loss of audiences and jeopardize financial success.

Before the emotional blowback from both viewers and other influencers responding to Stell's video had even had a chance to recede, another beauty-guru scandal rapidly began to unfold. In this case, the "truths" revealed emphasized the fragility of a beauty influencer's image and authenticity when that influencer's very character and social media history come into question. It began when an influencer posted a picture of himself with three friends, who happen to also be YouTube personalities, and, as a caption to this picture, which depicted the group making a rude hand gesture, the individual posted a statement mocking another popular and successful influencer and claiming that the members of the group were finding success without him. Now, that influencer being derided happened to be Jeffree Star, a very successful and wealthy influencer/business-owner with his own line of make-up. While Star was not identified in the post, followers familiar with the players involved and the troubled history among them quickly came to a conclusion about the intended target of the attack. Fans came to Star's defense and proceeded to launch their own attacks on those influencers involved in the post. Although Star is far from a controversial figure in the beauty community, having been in trouble for using racist language in the past, on-screen apologies to viewers and a YouTube series with Shane Dawson highlighting his vulnerability and even revealing his history of self-harming seemed to have won him back audience favor.[8] In an effort to avoid alienating fans now supportive of Star, these other influencers quickly went into damage-control mode, planning their own apologies for their fans. All of this later came out when the individual who originally posted the photo caption, Gabriel Zamora, "Gabby," revealed these behind-the-scenes plans in a video titled "My Truth" as a response to his feeling manipulated by others in the group. In an attempt to defend Star and lash back at the influencer group, fans combed through the social media histories of group members and shared racist posts some of them had made in the past. The affected individuals quickly found themselves scrambling to navigate their own public-relations nightmares. Apologies took on an even more serious tone, or attempted to, as influencers found themselves struggling to account for offensive behaviors. In a business in which retaining subscribers and a large fan base is essential for success, influencers do whatever it takes to keep viewers tuned in and following their posts. These individuals had a lot riding on their apologies, and, for two of them, it did not go well.

The two influencers involved in the scandal with the biggest names and followings were Manny MUA (aka Manny Gutierrez) and Laura Lee, both of whom have subscribers numbering in the millions and numerous collaborations with established makeup brands. Laura Lee's video apologizing for a racist comment posted around the time of the Trayvon Martin case was particularly controversial and received major criticism from viewers skeptical of her sincerity in what seemed an over-the-top performance.[9] Viewers derided her for her lack of sincerity and weighed in on the fate of her YouTube career moving forward, and, although she has since taken down her apology video, numerous other YouTubers posted videos recording their incredulous, often laughter-filled responses to her video or even made their own versions mocking her emotional post.

After Lee's apology video aired but before Manny took his turn to apologize, Zamora posted a much longer apology, walking fans through every step of the scandal in a seemingly candid and straightforward way. In his "My Truth"[10] video, Zamora apologizes for both the picture and caption he posted as well as some racist language he had used in his social media past. Unlike Lee's tearful (but tearless?) post, Zamora speaks to the camera in a calm, thoughtful way and even shares links to other works about the negative impact of racist language. As he proceeds with his approximately forty-eight-minute monologue, he takes responsibility for his past actions and his most recent offense and then lays out the various factors contributing to the incident and the attempted "clean-up" after the fact. He even accuses Manny of being the mastermind, and a fairly heartless one at that, behind their public-relations plan and describes Manny as "toxic" and the common denominator in a series of failed beauty-industry relationships. In contrast to the negative feedback Lee's apology garnered from supposed fans, viewers held up Zamora's apology as a model of transparency and authenticity, posting comments such as, "This felt like I was sitting with a friend, it felt honest and real. THIS is an apology video" (Sarah Jay); "Lol 48 minutes of a genuine apology from Gabriel vs 4 min apology with fake tears from Laura lee" (Jackie_MS); "I'm blown away. You owned it. You truly apologized. And I believe you" (dss1337); "And that's how it's done ladies and gents" (hailey passini); and "now this is a REAL apology" (anna g smith).[11] One commenter even posted the following breakdown of the four YouTubers involved with the original picture scandal after viewing some of their posted apologies: "gabriel? forgiven. laura? a snake. manny? two faced. nikita? who knows where she is. jeffree star?? APPrOvEd" (lucy).[12] Furthermore, Zamora actually increased the number of his subscribers substantially through the seeming authenticity of his video: "First video I have ever watched of yours. You just gained a subscriber. This is so humble and heartfelt and sincere. As humans we mess up and sometimes we need to make mistakes to, be able to grow. Thank you for owning up to yours, it shows so much about your character in such a positive way" (Destiny Quinn) and "This turned me into a subscriber. Before all this I had no clue who you were. I'm glad you are such a real raw person. Someone who can actually learn and take responsibility for their mistakes. Something you don't see all that often in the beauty community. I'm happy to become a new follower and fan of you. Stay true boo boo" (Kaurrie Golightly).[13] Zamora actually even converted some viewers who didn't care for him prior to this apology: "To be honest, I wasn't a huge fan of the 'Gabriel' I used to see, who came across as snobbish and petty and rude. Before this video, I saw your apology tweet, and brushed it off as an insincere bid to get people back on your side. But this Gabriel? The one I see here? I am LIVING for it. I am so impressed by your genuine desire to apologize without excuses, and to share your narrative, and to own up to your mistakes" (Coreen Wiggins).[14] Clearly, when it came to the test of honest apologies, Zamora passed, and Lee failed.

Naturally, these accusations and responses added even more pressure to Manny's video apology, which appeared a day after Zamora's and allowed Manny to respond to some of Zamora's accusations. While Manny did smartly choose not to go on the offensive in his video, titled "My Reality Check,"[15] and instead acknowledges that Zamora made some valid points and that he, Manny, has some personal issues to work on improving in his life, his subscriber numbers took a major hit at the time, and many viewers did not respond positively to his video, posting replies such as, "I use to love your videos I have followed for the longest time . . . good bye many" (Jackie Barajas), "Its funny he had to wait till after he watched Gabriel's video to apologize. He's just saying words" (christina jones), "Uhhhh this was painful to watch because the 'emotion' was so forced. Not genuine at all" (misc.saraii), and "All I'm hearing is 'please forgive me so I don't lose my career'" (Stephanie Rodriguez).[16] Some fans, so angry and seemingly feeling empowered and entitled to pass judgment, posted comments praising his reduction in subscribers. While both Manny and Lee took breaks from posting videos until after the backlash settled a bit, it was not long before Lee returned to posting new content and Manny began to receive more positive comments, asking him to come back to YouTube. This scandal and its resulting aftermath, however, emphasize the power of the viewer and the importance of authenticity, particularly when it comes to apologizing.

All of this, naturally, raises questions about the scale or barometer used to evaluate apologies, particularly in the world of social media and the YouTube platform. As one commenter indicates, there exists a whole genre of apology videos: "This is one of the most real apologies I've ever sat through. It's amazing that you explained this. Thank you" (10,000 Subscribers without Any Videos).[17] Having "sat through" numerous apologies seems to position and legitimize the viewer as a sort of judge or authority on the issue, particularly as there can be apology markers that viewers find appealing or alienating simply based on a history of basic human interactions. The public apology certainly is nothing new; celebrities, from actors to athletes, have been making them to salvage careers and a fanbase for decades, and apologies in politics have become the norm. Judging the sincerity of such apologies, then, has become the right, the job, of the public, often moderated or even directed by the media. One of the most famous public apologies came in 1998, when Bill Clinton offered his first admission of guilt and apology for his affair with Monica Lewinsky. However, as Jacoba Urist points out in her article "The Art and Science of Apologizing" written for *The Atlantic*, "many who study the psychology of apologies view the address as a four-minute primer on how not to apologize for something."[18] Urist cites research conducted by Aaron Lazare and others revealing that timing plays a major role in how an apology is viewed, an idea that viewer posts following these beauty-influencer apologies certainly supports. A study led by Roy Lewicki, Robert Lount, and Beth Polin identifies six common elements of an effective apology: "an expression of regret for the offense, an explanation of why the violation occurred, an acknowledgment of responsibility for the offense, a declaration of repentance, an offer of trust repair, and a request for forgiveness."[19] So how do we use these evaluative tools to assess these beauty gurus' videos, and exactly why did Manny and Lee's apologies fail so dramatically while Zamora's worked? A first "read" compels viewers to consider how gender may be a factor and to ask how the image of a woman apologizing sits with viewers differently than when it is a male apologizing. The stereotypical picture of a woman crying to the point of incoherency certainly can strike an alienating chord for both male and female viewers, and this gendered reading deserves more scrutiny, but other key components of their apologies complicate the effort to apply a potentially limiting, binary reading. Support for this comes in the fact that Manny's apology, much like Lee's, was summarily dismissed by viewers for its lack of sincerity, suggesting that Zamora's video stands out in significant ways. Zamora certainly remains calmer in his delivery than Lee, but then Manny remains calm as well. However, Zamora does admit to shooting his video multiple times until he felt able to record a version that was more levelheaded. This process suggests a degree of thoughtfulness and self-reflection lacking in the videos of the other two. What could seem crafted and inauthentic because of that editing actually ends up being effective given his confession and openness about that creative process. Ultimately, it seems to be this very thoughtfulness and transparency that speaks to his viewers so compellingly, for Zamora hits on all of Lewicki, Lount, and Polin's essential components, from expressing regret, offering a detailed explanation, and taking responsibility to repenting, taking steps to correct the situation, and asking for forgiveness. While Zamora could have craftily consulted such a list as a sort of manual on the art of apologizing, the video does not read this way, and its overwhelmingly positive response suggests that the research is right: people do naturally look for and connect with key elements in apologies.

The particular scandal that unfolded among these beauty influencers may not represent anything new in the way of drama and public apologies, but it does highlight some distinctive characteristics of this relatively new platform for the makeup tutorial as well as the "beauty community" as it is understood today. As Morgan Sung points out in her *Mashable* article "The Art of the YouTube Apology Video," "When an actor messes up, they typically have a team of managers, agents, and crisis managers to back them up with handcrafted personal statements apologizing for their actions. When a beauty guru messes up, they set up their tripods, get the tears going, and hit record."[20] While some of the more successful influencers do have managers, for the most part these individuals, eager to take advantage of a medium that can allow anyone to skyrocket to fame and fortune, rely on their own self-marketing and -presentation. In fact, it is this sense of spontaneity and accessibility that often contributes to the influencers' image of authenticity. The world of YouTube and modern social media in general has at least a limited democratizing effect in this way through the "demotic turn," which Graeme Turner defines as "referring to the increasing visibility of the 'ordinary person' as they have turned themselves into media content,"[21] giving anyone with access to a computer and a camera the opportunity for great economic success. However, it can mean that individual becomes all the more vulnerable as well. Furthermore, while celebrities and politicians certainly can suffer in future ticket sales and voting polls if they do not regain fans and supporters through effective apologies, in the world of the online beauty community, influencers feel the dramatic impact of viewer opinion and judgment with much more immediacy. As in the case of Laura Lee, who lost more than

200,000 subscribers after launching her apology video,[22] sponsors and beauty-industry companies can pull influencer products and collaborations, only to reinstate their financial backing when and if the influencer has passed through the scandal and regained the faith and support of a large enough fan base.

The viewer holds power not only in clicking or unclicking the "subscribe" button but also in the replies and comments posted below the influencer's initial video post, as the comments included here reveal. Fans in this way can exercise their power even more tangibly and participate in their own crucial part of the beauty community, in this case as judge and jury. In a September 2018 video by influencer Jackie Aina, in which she candidly describes the old beauty community, the "old YouTube" as "never coming back," as "deceased," as "dead," Aina points out that "YouTube is curated at the hands of people who watch."[23] One commenter responding to Manny's apology video even admitted to this power, stating, "the only reason why these influencers are successful is because of the subscribers. we choose who to support and i think we're fed up of lies that there's no room for second chances" (dirtypeach16).[24] In these ways, the viewer, the consumer, the fan, has tremendous power to promote or destroy the success of an influencer, and the fickleness of the fanbase, who can, as Aina also points out, turn on the influencers as they become "too" successful, is something these beauty gurus have to appease if they want that accessible, yet at times elusive, social and economic success. In ways, the world of the makeup tutorial and its beauty community resembles aspects of these other industries, from show business to politics, but it is also its own, new thing, a social media space in which authenticity and accessibility become marketable commodities measured by the content and style of their creators and the interest and engagement of their powerful fans and subscribers.

Following this and even more recent YouTube beauty dramas and viewer chastisements, English makeup artist and entrepreneur Wayne Goss took time on his YouTube channel to express his distaste for frequent online attacks cast by followers, critics, and fellow YouTubers, describing them as "public floggings."[25] These online acts of virtual violence can become quite aggressive and quickly reflect a sort of mob mentality. Such fan-critics often go after a public figure whom they believe has violated a sort of understood code, compromising integrity by promoting or pedaling a subpar product or, as evident in the case of Manny, Lee, and Zamora, disrespecting a particular group of followers, for example, which could suggest a positive function of this sort of policing by YouTube fans and channel subscribers. Beauty gurus and influencers must navigate a fine line between entertaining and informing viewers in order to build and maintain followers in what Rachel Berryman and Misha Kavka describe as "business through intimacy,"[26] something Florencia García-Rapp explores in her study of YouTube celebrity Bubzbeauty:

> Being authentic is essential to reach sustained viewer attention and engagement. For the analyzed community an authentic guru is someone "real." This implies following certain norms of behavior, but the notion that underlies them all is being genuine, true to yourself (spontaneous) and not in search of fame or money (premeditated).[27]

García-Rapp goes on to point out that "[a]lthough being authentic is often seen in opposition to self-branding and commercialization, it is relevant to note that self-promoting and online fame—together with the social and economic perks this entails—can also be seen as deserved and subsequently legitimized in the community."[28] This bestows significant power on the followers of these beauty gurus, as followers can launch a successful career, but, in that power they hold, they can also ensure the failure of an individual channel or even a product line created or promoted by the channel host. The successful beauty influencer, then, has to be trustworthy and knowledgeable in regard to makeup application and product lines as well as entertaining and engaging. At times, however, taking risks because of greater financial freedom or even out of a sense of social responsibility can appeal to viewers as another aspect of authenticity and audience engagement.

Some YouTube celebrities have become experts at maintaining their dual role as educator and entertainer, while others have based much of their online identities and credibility on distancing themselves from the drama that can arise when YouTubers, or their fans, go after other channel hosts or cultivate outrageous, sometimes venomous, online personas. The equivalent of tutorial "no spin zones" (unlike those previously discussed), these more moderate channels often get and hold onto followers because their hosts claim to only ever tell the truth and avoid all the nastiness, unlike some other hosts with whom they contrast themselves. Often, these YouTubers go so far as to project themselves not only as truth-sayers but claim to use their channels as platforms for social mindfulness. Stephanie Nicole, for example, is a beauty influencer known for her no-nonsense style and the intensive research she puts into prepping for many of her informative, often rather lengthy, videos. In June 2017, she participated in the YouTube BOMB makeup challenge initiated by two other YouTube channel hosts, Alyssa Forever and Alissa Ashley, "to help shed light on some maybe lesser known, minority-owned brands."[29] In this case, the acronym BOMB stands for Black-Owned Makeup Brands, and, at the start of her monologue, Nicole informs her viewers that the advertisement proceeds made from this particular video would all be donated to a local charity in California, where she lives, called United Roots, an organization whose mission is, as paraphrased by Nicole, "to engage and empower marginalized youth." The video proceeds to feature brands such as A.J. Crimson, Juvia's Place, Beauty Bakerie, Plain Jane, Blac Chyna, Coloured Raine, and Pat McGrath. In this way, Nicole participates in and advances a tutorial challenge geared at increasing viewer-consumer awareness and directing purchasing power to support potentially lesser known brands and minority entrepreneurs.

The second half of her approximately forty-five-minute review and makeup demonstration, however, features her discussing a recent controversy between Jackie Aina and Jeffree Star. In her monologue, what she refers to as "my blabberings" in the time-stamp section below her video, Nicole criticizes Jeffree Star for his racist language[30] and defends Jackie Aina's protest of Jeffree Star and his makeup line. While in this case Nicole does involve herself in what even she calls "drama," she does so with her typical straightforward, call-it-like-she-sees-it attitude, thereby maintaining her authority and trustworthiness as a "speaker of truth," only peripherally involved in the situation but compelled to comment because she refuses to support Jeffree Star's actions and instead chooses to step forward and "call him out." She even goes so far as to at least implicitly make the case that the makeup tutorial and social awareness/engagement are not, and should not be, mutually exclusive:

> If you're a commenter that says, "Stick to makeup" or something like that, perhaps you're as deep as a puddle and you can only talk about beauty products or your little pinhead would pop off, but that is not me. I'm always going to speak about things that are important to me. If you don't like that, you certainly don't have to watch me and you certainly don't have to be subscribed. The beauty of doing this as my hobby is I don't have to pander to anybody. It's quite liberating.[31]

This last part of her comment highlights the freedom she feels due to her not having to support herself financially through the success and kickbacks of affiliate links and subscribers in YouTube. At the time of this video, at least, she had another job and so refers to YouTube as merely her "hobby."[32] The implication of this is that she can speak the truth, or at least her truth, but those who have made YouTube their business may not feel as free to do so. In other words, those channel hosts for whom makeup tutorials represent their main source of income may try to avoid controversies that could alienate or offend their target audience, and their reviews of products could be less than honest out of fear of losing brand support, something consistently viewed as a sort of betrayal or violation of trust by viewer-subscribers, as revealed in the behind-the-scenes payments Stell later attempted to expose. This dynamic between intimacy and economics in the virtual communities surrounding makeup tutorials is something reflected here, and Nicole's and others' videos show the makeup tutorial as a space not just for product reviews and methods for makeup application; it is also a space where the sphere of an individual's influence can actually extend beyond beauty, reaching out to a built-in audience of followers to increase awareness and inspire change, sometimes with a little drama along the way.

A powerful example of this occurred in January 2018, with the much-anticipated launch of a new foundation line. Tarte's Shape Tape concealer was a long-time favorite among YouTube beauty influencers, so there was a lot of hype leading up to the company's release of its Shape Tape foundation. Less than a year prior to this launch, Fenty Beauty, Rihanna's makeup line, released its own foundation in what the Fenty website initially described as a "boundary-breaking range of 40 shades."[33] In dramatic contrast, the promising, highly anticipated launch of Tarte's Shape Tape foundation, with its limited shade range and resulting, non-inclusive image, met with immediate criticism from popular YouTubers, as evident in Alissa Ashley's review video, addressed to both viewers and the brand itself, in which she compellingly highlights the inequity of Tarte's limited shade range:

> I'm extremely disappointed in Tarte because you guys should know better as a brand and you should know that it is 2018, and it's time to be more inclusive. It is not that hard to get into the lab and at least try to make shades for deeper complexions . . . at this point it's a slap in the face because you releasing shades let's go ahead and check out the shade names, shall we? Fair sand, fair neutral, fair light neutral, light neutral, light sand, light medium neutral, light medium honey, medium honey, medium sand, medium neutral, medium tan honey, tan honey, deep honey, rich sand, and mahogany. There's literally three shades that could possibly work for people with a darker complexion, and every other single shade is a light shade, and even people who are light have spoken out about the fact that enough is enough and you guys need to be more inclusive.[34]

In a video recorded a day before Ashley's review but published on the same date, Jackie Aina (joined by Ashley) expresses similar disappointment and her larger concerns:

> This brand just embodies the exact opposite of everything that I stand for. Sorry, but they don't do anything that makes people feel included. I look on their Instagram and I don't see anyone who looks like me, remotely close to anyone who looks like me, rarely. This foundation launch just reinforced that for me. Like, there's no effort. If you can only do fifteen shades, I can give credit where due. I realize it's a big big job launching complexion products. I know it's expensive even for, you know, um, the brands like Tarte, and it's not cheap. It's it's, you know, there's a lot that goes into it, but they didn't even try.[35]

Jackie Aina's fans were quick to respond and show support of her critique. One commenter, Abigail Rose, further highlights that the root of the problem is, and should be, concerning to everyone:

> i was really looking forward to this launch bc I really enjoy the concealer . . . but really? such a disappointment. I don't have to be a POC [person of color] to see that this is absolutely ridiculous. does tarte really not have any black women on their team? or are they just being ignored? If Kylie jenner-the-culturalappropriator-and-business-snatcher can and is willing to make a half suitable shade range, a company as large and successful as tarte should hop aboard and appreciate the WOC [women of color],. smh [shaking my head].[36]

This non-inclusive product launch, emblematic of an inequity marking many makeup brands, and the eye-opening reviews, posted most powerfully by those directly impacted by the limited range and its implications, actually became a sort of rallying call, uniting viewers and consumers regardless of color to seek change and equity in something that may not have felt so close to home in the past. In this way, the makeup tutorial actually serves to represent or call for a higher authenticity in its creators and consumers, even opening hosts and viewers up to views and perspectives critical in understanding a greater cultural truth.

Ashley Klaty, in a tearful, follow-up video to a previous review of this foundation, states that she "messed up" and shares her regret in posting something that could have been viewed as supporting a non-inclusive line and brand. She goes on to say that she was not as informed as she should have been and that she will be "tak[ing] a break from Tarte"[37] until it improves the range of its color options, something brand representatives indicated would happen in the near future.[38] Viewers and fans showed support in their comments responding to her emotional video, one particular post from Bri Gilmore, a woman of color, stating, "OMG (crying smiley face) it's okay! (heart emoji) Don't cry, don't be sad! From what I hear the formula is amazing, you had it in your shade, it's not your fault! It's TARTE!"[39] Other beauty influencers offered similar explanations as to why they would not be reviewing or were, essentially, ashamed for having posted a review of the product. Nikkie de Jager of NikkieTutorials, a very established YouTube celebrity who has enjoyed multiple collaborations with well-known makeup brands, took down her review of the product, granted after severe criticism from her followers, and posted the following comment to Twitter: "I am putting my Tarte Shape Tape video offline. Thank you for showing me the importance of showcasing my voice. The Tarte shade range is an absolute mess and I should've spoken up about it more than I did."[40]

While this heightened engagement with and awareness of an inequality that permeates even the beauty industry seems like an entirely positive development, beauty influencer followers and even other channel hosts rightly complicated the situation further, compelling viewers and participants to examine even their own reactions to the situation. For example, under Jackie Aina's video review of the new Tarte foundation, two viewers posted comments further demonstrating the complexity of the situation and the power of perspective:[41]

> ChellyBooTV: I like how all the white influencers are jumping on the bandwagon as if they haven't been reviewing products that aren't inclusive . . . yall don't care stop being fake made.
>
> Zovesta Storm: I'm so sad because holy cow was I blind :(I saw all the variations in shades and was so happy I could get my own exact shade . . . and didn't even notice how there weren't many dark shades! So ashamed. Incredible how self absorbed we can be—we don't notice these things until they're pointed out![42]

Here we see questions of investment and legitimacy compelling viewers to acknowledge that this is not a new problem. Furthermore, the posts here expose what might be viewed as a sort of cultural appropriation of an issue to situate hosts (and even subscriber-commenters) as perhaps flawed but ultimately enlightened, thereby making them both accessible as "real" humans and deserving of continued support and trust for having "seen the light" regarding their limited perspectives and experiences. To ignore this harsh reality would cast a blind eye toward a crucial element of this complex social dynamic, but to deny the more hopeful potential of the situation would prevent embracing this opportunity and the makeup tutorial itself as a platform for increased mindfulness moving forward. On her own channel, in her earlier BOMB video, Stephanie Nicole combines her dual goal of supporting minority-owned makeup brands and criticizing another beauty guru for his racist actions with weighing in on this issue of authority when it comes to race and minority rights more broadly:

> People can talk about LGBT rights; they can talk about people of color's rights; we can talk about any issue without being one ourselves. I think the main important thing in that is that you're not talking over that community. Like, it's not my place to be morally outraged for someone else, but I can say when I see a disgusting act; I can say I don't agree with that and I don't support it.[43]

In addition to making a case for the value of hearing all voices speaking out against injustice, she goes on in the video to further complicate the issue by highlighting what she sees as the frequently economic, rather than overtly racist or moralistic, motives behind brand decisions regarding makeup shade ranges. The dialogue playing out, then, among commenters, between channel hosts, and within the interactive community as a whole, encapsulates the complexities of race in society and compels perhaps the typically passive viewer-consumer to either feel their perspective is being voiced and finding an audience or to become more invested in the problem even if they have not been touched by it personally before, now that they see a "friend," the beauty influencer with whom they feel they have formed a connection, dramatically impacted. Furthermore, by participating in this shared virtual community to which they belong (and which they likely seek to protect), they realize, perhaps most dramatically, their own power to direct change as consumers, who cast a vote with every click of a button or swipe of a credit card.

Even more recently, in January of 2020, further evidence of makeup tutorials offering social commentary and community while, at the same time, inviting potential viewer critique and judgment occurred when Nikkie de Jager posted her video "I'm Coming Out."[44] The makeup-vlogging, creative and commercial powerhouse that is NikkieTutorials has, as of February 2020, over thirteen million subscribers and has been a presence on YouTube since she was fourteen years old. As the video dramatically reveals, she is transgender and actually "transitioned on YouTube," without viewers ever realizing this truth, yet viewers generally responded not with a sense of betrayal but with support and encouragement: "what i'm hearing is that a trans woman dominated the makeup industry without anyones knowledge . . . i stan"[45] (lucas).[46] Nikkie admits to creating the video, at least at this point in time, to get in front of a blackmail threat, but this motivation and the years of not being open about her history, in this case, do not appear to violate her image of authenticity for viewers, as the comments to her video reveal: "Well, holy moly! I've been watching a looong time and I'd have never guessed it! Doesn't make any difference, I love you anyway" (Kathy Weaver); "Who the eff cares what's under her clothes (or what used to be under her clothes). It's not what her channel is about. She just empowered herself more by sharing more of herself, making her more of an icon than she already was" (Eileen Kenney); and "You've always been Nikki to me . . . man woman trans whatever it just a label what makes you you is your heart your personality and the way you love. Thats it. See you in your next video" (Jessica Ritchie).[47]

Rather than the dramatic revelation or its timing alienating viewers, comments further indicate that her situation, vulnerability, and empowering response further endeared her to audiences and even won her new audiences. Many viewers highlighted her being blackmailed as part of what intensified their sympathy and support: "I'm sad that you couldn't really do this the way you wanted to or even that you had to but at the end of the day we will stand by your side. You have always been the same person :) stay true to yourself always" (Meet the Rodgers) and "I'm sorry your hand was forced with this. I have nothing but more respect for you and your beautiful self!! Thank you for sharing your story. This will help SO many people!!" (chol1024).[48] The dramatic, almost click-bait nature of the title and the actual impactful content of the video even drew in new, and potentially unlikely, viewers as well:

"First time watching you. LOVED IT!!!!! I'm a gay 69 year old man. Can relate to so much of what you shared. Thanks for your bravery and sharing yourself. You are a beautiful women!!! Steven" (Steven Dexter) and "Seems like the most honest lady, in the true sense of the word, that I have every witnessed . . . I'm straight . . . and by watching this video message, I've learned a lot about respect, human rights, compassion and about myself . . . this video has inspired me to change my attitude, and be more considerate . . . thanks Nikkie" (wayne reynolds).[49] Clearly, this important personal moment for Nikkie became a personal moment for her viewers as well—one that connected them with her and with each other more meaningfully. Some viewers even reflected on the overwhelming support of her audience: "I'm so proud of this community" (Sweet Scribblez), a comment which received two million likes itself.[50] This episode embodies all of the distinctive qualities of the vlogging experience more broadly as well as elements of the makeup tutorial specifically, highlighting it as a digital space for establishing bonds through instructional content and a sense of vlogger authenticity that results in community creation and a platform for promoting relevant social commentary and change.

While I have focused on specific, representative examples of how the makeup tutorial platform functions as a sort of intersection of personal empowerment, dramatic entertainment, social criticism, and commerce, countless instances of similar episodes, some high drama and some more pragmatic in their social and physical application, certainly can be found. This policing and critiquing of the makeup industry and of one another becomes a way to critique society more broadly and further demonstrates the true power of makeup and the sort of self-marketing and -branding characteristic of the online tutorial. In this way, we see that makeup can be empowering for the individual; who can gain social and financial success as well as resist or redefine boundaries of beauty, gender, race, and identity through its application; as well as empowering for the viewing-posting community, which learns the value of diversity and the impact and importance of their shared voices and experiences through the online tutorial platform.

NOTES

1. In this chapter, I use the terms "influencer," "guru," "channel host," and "beauty vlogger" interchangeably to refer to makeup tutorial creators who have established themselves as amateur or professionally-trained authorities on the use and application of makeup. Much of their authority ultimately comes, however, from the legitimacy gained through the audiences that follow them on YouTube and other social platforms.

2. Alex Abad-Santos, "Laura Lee, Jeffree Star, and the Racism Scandal Upending the YouTube Beauty Community, Explained," *Vox*, August 31, 2018, https://www.vox.com/2018/8/28/17769996/laura-lee-jeffree-star-racism-subscriber-count.

3. Andrew Tolson, "A New Authenticity? Communicative Practices on YouTube," *Critical Discourse Studies* 7, no. 4 (2010): 286, DOI:10.1080/17405904.2010.511834.

4. Ibid., 286.

5. Marlena Stell, "My Truth Regarding the Beauty Community," YouTube Video, 8:55, August 27, 2018, https://www.youtube.com/watch?v=fBNZrvGLmyQ&t=18s.

6. According to Federal Trade Commission (FTC) regulations, content creators on YouTube must disclose when they are being compensated for a review or are posting sponsored content. However, vloggers do not always abide by these guidelines, and exactly how this information must be shared with viewers and the degree to which this is policed is not always clear, though the FTC did release a guide in 2019 titled "Disclosures 101 for Social Media Influencers" that may aid in ensuring such transparency.

7. Alison Hearn, "Insecure: Narratives and Economies of the Branded Self in Transformation Television," *Continuum* 22, no. 4 (2008): 497, DOI:10.1080/10304310802189972.

8. Shane, "The Secret World of Jeffree Star," YouTube Video, 42:29, August 1, 2018, https://www.youtube.com/watch?v=xUf2-sjGqQw&t=927s. Since then, both Shane Dawson and Jeffree Star have become the center of their own controversy, further highlighting the precariousness of vloggers' images and popularity.

9. While Lee removed the original apology video, numerous videos are available that include parts of her apology or even the whole video, but it is typically paired with on-screen commentary or even presented in a split-screen format featuring viewers' shocked, often comical reactions to her apology.

10. Gabriel Zamora, "My Truth," YouTube Video, 48:56, August 21, 2018, https://www.youtube.com/watch?v=QWnmPEHzRrk&t=126s.

11. Ibid.

12. Ibid.

13. Ibid.

14. Ibid.

15. Manny MUA, "My Reality Check," YouTube Video, 25:26, August 22, 2018, https://www.youtube.com/watch?v=s86Ja0LyNFI .

16. Ibid.

17. Zamora, "My Truth."

18. Jacoba Urist, "The Art and Science of Apologizing," *The Atlantic*, February 23, 2016, https://www.theatlantic.com/science/archive/2016/02/how-to-apologize/470457/.

19. Roy J. Lewicki, Beth Polin, and Robert B. Lount Jr., "An Explanation of the Structure of Effective Apologies," *Negotiation and Conflict Management Research* 9, no. 2 (April 2016): 177–196, https://doi-org.ezproxy.libproxy.db.erau.edu/10.1111/ncmr.12073.

20. Morgan Sun, "The Art of the YouTube Apology Video," *Mashable*, August 23, 2018, https://mashable.com/article/youtube-apology-video-laura-lee-gabriel-zamora-jeffree-star/#TtZ4RFLqfSqz.

21. Graeme Turner, *Ordinary People and the Media: The Demotic Turn* (London: Sage Publications, 2009), 2.

22. Geoff Weiss, "Laura Lee Apologizes for Racist Tweets Amid Loss of 240,000 Subscribers in Roughly 1 Week," *Tubefilter*, August 20, 2018, https://www.tubefilter.com/2018/08/20/laura-lee-apologizes-subscribers-loss/.

23. Jackie Aina, "My 1st Mukbang!!! Missing the Old YouTube? Why YouTubers Aren't Growing," YouTube Video, 17:37, September 30, 2018, https://www.youtube.com/watch?v=4R81qBerF3Q.

24. Manny MUA, "My Reality Check."

25. Wayne Goss, "In Defence of Tati and Halo Beauty," YouTube Video, 11:38, 6 March 6, 2018, https://www.youtube.com/watch?v=WzmVFAUm6WQ&t=29s.

26. Rachel Berryman and Misha Kavka, "'I Guess a Lot of People See Me as a Big Sister or a Friend': The Role of Intimacy in the Celebrification of Beauty Vloggers," *Journal of Gender Studies*, 26:3, (2017): 307, DOI:10.1080/09589236.2017.1288611.

27. Florencia García-Rapp, "'Come Join and Let's Bond': Authenticity and Legitimacy Building on YouTube's Beauty Community," *Journal of Media Practice*, 18:2–3, (2017): 124, DOI: 10.1080/14682753.2017.1374693.

28. Ibid., 126.
29. Stephanie Nicole, "BOMB | Using All Black Owned Makeup Brands," YouTube Video, 43:18, 26 June 2017, https://www.youtube.com/watch?v=mqpNm_7TEQE&t=177s.
30. Such episodes and others are part of what has made Star such a controversial figure and what later apology videos and his YouTube series with Shane Dawson tried to address to some extent.
31. Ibid.
32. In the years since posting this video, Nicole has become less active on YouTube, at least as of early 2020, presumably to focus more on her career outside of YouTube.
33. The line has since been further expanded to include fifty shades as of early 2020.
34. Alissa Ashley, "New Tarte Shape Tape Foundation . . . Are They Serious?," YouTube Video, 14:11, January 17, 2018, https://www.youtube.com/watch?v=WNs7fkbANM8&t=514s.
35. Jackie Aina, "Black Girls React to Tarte Shape Tape Foundation | Jackie Aina," YouTube Video, January 17, 2018, https://www.youtube.com/watch?v=4cXsgT3ZcL8&t=265s.
36. Ibid.
37. Ashley Klaty, "I Messed Up | Tarte Shape Tape Foundation," YouTube Video, 6:59, January 20, 2018, https://www.youtube.com/watch?v=ZEIpDBc6fL8.
38. Tatiana Bido, "Tarte Just Launched a Foundation and People Are Not Happy," *Newbeauty*, January 18, 2018, https://www.newbeauty.com/blog/dailybeauty/11839-tarte-shape-tape-foundation-controversy/.
39. Klaty, "I Messed Up."
40. NikkieTutorials, Twitter Post, January 17, 2018, 4:13 AM, https://twitter.com/nikkietutorials/status/953601109893025794?lang=en.
41. Comments are no longer visible or enabled for Aina's "Black Girls React to Tarte Shape Tape Foundation | Jackie Aina" video.
42. Aina, "Black Girls React to Tarte."
43. Stephanie Nicole, "B.O.M.B."
44. NikkieTutorials, "I'm Coming Out," YouTube Video, 17:13, January 13, 2020, https://www.youtube.com/watch?v=QOOw2E_qAsE.
45. "Stan" is a slang term that has come to mean being a strong supporter or fan of someone or something.
46. Ibid.
47. Ibid.
48. Ibid.
49. Ibid.
50. Ibid.

BIBLIOGRAPHY

Abad-Santos, Alex. "Laura Lee, Jeffree Star, and the Racism Scandal Upending the YouTube Beauty Community, Explained." *Vox*, August 31, 2018. https://www.vox.com/2018/8/28/17769996/laura-lee-jeffree-star-racism-subscriber-count.

Aina, Jackie. "Black Girls React to Tarte Shape Tape Foundation | Jackie Aina." YouTube Video, January 17, 2018. https://www.youtube.com/watch?v=4cXsgT3ZcL8&t=265s.

———. "My 1st Mukbang!!! Missing the Old YouTube? Why YouTubers Aren't Growing." YouTube Video, 17:37, Sept. 30, 3018. https://www.youtube.com/watch?v=4R81qBerF3Q.

Ashley, Alissa. "New Tarte Shape Tape Foundation . . . Are They Serious?" YouTube Video, 14:11, January 17, 2018. https://www.youtube.com/watch?v=WNs7fkbANM8&t=514s.

Berryman, Rachel and Misha Kavka. "'I Guess a Lot of People See Me as a Big Sister or a Friend': The Role of Intimacy in the Celebrification of Beauty Vloggers." *Journal of Gender Studies* 26:3, (2017): 307–320, DOI:10.1080/09589236.2017.1288611.

Bido, Tatiana. "Tarte Just Launched a Foundation and People Are Not Happy." *Newbeauty*, January 18, 2018. https://www.newbeauty.com/blog/dailybeauty/11839-tarte-shape-tape-foundation-controversy/.

Fenty Beauty. "Fenty Beauty by Rihanna." Accessed August 9, 2018. https://www.fentybeauty.com/.

García-Rapp, Florencia. "'Come Join and Let's Bond': Authenticity and Legitimacy Building on YouTube's Beauty Community." *Journal of Media Practice* 18:2–3, (2017): 120–137, DOI:10.1080/14682753.2017.1374693.

Goss, Wayne. "In Defence of Tati and Halo Beauty," YouTube Video, 11:38, March 6, 2018. https://www.youtube.com/watch?v=WzmVFAUm6WQ&t=29s.

Hearn, Alison. "Insecure: Narratives and Economies of the Branded Self in Transformation Television." *Continuum* 22, no. 4 (2008). 495–504, DOI:10.1080/10304310802189972.

Klaty, Ashley. "I Messed Up | Tarte Shape Tape Foundation," YouTube Video, 6:59, January 20, 2018. https://www.youtube.com/watch?v=ZEIpDBc6fL8.

Lewicki, Roy J., Beth Polin, and Robert B. Lount Jr. "An Explanation of the Structure of Effective Apologies." *Negotiation and Conflict Management Research* 9, no. 2 (April 2016): 177–196, https://doi-org.ezproxy.libproxy.db.erau.edu/10.1111/ncmr.12073.

Manny MUA. "My Reality Check." YouTube Video, 25:26, August 22, 2018. https://www.youtube.com/watch?v=s86Ja0LyNFI.

Nicole, Stephanie. "B.O.M.B. | Using All Black Owned Makeup Brands," YouTube Video, 43:18, 26 June 2017. https://www.youtube.com/watch?v=mqpNm_7TEQE&t=177s.

NikkieTutorials. "I'm Coming Out." YouTube Video, 17:13, January 13, 2020. https://www.youtube.com/watch?v=QOOw2E_qAsE.

———. Twitter Post, January 17, 2018, 4:13 AM. https://twitter.com/nikkietutorials/status/953601109893025794?lang=en.

Shane. "The Secret World of Jeffree Star." YouTube Video, 42:29, August 1, 2018. https://www.youtube.com/watch?v=xUf2-sjGqQw&t=927s.

Stell, Marlena. "My Truth Regarding the Beauty Community." YouTube Video, 8:55, August 27, 2018. https://www.youtube.com/watch?v=fBNZrvGLmyQ&t=18s.

Sung, Morgan. "The Art of the YouTube Apology Video." *Mashable*, August 23, 2018. https://mashable.com/article/youtube-apology-video-laura-lee-gabriel-zamora-jeffree-star/#TtZ4RFLqfSqz.

Tolson, Andrew. "A New Authenticity? Communicative Practices on YouTube." *Critical Discourse Studies* 7, no. 4 (2010): 277–289, DOI:10.1080/17405904.2010.511834.

Turner, Graeme. *Ordinary People and the Media: The Demotic Turn*. London: Sage Publications, 2009.

Urist, Jacoba. "The Art and Science of Apologizing." *The Atlantic*, February 23, 2016. https://www.theatlantic.com/science/archive/2016/02/how-to-apologize/470457/ .

Weiss, Geoff. "Laura Lee Apologizes for Racist Tweets Amid Loss of 240,000 Subscribers in Roughly 1 Week." *Tubefilter*, August 20, 2018. https://www.tubefilter.com/2018/08/20/laura-lee-apologizes-subscribers-loss/.

Zamora, Gabriel. "My Truth." YouTube Video, 48:56, August 21, 2018. https://www.youtube.com/watch?v=QWnmPEHzRrk&t=126s.

Chapter Two

The Popularity of Fenty Beauty and How It Reflects the Online Beauty Community

April Wilson

In this age of vlogger celebrity, where marketing and community are closely tied to social influence, many of us now turn to online personalities, often dubbed as "influencers,"[1] when deciding whether to buy a product, and this is especially true for the beauty community. If you were to click on YouTube right now and click on a review of a foundation, more often than not you may notice the YouTuber mention the shade range of the product, particularly the number of shades available. More and more frequently, when companies release a foundation range they stick to the "Fenty 40" rule in regard to how many shades they will have available because, as Kristina Rodufulo points out, "For New Foundation Ranges, 'Fenty 40' Is the Magic Number."[2]

Famously, singer Rihanna's beauty company, Fenty Beauty, launched in 2017 with forty shades of foundation, which was deemed a bold move for a new company at the time: "The shades will center Fenty Beauty as a leader in diverse foundation ranges."[3] Typically, when launching a foundation range, companies will launch twenty, at the most thirty, shades and expand if the range is popular. YouTuber Patricia Bright, who reviewed the collection when it launched in the United Kingdom, commented on how forty shades was a lot to start off with: "And Rihanna was like you know what I'm going to launch with foundation. The hardest thing to launch with. There's 40 shades. Literally 40 shades of foundation. There are other brands that have 40 shades, Lancôme has literally 40 shades plus more and shade matching but to start off with 40 shades that is a lot."[4] Rihanna decided to launch with forty shades of foundation in what was deemed a political move in the world of makeup "so that women everywhere would be included,"[5] which was clear right from the first video preview of the campaign that featured women of a large variety of ethnicities and skin tones.[6] Press coverage of the trailer highlighted this, focusing on "The Campaign's Diverse Stars,"[7] especially as a lot of the models were also unknown at the time: "It seems Rihanna has gone above and beyond in casting diverse models, some who might be new to the game, so not every Fenty Beauty model has been identified in this story as of press time."[8]

However, Fenty Beauty, as many commenters have reflected on, was not the first foundation range to have forty shades: "M.A.C had 43 existing shades of its Pro Longwear Foundation when Fenty launched. Maybelline expanded its Fit Me line of foundation 16 shades in May 2017, bringing the total up to 40. Plus, Make Up For Ever's Ultra HD Foundation dropped back in 2015 with 40 shades."[9] There were, though, important distinctions that made Fenty Beauty stand out from the crowd. Firstly, it's important to note that MAC,[10] Maybelline,[11] and Makeup Up For Ever[12] are not cruelty free, whereas Fenty Beauty is, and their Pro Filt'r foundation is also suitable for vegans,[13] which is of increasing importance to consumers. In Great Britain, for example, the number of vegans went from 150,000 in 2014 to 600,000 in 2018.[14] Significantly, there is also a growing amount of people who are becoming more concerned about what goes into making their favorite products: "Over half (56 percent) of Brits adopt vegan buying behaviours such as buying vegan products and checking if their toiletries are cruelty-free."[15]

Cruelty-free and vegan products have become popular topics, and, unsurprisingly, there has been a spike in popularity on Google for the word "veganism": "In 2008, the word 'veganism' had a popularity score of only 17 but it has increased to 88 only 10 years later."[16] Understandably, this spike in popularity means that YouTubers (whether they are necessarily completely cruelty free or not) want to be able to highlight cruelty-free or vegan products whenever they can to their viewers as they know it is important information for them.

The price range of Fenty Beauty's foundation is also significant, as it is not at the top of that competitor set, priced at $34,[17] compared to MAC, priced at $36;[18] Maybelline, (a well-known drug store makeup company), priced at $7.99;[19] and Makeup Up For Ever, priced at $43.[20] Therefore, compared to its immediate higher end competitors, Fenty Beauty has positioned itself at a lower price point but with just as much of a shade range available: "And at $34 a pop, Fenty Beauty foundation lands in a price point sweet spot: More expensive than what you could grab at CVS, but far less costly than what you'd find at a luxury brand's counter."[21] With the online beauty community bridging the gap between drug store, lower cost makeup and high end, more expensive makeup, and with popular creators and online beauty publications often posting side-by-side comparisons of low cost and higher end makeup,[22] the barrier between drug store and high end has been greatly lifted, with many now diversifying their makeup collections to include both. By situating themselves at the middle point pricewise, Fenty Beauty ensures that they could easily fit into a lot of different personal makeup collections.

Secondly, shade range has not always historically been at the forefront of the beauty industry's attention, along with the inclusion of black women in the world of beauty. When black women were marketed to, it was often with products to alter their appearance to white European standards of beauty (lighter skin, straighter hair). This can be seen by how, according to Shawna Collins, "The two main product categories advertised between 1920 and 1960 were skin lighteners and hair straighteners."[23] Although the situation facing the beauty industry in 2017 was a lot different than between 1920 and 1960, the brand still launched in an industry famous for its historical lack of inclusion of darker skinned women: "For a long time the beauty industry has neglected women of colour as consumers."[24]

Fenty Beauty's launch, however, signaled a wake-up call, and the brand Make Up For Ever, trying to market off the success of Fenty Beauty, wrote the following Instagram post after their launch: "40 shades is nothing new to us. . . . Since 2015, the #ultraHDfoundation released 40 shades for everyone's unique skin tone understanding the difference between red and yellow undertones. With expertise, time and passion—we shall continue to develop and improve our products for pros, for you, for everyone."[25] Rihanna famously responded in the comments saying, "lol. Still ashy,"[26] and "shook,"[27] therefore dismissing their claims that the brand caters to different undertones. Rihanna's claim in particular refers to foundation tones for black women; online many women have referred to foundation products with undertones that do not match their skin tone as making them look "washed out" or "ashy": "That's when I learned that foundation oxidizes, and on dark skin, that means it can look especially chalky and ghostlike;"[28] "Some cosmetic companies simply take a shade for white skin and add red tones to darken it for black consumers. This is why women of color are sometimes left with foundations that causes their skin to appear grey and ashy."[29] In a video examining Fenty Beauty, a reporter for the American news and entertainment website *Vox* comments on how "finding deeper shades that actually offer the right undertones for women of color has been incredibly hard."[30]

The significance of the undertone range offered by Fenty Beauty was not unnoticed by YouTube, as YouTuber Stephanie Nicole (who is famous for her in-depth, researched product reviews) comments in her review of Fenty Beauty:

> It's not so much that other makeup brands haven't had other offerings before because MAC does have quite a few foundations . . . but the big deal with that is even when they have darker shades . . . their undertones can be very wrong

> in those and it can make people of color look kind of red or very orange. These foundations from the reviews . . . I've been seeing are saying that the undertones match them perfectly.[31]

Data as well appears to back Fenty Beauty, as reporters from *The Pudding* measured the inclusivity of other lines of foundation in the United States in comparison to Fenty Beauty by recording the hexadecimal color code used to represent each available shade on the brand's website and then used Photoshop to extract the lightness values, which they then plotted to see whether a foundation line catered to lighter or darker skin tones.[32] The results were positive for Fenty Beauty, as they found that it does, in fact, have a wider range of shades than rival Make Up For Ever and has a wide assortment of shades in both the lightest skin tone range and the darkest skin tone range.[33]

This data was also backed up by reviews, as YouTuber Nyma Tang, who is known for her series #thedarkestshade on her YouTube channel "where she tests out and reviews the darkest shade of makeup that a brand or line carries,"[34] reviewed the darkest shade in Fenty Beauty's range. Although the shade did not match her exactly, she praised the company for coming out with such a diverse shade range and a product that was usable for her: "Fenty Beauty launched with 40 different foundation shades, which is pretty awesome . . . for me it's amazing to see as some companies, even still to this day, I still can't wear some of these companies' foundations . . . and for Fenty Beauty . . . to come out with something I can actually work with I am very happy and very pleased to see that."[35] Nyma started her series #thedarkestshade in order to address the issue in the beauty industry of the darker side of the spectrum being left out completely: "I was compelled to [make these videos] because I felt like, if I didn't do it, the darkest side of the spectrum is going to keep going unnoticed. I hope that companies notice that when you release products like this, you have to include everybody,"[36] as well as to provide other women with darker skin "accurate, unbiased information about complexion products that will (or won't) work for them."[37] For Nyma, Fenty Beauty represented a brand listening in and offering more inclusion through a launch that would work for every complexion, making it truly inclusive: "When I went to Sephora to pick up this foundation, I saw other dark skinned girls in Sephora getting matched . . . and it literally melted my heart . . . it was so awesome to see a huge launch, probably one of the biggest launches of the year, and there was girls in there that looked like me that were able to get matched for it."[38] It is, however, important to note that representation in makeup launches is specifically referring to mainstream makeup brands, those which are easily accessible in big beauty stores like Sephora (which is true for Fenty Beauty in the United States), as there is also a growing and popular community of black-owned makeup brands (that cater both specifically to black women and to everyone) who have risen to prominence using social media.

YouTube, in particular, is instrumental in making these brands recognized, as two YouTubers, Alissa Ashley and Alyssa Forever, are credited with starting the BOMB (Black-Owned Makeup Brands) makeup challenge.[39] The challenge aims to show support for black- and minority-owned makeup companies by YouTubers trying out new makeup products from black-owned makeup brands. YouTuber Jackie Aina is often credited with popularizing the challenge, where she made it clear that she was directing the challenge to all "Non-Black YouTubers"[40] through the title of her video. However, in the description of the video, she also mentions that her challenge is for everyone: "The same applies to black YouTubers!"[41]

Challenges like these were great for raising the profile of smaller black-owned brands; however, they did not tap into the consumer who wanted black-owned and diverse makeup to be more visible in the mainstream beauty community. Although there are brands like indie company Juvia's Place, owned by Nigerian-born Chichi Eburu and which is described as "the fastest growing black-owned cosmetics brand on the market,"[42] (having had mainstream success and even launching a UK website in 2018),[43] Fenty Beauty marked the moment that any woman could walk into a store and be able to find a product that represented her.

That said, Fenty Beauty, when it launched, did still have some accessibility issues for consumers outside the United States. Within the United Kingdom, for example, Fenty Beauty was only available to purchase in person and online through Harvey Nichols, but the company only had seven physical stores within the UK and Ireland.[44] However, although Fenty Beauty only originally launched in seventeen countries (simultaneously, which is, in fact, a large undertaking for a new brand[45]), Fenty Beauty has continued to expand globally since the launch, launching in Qatar, Bahrain, and Kuwait in September 2017 and in Saudi Arabia in April 2019.[46] International shipping is also available from the Fenty Beauty website to 127 countries.[47] Fenty Beauty has also since expanded in the United Kingdom and is now sold in health, beauty, and pharmacy retailer Boots, launching in thirty-two stores nationwide,[48] making it a lot more accessible to the UK beauty consumer.

In order to give the brand a global feel, Fenty Beauty has also utilized social media tactics, in particular, utilizing the more "interactive and dynamic web experience"[49] of Web 2.0, which is "focused on the ability of people to collaborate and share information online via social media, blogging and Web-based communities,"[50] in comparison to the static HTML pages of the first stage of the internet.[51]

Fenty Beauty created this "interactive and dynamic web experience"[52] by forming a community based on marketing to everyone and not focusing on a particular demographic. Rihanna herself said the focus of the company was to be inclusive for everyone: "There needs to be something for a dark-skinned girl; there needs to be something for a really pale girl; there needs to be something in-between."[53] This was something backed on social media by a review of the foundation by Krystal Robertson, who describes herself as albino. She praised the company, in particular, for the undertones of the product, highlighting how foundations "always end up orange"[54] on her, as "I'm albino I have no pigment."[55] What is also significant is that Robertson was not even using the lightest shade available, stating how she used "Shade #110. And I think they even have a shade lighter than this."[56]

Both Rihanna and Fenty Beauty proceeded to share the review on their Instagram stories; Rihanna accompanied it with a heart emoji, whereas Fenty Beauty accompanied the post with the hashtag #TheNewGenerationOfBeauty.[57] The use of "new generation" in the hashtag emphasizes that Fenty Beauty is highlighting and marketing to a new generation of consumers, which is essentially anyone, no matter their skin tone. As shown by Robertson's post, they have taken everyone into account, and it is this inclusivity that also lines up with the popular feminist theory of intersectionality, which "has enjoyed a resurgence in popular and academic feminism."[58]

Intersectionality is "the key analytic framework through which feminist scholars in various fields talk about the structural identities of race, class, gender, and sexuality."[59] Coined by Kimberlé Crenshaw in 1989 in her pioneering paper "Demarginalizing the Intersection of Race and Sex: A Black Feminist Critique of Antidiscrimination Doctrine, Feminist Theory and Antiracist Politics," the term intersectionality argues that the "problematic consequence of the tendency to treat race and gender as mutually exclusive categories of experience and analysis"[60] leads to black women being "theoretically erased."[61]

Crenshaw's argument was that a black woman will be treated differently than a white woman, as she will be discriminated against for both her gender and her race.[62] While Crenshaw's ideas about race and gender were not new and have been discussed since the beginning of feminism, this was something she herself acknowledged, making it clear that "she popularized the term 'intersectionality' but not the concept."[63] Since then, the term intersectionality has now also been further developed "to talk about other different experiences, such as someone's class, wealth, disability status, weight, sexuality, and other identities (like, for example, if one is transgender or intersex or identifies outside the gender binary)."[64]

While Rihanna's makeup line does not explicitly market itself as a vehicle for intersectional feminism, by marketing itself as a product that appeals to people who have felt excluded and not catered to in the makeup industry, it sets itself up as a company that takes other experiences into account—a key defining feature of intersectionality. By listening to consumers' experiences and showcasing them, like it does with Robertson (who, because of her albinism had struggled with her experience with beauty products), Fenty Beauty is creating a place for these women to be heard, something further highlighted by the experience of YouTubers like Nyma Tang, who felt Fenty Beauty was taking her experience into account, something a lot of the other companies she reviewed had not done.[65]

SEPARATING ART FROM THE ARTIST IN WEB 2.0

The dual posting of Robertson's story by both Rihanna and Fenty Beauty also shows just how involved Rihanna is with her company as well as how invested she is, something which has become more and more prevalent on social media with makeup brand owners often using their personal platform to engage those invested in the brand.

Notable examples include Claudia Norvina Soare from Anastasia Beverely Hills, daughter of the founder of the company, Anastasia Soare, who describes herself in the following way: "I'm the president of the company. I started at the front desk of the salon. I make all the makeup. Obviously, I run everything by my mom first. She has to love it and approve it. But I make the makeup, and she makes the brow."[66] It was also Norvina who pushed for the brand to have a social media presence, as her mother, Anastasia Soare, points out: "My daughter was the one actually who believed in social media—she pushed me to get into Instagram, Snapchat, and everything else."[67] Not only has this resulted in a palette called "Norvina," which Norvina describes as her "very first namesake,"[68] but Norvina also regularly posts on her personal Instagram about the brand and her journey as a creator: "I absolutely love her so much RIVIERA . . . 2019 is a creative evolution for me as a creator, I feel comfortable to grow and supported by all of you guys to show you more of me."[69]

Another notable example is Kat von D, who initially gained fame as a tattoo artist before launching her makeup brand and who often posts announcements about her makeup page on Instagram.[70] However, the link between her as a person and her brand has also caused her issues in the past, as she announced on Instagram (in a now deleted post) that she would not be vaccinating her baby, causing people to boycott her brand.[71]

Kat Von D later responded to the criticism, as well as rumors that had circulated online about her and her family being Nazis in a video on her YouTube channel (although, in regards to the anti-vaccination comments, this came more than six months after her initial Instagram post that incited the controversy):

> I am not an anti-vaxxer, what I am is a first time mother, I'm one of those moms that reads everything . . . back when I was pregnant someone asked me on Instagram if we were vaccinating our baby and after doing a bunch of

> research . . . naturally I experienced some hesitancy . . . if I'd have known that I would have let so many people down with that I would have never, never shared where we were at with that at that time. Since then, we have decided as parents to consult with our pediatrician and let him educate us and guide us . . . I have learnt my lesson and I've decided not to make . . . any of our baby's health records public.[72]

Response to the video was mixed on social media (although there were no direct comments made on the YouTube video as Kat Von D chose to turn off the commenting feature for the video), with some supporting the star and some criticizing her for not fully addressing the anti-vaccination rumors.[73]

With the gap between creations and creator becoming smaller in this Web 2.0 landscape, using a personal Instagram account to make a makeup company more "human" can be a useful tool, but, as seen in the above example with Kat Von D, it can also be a risky one. Interestingly, Kat Von D announced she would no longer be involved with her namesake makeup line in early 2020, selling off her shares to the brand's parent company Kendo, in order to focus on other endeavors.[74]

Rihanna's history and the public perception of her, then, is paramount to her success, and in recent years she has become famous for her alternative and distinctive "badgirlriri" fashion choices (Rihanna's Instagram name often being used in discussions about her[75]) and for gracing best dressed lists. Rihanna is widely believed to have emerged as a fashion icon since the debut of her album *Good Girl Gone Bad*, which, like albums of many artists before her (such as Christina Aguilera), aimed to dispel her previous good girl image:[76] "We figured *Good Girl Gone Bad* was the perfect title because it showed people I'm my own [person] now. Not doing what anyone wants me to do. I'm not the innocent Rihanna anymore. I'm taking a lot more risks and chances. I felt when I cut my hair, it shows people I'm not trying to look or be anybody else."[77] Many credit the album and its single "Umbrella" with making Rihanna as famous as she is today: "Ten Years Ago, 'Umbrella' Turned Rihanna into a Pop Icon;"[78] "*Good Girl Gone Bad* Transformed Rihanna from a Popstar to an Icon."[79] Since the release of the album, she has also become known for her "bad girl" image, both by her actions at award ceremonies but also on social media: "She's puffed joints on Snapchat, swigged from flasks at the Grammys and wielded guns in video clips."[80]

However, what is also a trademark of Rihanna's style is that, as fashion designer and film director Tom Ford describes it, it is "constantly evolving."[81] While in the *Good Girl Gone Bad* stage of her career she would often wear a "fetish-shaded new look: leather, bra tops, bondage straps, thigh-high boots and a distinctive, provocatively sexual, heavy-lidded, head-thrown-back stance,"[82] this is not a style that Rihanna fiercely kept to, and she became known as someone who was happy to experiment with fashion and did not take it too seriously: "Rihanna has fun with her clothes."[83]

Alongside her own personal style, Rihanna has had numerous successful fashion collaborations with famous brands, including teaming up with Emporio Armani Underwear and Armani Jeans to create her first fashion line, comprised of denim and lingerie, in 2011;[84] "high street" retailer River Island;[85] the underwear company Stance, where she is billed as a contributing creative director;[86] and high-end designer brand Dior to create a line of futuristic sunglasses;[87] (she was also later named as the new face of Dior and is the first black spokeswoman for the brand).[88]

One of her most famous collaborations is with the sports brand Puma, with her sneakers often selling out within a matter of hours.[89] In fact, she was named the new creative director for Puma's women's collection and global ambassador for the brand in 2014.[90] In 2016 she went on to design an original collection for Puma, which was unveiled at New York Fashion Week and met with rave reviews.[91] The focus on her style and fashion has even led figures like Charles, Prince of Wales, to call Rihanna a "global style icon"[92] in a speech he delivered at an evening reception hosted by the governor general in Barbados.

Rihanna herself has also branched out into her own fashion lines, launching a lingerie and nightwear line called Savage x Fenty in May 2018[93] and her own clothing line Fenty a year later in May 2019.[94] Both brands are notably mentioned as being size inclusive with Savage x Fenty offering sizing from XS to XXXL[95] and Fenty being described as inclusive for a luxury fashion brand going up to a French size 46, equivalent to a UK 18.[96]

Alongside her influence on the world of fashion and her "bad girl image," Rihanna is also known for her philanthropy, starting her own charity, The Believe Foundation, in 2006[97] and in 2012 founding the Clara Lionel Foundation (CLF),[98] which holds an annual Diamond Ball event.[99] In 2017, Rihanna was named as the Harvard University Humanitarian of the Year for her charitable work,[100] including the funding of a "state-of-the-art center for oncology and nuclear medicine to diagnose and treat breast cancer at the Queen Elizabeth Hospital in Bridgetown, Barbados,"[101] and for her work widening access to education for children.[102]

Rihanna presents herself as the "cool girl" whose fashion and style are seemingly effortless but also as someone who genuinely cares about the world and uses her fame and fortune to give back. With many looking up to Rihanna as an icon, it was not unexpected that any makeup range of hers would be a success and that she would try to use her influence in a positive way (evident in the diverse shade range with which the brand launched).

At the same time, her image as someone who is unafraid to take risks means it also was not unexpected for her to use social media to respond to criticism thrown at her brand, like her comments on Instagram to Make Up

For Ever. This is also something that she has done with potential customers as well, responding to a comment made on Instagram that suggested she had taken six months (the brand had only launched three months prior) to restock the darker shades of her foundation (which sold out days after their release).[103] She responded by saying, "Sis. we overstocked for 4 months plus. But what can I do when errbody luh da kid?! . . . also what's your shade sis?"[104] By explaining that the reason for the need for a restock was not due to a lack of planning but the unexpected demand for the product, she humanizes the brand and highlights its success. It is also her "tongue in cheek" attitude on social media (which her bad girl image has caused people to expect) that has led many people to cheer her on for such comments, as well as the knowledge that the reason the darker shades sold out was because many darker skinned women were excited to get their hands on a product that catered to them.

Alongside Rihanna's online presence, Rihanna and Fenty Beauty have crafted a Fenty Beauty community that also uses Instagram to support other people who are interested in Fenty's products. When one fan, Grace Boye, commented on a picture on Fenty Beauty's Instagram of blogger Aysha Harun wearing Fenty Beauty's red lip paint Stunna, she lamented, "I want to try this out soo bad. I've been told Red doesn't suit me . . . my lips are too big."[105] Many people in the comment section quickly came to her defense, including Fenty Beauty, which wrote, "this red is for EVERYONE," accompanied by emojis of women of different skin tones.[106] The company later posted a screenshot of the interaction, commenting, "The #FENTYBEAUTY sisterhood is real!!"[107] The post was then commented on by Rihanna, who showed her support through love heart emojis in the comment section.[108] Later on, Fenty Beauty reached out to Boye to send her the Stunna lip paint,[109] which resulted in her posting an image of herself wearing the product on Instagram and thanking everyone for their support and saying that she now embraces her big lips: "Yes, I was called 'Big lips' before, but now as I embrace my blackness, my African Culture, I accept who I am."[110]

THE YOUTUBE BEAUTY COMMUNITY

Considering Fenty Beauty in the context of the YouTube beauty community shows the lasting legacy of the brand. One such example is the YouTuber staple the "haul," which has evolved into various incarnations, including what is dubbed a "PR haul," in which a YouTuber will unwrap, live on screen, the products they have been sent by brands. Alongside a "PR haul," it is also likely that the YouTuber will post a separate video showcasing, testing, or reviewing the new product, often showing the PR package while doing so. Because of this, brands often send over the whole shade range for a product, despite the fact that the YouTuber will only feasibly get wear out of one or, at most, a few of the shades they are sent.

Popular YouTuber Jeffree Star (over 13 million subscribers)[111] explains this phenomenon in a collaboration video—("A YouTube collaboration is any collaborative effort made by two or more vloggers on YouTube to gain more exposure and grow their audience by working together")[112]—with Shane Dawson (over 21 million subscribers)[113], in which he declutters his makeup collection (decluttering videos, although they have been popular for years on the platform, have reached a peak in popularity with the success of *Tidying Up with Marie Kondo* on Netflix in January 2019)[114]. The video, "Getting Rid of $1,000,000 of Makeup w. Shane Dawson," as the title suggests, highlights the cost of products sent to individuals involved in the YouTube beauty community: "So when a brand has a new launch they want it to show up at your house, they want you to show it to your audience . . . but that's the game. They also want you to show to your audience that they have a shade range."[115]

This is something that Jeffree Star seems keen to share in an effort to educate Shane Dawson, who started to show an interest in beauty[116] after their extremely popular collaboration series *The Secret World of Jeffree Star*; (the five part series "had more than 70 million views in the first two weeks").[117] The two (Jeffree Star and Shane Dawson) have since collaborated again on *The Beautiful World of Jeffree Star* series, which documented the two stars collaborating on a makeup collection and merchandise line together through Jeffree Star's makeup company, Jeffree Star Cosmetics, and merchandise brand, Killer Merch. The series was unique for showing the background of what goes into a makeup release as well as including key business meetings with higher-ups within the beauty industry, as well as the costs and profits involved.[118] The collection was a massive success, despite issues with the website on launch day,[119] and was distinctly described as "breaking the internet" by media outlets.[120]

However, Jeffree Star's initial collaboration with Shane Dawson was, in fact, part of a wider series of documentaries by Shane Dawson exposing the secret life of high-profile YouTubers, which has been accused of "carv[ing] out a redemption arc for their problematic or outright disturbing behavior."[121]

This is something that could be said to apply to Jeffree Star, whose redemption arc on the platform reflects the dynamics of the YouTube beauty space. For many, Jeffree Star is someone they take issue with for talking about shade range because of his past racist comments, which resurfaced after YouTuber Stephanie Nicole mentioned them in her review of his "Beauty Killer" eye shadow palette.[122] In particular, he has famously been criticized for a sketch posted on his MySpace account (the platform where he initially gained fame) in which he jokes about bleaching a black woman's skin so her foundation shade would match:

> Sharolaid: You say black folk cannot wear MAC cosmetics, and you splash acid on her face!
>
> Jeffree Star: Well maybe if she wasn't wearing the wrong foundation, I wouldn't have to splash no battery acid. I wanted to lighten her skin tone, girl.[123]

Jeffree Star did post an apology video about his past comments on his YouTube channel,[124] building up a narrative in which he "transitions from being an upstart underdog into a massive success story into the community's best friend, despite his controversial past"[125] by explaining that his past actions were caused by his seeking attention and lashing out as a result of the abuse he used to receive every day because he looked different, though at the same time making it clear what he did and said was wrong.[126]

However, the YouTube community was not entirely convinced he was sorry about his actions,[127] especially since he also filed copyright strikes against other channels who spoke about the controversy, including Kat Blaque, an American YouTuber and activist.[128] Her video entitled "Is Jeffree Star Racist?," however, was not a video that outright condemned Star, and she, in fact, commented that it can be difficult to be judged on comments made in your past: "Very few people understand what it's like being visible for over ten years online. If we all had every single foolish and disgusting thing, that we've ever said, recorded online forever we'd all probably cringe at the things we used to say."[129]

In addition to his apology video, Jeffree Star has sought to defend his position in the beauty community by becoming a voice and advocate for increased shade ranges, praising Fenty Beauty for its shade range and criticizing Tarte Cosmetics for not catering to dark skin tones.[130] Star also criticized Givenchy when it brought out twenty different foundation shades, only two of which catered to women of darker skin tones, and said he would not be reviewing the line.[131] However, recently both Jeffree Star and his frequent collaborator Shane Dawson have been criticized for both their past racist and offensive content and behavior towards other influencers, which resulted in long-time partner Morphe Cosmetics announcing they were going to no longer sell Jeffree Star Cosmetics and Morphe seemingly removing Shane Dawson and Jeffree Star's makeup collection from their stores.[132]

In this YouTube beauty sphere, brands like Fenty Beauty become causes for YouTubers to rally behind to show they are "being better," despite any controversies they may have had in their past. Fenty Beauty positions itself as the perfect brand to rally behind because it does not have a history of controversy and because it is a brand that has demonstrated, both in the amount of foundation shades it launched and the community it has created online (through the targeted use of social media), that it is an inclusive, positive brand.

However, support from Fenty Beauty often goes above and beyond average online devotion for a makeup company, and this is because, as Stephanie Nicole explains, the line resonates deeply with people because of the broad shade range it makes available: "I find a lot of people to be very defensive of this line. That's because it's the first time that a lot of people of color have felt included in a launch, which I totally see you, I hear you."[133] In fact, when Fenty Beauty launched, ardent fans of the line were quick to respond to any criticism of the brand and often would compare the launches of other products to the brand. Huda Beauty, a cosmetics line owned by Huda Kattan, who achieved popularity through Instagram and was named as one of *Forbes*'s top ten beauty influencers in 2017,[134] launched her foundation line #FauxFilter on October 1, 2017, a month after the launch of Fenty Beauty. The twenty-five-shade-range collection was criticized because of its similar name to Rihanna's foundation, and many Fenty fans accused Huda Beauty of copying.[135] However, fans of Huda Beauty quickly came to the defense of the line, pointing out "that the beauty blogger [Huda Kattan] had been developing her foundation for years and it would have been impossible for her to create such an expansive product line in only a month's time."[136]

Whether time will change this consumer support, however, is uncertain, as Fenty Beauty itself came under fire in 2018 for their Morrocan Spice eye shadow palette, which was accused of cultural appropriation.[137] Cultural appropriation can be defined as "Members of one culture . . . tak[ing] for their own, for their own use, items produced by a member or members of another culture."[138] Fenty Beauty was accused of this by Ruqaya Izzidien in *The New Arab* because she felt the palette did "nothing to acknowledge true Moroccan culture."[139] Other outlets also accused the palette of being "orientalist," which can be defined as "a way of seeing that imagines, emphasizes, exaggerates and distorts differences of Arab peoples and cultures as compared to that of Europe and the U.S.,"[140] and criticized Fenty Beauty for not using Moroccan models in the advertisement.[141] In 2019, Fenty Beauty came under fire again after revealing a highlighter called "Geisha Chic," which many highlighted as being insensitive toward the Asian community.[142] The brand, however, apologized for the misstep and personally messaged an Instagram user who commented about the inappropriateness of the name of the product and removed the product for sale until it was renamed, gaining praise for their handling of the mistake in the community.[143]

THE "FENTY 40" EFFECT

After the success of Fenty Beauty, particularly how popular the range was with darker skinned women, which even caused a shortage of the darker shades,[144] more and more brands started to expand their foundation ranges and focus their campaigns on diversity. Just a week after Fenty Beauty launched, the brand Cover FX started a campaign called #NudeIsNotBeige on social media, highlighting how they expanded their foundation range in 2015.[145] Since the launch of Fenty Beauty, numerous different brands, from long-standing industry brands such as CoverGirl (with web series creator Issa Rae and celebrity cook Ayesha Curry as stars of the campaign)[146], Revlon, and Estée Lauder[147] (which expanded its range from forty-two shades to fifty-six), to cult favorites like Smashbox and Tarte,[148] the conscience-focused company Lush,[149] social media darlings ColourPop[150] and NYX,[151] and even luxury brand Dior,[152] have expanded their foundation lines to include forty foundations or more. Popular brands also teamed up with popular YouTube makeup artists to develop their foundation range, with one of brand Too Faced's founders, Jerrod Blandino, announcing through an Instagram photo "featuring black and brown models that he would be teaming up with black YouTube makeup artist Jackie Aina."[153] In comparison, since its launch Fenty Beauty has expanded to fifty shades of foundation alongside a new range of fifty shades of concealer,[154] although coverage of Fenty Beauty still focuses on the golden "Fenty 40" rule.

Fenty Beauty, then, highlights a growing trend that has built up from the YouTube beauty space where brands now have to think carefully about each aspect of their product and consider all their customers. The community will not accept people trying to "do better;" they now have to "be better." In what has become a community where creators and brands now face accountability for their actions (racist tweets that resurfaced from YouTuber Laura Lee being a prime example, as they resulted in her being dropped from all her major sponsorship deals,[155] a situation only exacerbated by her disastrous apology video that received major backlash online)[156], Fenty Beauty has revealed itself to be industry leading, with *Time* magazine even naming Fenty's foundation one of its best inventions of 2017.[157]

Instead of fracturing its customer base, Fenty Beauty presents a united front, a Fenty Beauty community (#FentyBeauty sisterhood), which is especially important in an increasingly fractured YouTube. Significantly, this sisterhood is working to change attitudes toward beauty and to whom companies should market. By reposting customers like Robertson, who had been neglected because of her very fair skin, as well as celebrating women like Boye, who was bullied for her naturally full lips,[158] despite the fact that full lips are now in trend because of influencers like Kylie Jenner[159] (however, significantly, Boye was treated differently online when she wore bright lipstick as a black woman with full lips), Fenty Beauty showcases and, importantly, has empowered a #NewGeneration of beauty that previously had been neglected.

Before "Fenty 40," how many shades of foundation a company offered was not deemed a political move but, in a post-"Fenty 40" world, it now can make or break a company's relationship with its consumers. Importantly, the power dynamic has shifted back to consumers, especially as online reviews (particularly those on YouTube) can make or break a brand or a product launch; for example, the launch of Anastasia Beverly Hills' Subculture palette was marred by negative backlash online, with many commenting that the eye shadows were powdery and difficult to blend.[160]

While Fenty Beauty has had some controversies, for now it appears to have walked away unscathed with many still quick to defend the beauty brand fiercely online.[161] This positions Fenty Beauty as a "safe" brand to like and use in the online community, and the way it has been celebrated by different figures within the industry shows that the online community is looking for a more intersectional beauty industry. Here's hoping the "Fenty 40" rule continues to inspire more change.

NOTES

1. "influencer," Cambridge Dictionary, accessed December 22, 2019, https://dictionary.cambridge.org/dictionary/english/influencer.
2. Kristina Rodulfo, "For New Foundation Ranges, 'Fenty 40' Is the Magic Number," *Elle*, May 31, 2018, https://www.elle.com/beauty/makeup-skin-care/a20967710/makeup-companies-40-foundation-shades-fenty-beauty-influence/.
3. Ashley Weatherford, "Rihanna's Beauty Line Will Include 40 Foundation Shades," *The Cut*, September 5, 2017, https://www.thecut.com/2017/09/rihanna-fenty-beauty-40-foundation-shades-pro-filtr.html.
4. Patricia Bright, "OK FENTY BEAUTY . . . YOU HAD TO GO THERE, REALLY? FIRST IMPRESSIONS!," YouTube video, September 9, 2017, https://www.youtube.com/watch?v=NZ-iP-Xxqss.
5. Fenty Beauty," Fenty Beauty, accessed March 18, 2019, https://www.fentybeauty.com/about-fenty.
6. Robyn Rihanna Fenty (@badgalriri), "This is @FentyBeauty. Head to a @sephora, #sephorainJCP or @harveynichols store to get an exclusive behind-the scenes look!," Instagram video, September 1, 2017, https://www.instagram.com/p/BYgX7EAjNF6/?utm_source=ig_embed.
7. Shea Simmons, "Who are the Models in the Fenty Beauty Video? The Internet Is Obsessed with the Campaign's Diverse Stars," *Bustle*, September 1, 2017, https://www.bustle.com/p/who-are-the-models-in-the-fenty-beauty-video-the-internet-is-obsessed-with-the-campaigns-diverse-stars-80510.
8. Ibid.
9. Rodulfo, "For New Foundation Ranges."
10. "MAC," Cruelty Free Kitty, accessed March 18, 2019, https://www.chicagomanualofstyle.org/tools_citationguide/citation-guide-1.html.
11. "Maybelline," Cruelty Free Kitty, accessed March 18, 2019, https://www.crueltyfreekitty.com/brand/maybelline/.

12. "Make Up For Ever," Cruelty Free Kitty, accessed March 18, 2019, https://www.crueltyfreekitty.com/brand/make-up-for-ever/.
13. "Fenty Beauty FAQ's," Fenty Beauty, accessed March 18, 2019, https://www.fentybeauty.com/faq.html.
14. "Statistics," The Vegan Society, accessed March 18, 2019, https://www.vegansociety.com/news/media/statistics.
15. "Statistics," The Vegan Society.
16. Lora Jones, "Veganism: Why Is It on the Up?," *BBC*, June 18, 2018, https://www.bbc.co.uk/news/business-44488051.
17. "PRO FILT'R," Fenty Beauty, accessed March 25, 2019, https://www.fentybeauty.com/pro-filtr/soft-matte-longwear-foundation/FB30006.html?dwvar_FB30006_color=FB0340.
18. "PRO LONGWEAR NOURISHING WATERPROOF FOUNDATION," MAC, accessed March 25, 2019, https://www.maccosmetics.com/product/13847/35126/products/makeup/face/foundation/pro-longwear-nourishing-waterproof-foundation.
19. "Fit Me Foundation," Maybelline, accessed March 25, 2019, https://www.maybelline.com/face-makeup/foundation-makeup/fit-me-matte-poreless-foundation/fair-porcelain.
20. "Make Up For Ever—Ultra HD Invisible Cover Foundation," Sephora, accessed March 25, 2019, https://www.sephora.com/product/ultra-hd-invisible-cover-stick-foundation-P398775.
21. Jessica M. Goldstein, "Rihanna Is Marketing Her Makeup to Everyone—And It's Paying Off," *Think Progress*, September 14, 2017, https://thinkprogress.org/fenty-beauty-rihanna-caf1fe83a641/.
22. Victoria Jowett, "One of These Makeup Looks Cost £500 More than the Other—Can You Tell Which?," *Cosmopolitan*, July 11, 2017, https://www.cosmopolitan.com/uk/beauty-hair/a10282481/high-end-vs-cheap-makeup-review/.
23. Shawna Collins, "Dark Shades Don't Sell": Race, Gender, and Cosmetic Advertisements in the Mid-Twentieth Century United States" (MA diss., McMaster University, 2018), 4.
24. *Vox*, "How Beauty Brands Failed Women of Color," YouTube video, November 14, 2017, https://www.youtube.com/watch?v=v5e4gwDGrNk.
25. Make Up For Ever (@makeupforeveroffical), "40 shades is nothing new to us—Since 2015, the #ultraHDfoundation released 40 shades for everyone's unique skin tone understanding the difference between red and yellow undertones," Instagram photo, September 25, 2017, https://www.instagram.com/p/BZegQavhi5e/?utm_source=ig_embed.
26. Ibid.
27. Ibid.
28. Monica Perry, "5 Ways to Avoid This Weird but Common Foundation Issue," *Allure*, April 5, 2016, https://www.allure.com/story/dark-skin-foundation-tips.
29. *Makeup for Melanin Girls*, "Bye Ashy: How to Find Your Right Foundation Shade Using Undertones," January 2, 2018, https://makeupformelaningirls.com/blogs/community/bye-ashy
-how-to-find-your-right-foundation-shade-using-undertones.
30. *Vox*, "How Beauty Brands Failed Women of Color."
31. Stephanie Nicole, "Fenty Beauty Review (#2 Billion & 3) | Demo w/ Wear Check In | Swatches," YouTube video, September 22, 2017, https://www.youtube.com/watch?v=dLj95bKMb_c.
32. Jason Li, Amber Thomas, and Divya Manian, "Beauty Brawl—How Inclusive Are Beauty Brands around the World?," *The Pudding*, June, 2018, https://pudding.cool/2018/06/makeup-shades/.
33. Ibid.
34. Alle Connell, "Nyma Tang Tries the Darkest Shades in Makeup for an Important Reason," *Revelist*, July 14, 2017, http://www.revelist.com/bloggers/nyma-tang/8404/nyma-has-a-seriously-amazing-series-on-youtube-called-the-darkest-shade-where-she-tests-out-and-reviews-the-darkest-shade-of-makeup-that-a-brand-or-line-carries/3.
35. Nyma Tang, "Fenty Beauty Pro Filt'r Foundation Review|| Nyma Tang #thedarkestshade," YouTube video, 11 September, 2017, https://www.youtube.com/watch?v=hQbeB0YXLhs&t=1s.

36. Connell, "Nyma Tang."
37. Ibid.
38. Tang, "Fenty Beauty."
39. Natalie Lukatitis, "This Challenge Is Putting Unknown Beauty Brands on the Map," *Marie Claire*, October 16, 2017, https://www.marieclaire.co.uk/beauty/make-up/bomb-challenge-440479.
40. Jackie Aina, "Calling ALL Non-Black YouTubers! New Makeup Challenge!," YouTube video, July 26, 2016, https://www.youtube.com/watch?v=3wUc3srYfPI.
41. Ibid.
42. Laura Capon, "The World's Most Pigmented Eyeshadow Palette is FINALLY Launching in the UK," *Cosmopolitan*, July 18, 2018, https://www.cosmopolitan.com/uk/beauty-hair/makeup/a22331747/juvias-place-eyeshadow-palette-uk/.
43. Ibid.
44. "THE COMPANY," Harvey Nichols, accessed March 25, 2019, https://www.harveynichols.com/about/the-company/.
45. "Rihanna Launches Fenty Beauty, a Global Makeup Brand, in 17 Countries," Cision PR Newswire, accessed March 25, 2019, https://www.prnewswire.co.uk/news-releases/rihanna-launches-fenty-beauty-a-global-makeup-brand-in-17-countries-643185393.html.
46. Camille Augistin, "Rihanna's Fenty Beauty to Make Monetary Waves in Saudi Arabia," *Vibe*, April 7, 2018, https://www.vibe.com/2018/04/rihannas-fenty-beauty-launches-in-saudi-arabia.
47. "FENTY BEAUTY SHIPPING INFORMATION," Fenty Beauty, accessed March 25, 2019, https://www.fentybeauty.com/shipping-info.html.
48. Chantelle Symester, "Fenty Beauty Boots Store Locations That Will Stock Rihanna's Make Up Range from TODAY," *The Daily Mirror*, May 9, 2019, https://www.mirror.co.uk/3am/style/3am-fashion-celebrity-beauty/fenty-beauty-oots-store-locations-15019828.
49. "Web 2.0," Techopedia, accessed March 21, 2019, https://www.techopedia.com/definition/4922/web-20.
50. Ibid.
51. Ibid.
52. Ibid.
53. Cat Quinn, "Rihanna's Fenty Beauty Products Drop Today—& We Tried Them First," Refinery29, September 7, 2017, https://www.refinery29.com/en-us/2017/09/171310/rihanna-fenty-beauty-sephora-new-products-2017.
54. Krystal Robertson (@acondria), "@badgalriri #SlayedMyLife 2 Happy . . . what a wonderful day!!!! @fentybeauty #ThankYouAll," Instagram photo, 17 September, 2017, https://www.instagram.com/p/BZIPYk-gBF4/?utm_source=ig_embed&utm_campaign=embed_loading_state_control.
55. Ibid.
56. Ibid.
57. Meghan Decker, "This Albino Woman's Review on the Fenty Beauty Shade Range Is Going Viral," Refinery29, September 18, 2017, https://www.refinery29.com/amp/en-us/2017/09/172688/fenty-beauty-foundation-inclusive-tones-albino-photo.
58. Bim Adewunmi, "Kimberlé Crenshaw on Intersectionality: 'I Wanted to Come Up with an Everyday Metaphor that Anyone Could Use,'" *New Statesman*. April 2, 2014, http://www.newstatesman.com/lifestyle/2014/04/kimberl-crenshaw-intersectionality-i-wanted-come-everyday-metaphor-anyone-could.
59. Britney Cooper, "Intersectionality," in *The Oxford Handbook of Feminist Theory*, ed. Lisa Disch and Mary Hawkesworth (New York: Oxford University Press, 2016), 385.
60. Kimberlé Crenshaw, "Demarganializing the Intersection of Race and Sex: A Black Feminist Critique of Antidiscrimination Doctrine, Feminist Theory and Antiracist Politics," *University of Chicago Legal Forum*, no.1 (1989): 139.
61. Ibid.
62. Kimberlé Crenshaw, "Demarganializing the Intersection of Race and Sex: A Black Feminist Critique of Antidiscrimination Doctrine, Feminist Theory and Antiracist Politics," 139–167.

63. Jenée Desmond-Harris, "To Understand the Women's March on Washington, You Need to Understand Intersectional Feminism," *Vox,* January 21, 2017, https://www.vox.com/identities/2017/1/17/14267766/womens-march-on-washington-inauguration-trump-feminism-intersectionaltiy-race-class.

64. April Wilson, "Feminism and Activism in the 2017 Pepsi Advertisement: Can Anything Be Gained by Them Becoming a Staple of Popular Culture?" (MA diss., University of Hertfordshire, 2017), 26.

65. Connell, "Nyma Tang."

66. Renee Jacques, "5 Surprising Things You Didn't Know about Anastasia Beverly Hills," *Allure*, December 29, 2015, https://www.allure.com/story/history-of-anastasia-beverly-hills.

67. Alyssa Reeder, "Anastasia Soare, Founder, Anastasia Beverly Hills," *Into the Gloss*, May 19, 2015, https://intothegloss.com/2015/06/anastasia-soare-founder-anastasia-beverly-hills/.

68. Norvina, "NORVINA Presents: ABH Norvina Palette," YouTube video, July 28, 2018, https://www.youtube.com/watch?v=SD60paoggNo.

69. Claudia Norvina Soare (@norvina), "What can I say I absolutely love her so much RIVIERA is a getaway in a palette", Instagram photo, February 26, 2019, https://www.instagram.com/p/BuU31wch4Pw/.

70. Kat Von D (@thekatvond), "So excited to finally announce that @jackiecruz will be the face [and eyes] of our new @katvondbeauty GO BIG OR GO HOME MASCARA!," Instagram photo, March 20, 2019, https://www.instagram.com/p/BvPMT1oFRYP/.

71. Alex Archambault, "Kat Von D Said She Won't Vaccinate Her Baby—And People Are So Outraged They're Boycotting Her Beauty Line," *Insider*, June 11, 2018, https://www.thisisinsider.com/kat-von-d-not-vaccinating-baby-doctor-says-bad-idea-2018-6.

72. thekatvond, "I am NOT a Nazi. I am NOT Anti-vaxx," YouTube video, March 14, 2019, https://www.youtube.com/watch?v=pc1K_MXe1M4.

73. Ellie Bate, "Kat Von D Denied Accusations She's a Nazi and an Anti-vaxxer after People Boycotted Her Makeup Line," *Buzzfeed*, March 18, 2019, https://www.buzzfeed.com/eleanorbate/kat-von-d-nazi-anti-vaxxer-accusations-video.

74. Thatiana Diaz, "KVD Beauty Says Its Name No Longer Stands for Kat Von D," Refinery29, January 28, 2020, https://www.refinery29.com/en-us/2020/01/9317417/kvd-vegan-beauty-brand-brand-initials-meaning-rebranding.

75. Tallie Spencer, "Rihanna Shows Up and Shows Out in Cheetah Print at Beyonce and Jay-Z's Oscars Afterparty," *Billboard*, February 25, 2019, https://www.billboard.com/articles/columns/hip-hop/8500082/rihanna-oscar-afterparty-beyonce-jayz-cheetah-dress.

76. Shaheem Reid, "Rihanna Loses Good Girl Image, Thanks to Jay-Z, Justin, Timberland, Ne-Yo," *MTV News*, May 1, 2007, http://www.mtv.com/news/1558496/rihanna-loses-good-girl-image-thanks-to-jay-z-justin-timbaland-ne-yo/.

77. Ibid.

78. Mikhael Agafonov, "Ten Years Ago, 'Umbrella' Turned Rihanna into a Pop Icon," *Dazed*, March 29, 2017, http://www.dazeddigital.com/music/article/35332/1/rihanna-umbrella-10th-anniversary-retrospective.

79. Sam Murphy, "'Good Girl Gone Bad' Transformed Rihanna from a Popstar to an Icon," *Interns*, June 6, 2017, https://theinterns.net/2017/06/06/good-girl-gone-bad-transformed-rihanna-from-a-popstar-to-an-icon/.

80. Sam Murphy, "'Good Girl Gone Bad' Transformed Rihanna from a Popstar to an Icon."

81. Jess Cartner-Morley, "Rihanna: The Pop Star Who Became a Fashion Powerhouse," *The Guardian*, September 15, 2017, https://www.theguardian.com/fashion/2017/sep/15/rihanna-pop-star-fashion-powerhouse-beauty-brand.

82. Ibid.

83. Ibid.

84. Ella Alexander, "Rihanna Designs," *Vogue*, November 22, 2011, https://www.vogue.co.uk/gallery/rihanna-launches-armani-fashion-collection.

85. MTV, "Rihanna Launches Collection at LFW," accessed 25 March, 2019, http://www.mtv.co.uk/rihanna/news/rihanna-launches-collection-at-lfw.

86. BallerStatus, "Rihanna Teams Up with Stance for Sock Collection," accessed March 25, 2019, https://www.ballerstatus.com/2015/07/15/rihanna-teams-up-with-stance-for-sock-collection/.
87. Carver Low, "Rihanna Partners with Dior to Create Sunglass Collection," *HotNewHipHop*, May 25, 2016, https://www.hotnewhiphop.com/rihanna-partners-with-dior-to-create-sunglass-collection-news.21830.html.
88. Avery Thompson, "Rihanna Is the New Face of Dior: First Black Spokesperson for the Brand," *Hollywood Life*, March 14, 2015, https://hollywoodlife.com/2015/03/14/rihanna-dior-campaign-first-black-woman/.
89. Amira Mercer, "How Rihanna's Puma Creeper Became the Year's Must-Have Shoe," *Vanity Fair*, May 25, 2016, https://www.vanityfair.com/style/2016/05/rihanna-puma-creeper-shoe.
90. Vanessa Friedman, "Puma Explains Its New Creative Director: Rihanna," *New York Times*, December 17, 2014, https://runway.blogs.nytimes.com/2014/12/17/puma-creative-director-rihanna/.
91. Jessica Dafoe, "Puma Sales Skyrocket Thanks to Kylie Jenner and Rihanna, Kylie Not Backing Down Despite Kanye's Competition," *Inquisitr*, April 30, 2016, https://www.inquisitr.com/3048389/puma-sales-sky-rocket-thanks-to-kylie-jenner-and-rihanna-kylie-not-backing-down-despite-kanyes-competition/#sGEc5imGk1dZLPpK.99.
92. Olivia Petter, "Prince Charles Names Rihanna a 'Global Style Icon' on Barbados Visit," *The Independent*, March 21, 2019, https://www.independent.co.uk/life-style/prince-charles-rihanna-barbados-visit-bajan-global-style-icon-a8831856.html.
93. Steff Yotka, "Everything You Need to Know about Rihanna's Savage x Fenty Launch," *Vogue*, May 9, 2018, https://www.vogue.com/article/rihanna-savage-x-fenty-lingerie-launch-details.
94. Channing Hargrove, "Rihanna's Fenty Line Brings Some Much Needed Inclusivity to the Luxury Space," Refinery29, 22 May, 2019, https://www.refinery29.com/en-gb/2019/05/233437/rihanna-fenty-fashion-line.
95. Sarah Young, "Rihanna Launches Size-Inclusive Savage x Fenty Valentine's Day Collection," *The Independent*, 9 January, 2019, https://www.independent.co.uk/life-style/fashion/rihanna-savage-fenty-lingerie-underwear-valentines-day-lookbook-size-inclusive-a8719076.html.
96. Hargrove, "Rihanna's Fenty."
97. Sutheshna Mani, "Rihanna's Charities Prove Rihanna's More than Just a Singer," *Entity*, March 13, 2017, https://www.entitymag.com/rihannas-charities-more-just-singer/.
98. Clara Lionel Foundation, "Mission/Vision of CLF," accessed 24 March, 2019, https://web.archive.org/web/20160501082735/http://claralionelfoundation.org/about/mission-vision-of-clf/.
99. Clara Lionel Foundation, "Diamond Ball," accessed 24 March, 2019, https://web.archive.org/web/20160419215626/http://claralionelfoundation.org/diamond-ball/.
100. *The Harvard Gazette*, "Rihanna named Humanitarian of Year," accessed March 25, 2019, https://news.harvard.edu/gazette/story/2017/02/rihanna-named-humanitarian-of-year/.
101. Ibid.
102. Ibid.
103. Jason Pham, "Rihanna Hits Back at Instagrammer Who Criticized How She Runs Fenty Beauty," *Stylecaster*, March 24, 2018, https://stylecaster.com/beauty/rihanna-fenty-beauty-clap-back/.
104. Ibid.
105. Patrice Peck, "People Love What Rihanna's Makeup Company Did for a Woman Who Thought Her Lips Were 'Too Big' for Red Lipstick," *BuzzFeed*, December 4, 2017, https://www.buzzfeed.com/patricepeck/the-fenty-beauty-sisterhood-is-real?utm_term=.lb8O6x8jlj#.iy3qO4RZzZ.
106. Ibid.
107. Ibid.
108. Ibid.
109. Ibid.

110. Grace Boye (@n0bleprincess), "Thank you all for your support," Instagram photo, December 8, 2017, https://www.instagram.com/p/BcdI77rgXxd/?utm_source=ig_embed.

111. "jeffree star," YouTube channel, accessed March 18, 2019, https://www.youtube.com/user/jeffreestar.

112. "What Is a YouTube Collaboration and How to Make It Work," Vlog Nation, accessed March 25, 2019, https://www.vlognation.com/how-to-make-youtube-collab/.

113. "shane," YouTube channel, accessed March 18, 2019, https://www.youtube.com/user/shane.

114. AJ Willingham and Andrea Diaz, "Netflix Has People (Serenely) Bulldozing Their Closets, and Thrift Stores are Riding the Wave," *CNN*, January 14, 2019, https://edition.cnn.com/2019/01/12/entertainment/marie-kondo-konmari-tidying-up-netflix-trnd/index.html.

115. jeffreestar, "Getting Rid of $1,000,000 of Makeup w. Shane Dawson," YouTube video, March 8, 2019, https://www.youtube.com/watch?v=MbtesOrC5t4.

116. Laura Capon, "Update—A Shane Dawson x Jeffree Star Eyeshadow Palette is Actually Coming, According to Shane's Instagram," *Cosmopolitan*, December 13, 2018, https://www.cosmopolitan.com/uk/beauty-hair/makeup/a23643955/shane-dawson-jeffree-star-eyeshadow-palette/.

117. Mark Lugris, "Jeffree Star and Shane Dawson Are Working on a New Series," *The Talko*, February 25, 2019, https://www.thetalko.com/jeffree-star-shane-dawson-are-working-on-new-series/.

118. Alex Cosey and Jihee Junn, "Why the Shane Dawson and Jeffree Star YouTube Series Is a Big Deal," *The Spinoff*, November 23, 2019, https://thespinoff.co.nz/media/23-11-2019/why-the-shane-dawson-and-jeffree-star-youtube-series-is-a-big-deal/.

119. Paige Leskin, "The Frenzy Around YouTubers Jeffree Star and Shane Dawson's Makeup Collection Crashed the Website, and People are Freaking Out," *Business Insider*, November 1, 2019, https://www.businessinsider.com/youtube-jeffree-star-shane-dawson-cosmetics-makeup-palette-website-crash-2019-11?r=US&IR=T.

120. Paige Gawley, "Shane Dawson and Jeffree Star's 'Conspiracy' Collection Drops and Breaks the Internet," *Entertainment Tonight*, November 1, 2019, https://www.etonline.com/shane-dawson-and-jeffree-stars-conspiracy-collection-drops-and-breaks-the-internet-135489.

121. Julia Alexander, "Shane Dawson Could Use Jake Paul Doc to Address YouTube's Big Issue," *Polygon*, September 25, 2018, https://www.polygon.com/2018/9/25/17902866/shane-dawson-jake-paul-documentary-series-episode-1-david-dobrik-drama-vlog.

122. Stephanie Nicole, "Jeffree Star Beauty Killer Palette, Ice Cold Skin Frost and Brand Review," YouTube video, June 12, 2016, https://www.youtube.com/watch?v=N1qdgArqOSI.

123. Kat Blaque, "IS JEFFREE STAR RACIST?," YouTube video, July 29, 2016, https://www.youtube.com/watch?v=7bSE0avpj-A.

124. jeffreestar, "RACISM.," YouTube video, June 20, 2017, https://www.youtube.com/watch?v=Su6FeI7lHVg.

125. Alex Abad-Santos, "Laura Lee, Jeffree Star, and the Racism Scandal Upending the YouTube Beauty Community, Explained," *Vox*, August 31, 2018, https://www.vox.com/2018/8/28/17769996/laura-lee-jeffree-star-racism-subscriber-count.

126. jeffreestar, "RACISM."

127. Nicky Idika, "Jeffree Star Just Apologized for His Racist Past but the Internet Isn't Convinced," *Popbuzz*, June 21, 2017, https://www.popbuzz.com/internet/youtubers/jeffree-star-apology/.

128. Blaque, "IS JEFFREE STAR?"

129. Ibid.

130. Abad-Santos, "Laura Lee."

131. Chelsea Ritschel, "GIVENCHY CRITICISED FOR FOUNDATION LINE WITH LIMITED SHADE RANGE: 'THIS IS EMBARASSING,'" *The Independent*, February 22, 2019, https://www.independent.co.uk/life-style/givenchy-foundation-makeup-shades-new-color-diversity-dark-skin-a8793066.html.

132. Alex Peters, "Jeffree Star Dropped by Morphe After Years of Controversy," Dazed Beauty, July 11, 2020, https://www.dazeddigital.com/beauty/head/article/49794/1/jeffree-star-dropped-by-morphe-after-years-of-controversy.

133. Nicole, "Fenty Beauty."
134. "Top Beauty Influencers," *Forbes*, accessed March 25, 2019, https://www.forbes.com/top-influencers/beauty/#4f79004a3378.
135. Brianna Arps, "Rihanna Fans Are Accusing a Beauty Blogger of Copying Fenty Beauty's Foundation Line," *Insider*, October 4, 2017, https://www.thisisinsider.com/rihanna-fenty-beauty-huda-kattan-foundation-2017-10.
136. Ibid.
137. Ruqaya Izzidien, "Rihanna's Morroccon Spice Eyeshadow: Shades of Cheap Arab Tokenism," *The New Arab*, July 18, 2018, https://www.alaraby.co.uk/english/comment/2018/7/13/rihannas-moroccan-spice-eyeshadow-shades-of-cheap-arab-tokenism.
138. James O. Young, *Cultural Appropriation and the Arts* (Chichester: Wiley-Blackwell, 2010), 5.
139. Izzidien, "Rihanna's Morroccon."
140. "What is Orientalism?," Reclaiming Identity: Dismantling Arab Stereotypes, accessed March 25, 2019, http://arabstereotypes.org/why-stereotypes/what-orientalism.
141. Faima Baker, "Fenty Beauty Criticised for Not Using Models from Morocco for Moroccan Spice Line," *Metro*, July 27, 2018, https://metro.co.uk/2018/07/27/fenty-beauty-criticised-for-not-using-models-from-morocco-for-moroccan-spice-line-7764521/.
142. Sabrina Barr, "Rihanna's Fenty Beauty Apologises after 'Geisha Chic' Highlighter Sparks Controversy," *The Independent*, April 2, 2019, https://www.independent.co.uk/life-style/fashion/rihanna-fenty-beauty-geisha-chic-highlighter-makeup-remove-apology-a8850526.html.
143. Ibid.
144. Krissy Turner, "I've Been Wearing Fenty Beauty by Rihanna for Three Months, and Here's What I Think," *The Telegraph*, January 10, 2018, https://www.telegraph.co.uk/beauty/make-up/wore-fenty-beauty-rihanna-make-up-every-day-week-happened/.
145. Cheryl Wischhover, "The Fenty Effect Means Everyone Offers 40 Foundation Shades Now," *Racked*, May 30, 2018, https://www.racked.com/2018/5/30/17409524/fenty-effect-foundation-40-shades.
146. Sangeeta Singh-Kurtz, "How Rihanna Forced the Beauty Industry to Acknowledge a World Beyond the Rich and White," *Quartzy*, June 17, 2018, https://qz.com/quartzy/1304635/how-rihanna-forced-the-beauty-industry-to-acknowledge-a-world-beyond-the-rich-and-the-white/.
147. Ibid.
148. Ibid.
149. Kayla A. Greaves, "As Rihanna's Fenty Effect Sets New Standards, Why Do Some Brands Still Refuse to Create Wider Shade Ranges?," *Fashion Magazine*, October 2, 2018, https://fashionmagazine.com/beauty/fenty-effect-40-foundation-shades/.
150. Singh-Kurtz, "How Rihanna."
151. Greaves, "As Rihanna's Fenty."
152. Singh-Kurtz, "How Rihanna."
153. Ibid.
154. Nicola Dall'Asen, "Fenty Is Expanding the Pro Filt'r Foundation Range—Here Are All 10 New Shades," *Revelist*, January 3, 2019, https://www.revelist.com/beauty-news-/new-fenty-foundation-shades/14382.
155. Erica Steiner, "YouTuber Laura Lee Dropped from Every Major Sponsorship over Racist Tweet," *Blast*, August 22, 2018, https://theblast.com/laura-lee-dropped-partnerships-ulta-racist-tweet/.
156. Morgan Sung, "The Art of the YouTube Apology Video," *Mashable UK*, August 24, 2018, https://mashable.com/article/youtube-apology-video-laura-lee-gabriel-zamora-jeffree-star/?europe=true#hFo4DqNHnSqI.
157. Time Staff, "The 25 Best Inventions of 2017," *Time*, November 16, 2017, http://time.com/5023212/best-inventions-of-2017/.
158. Peck, "People Love."
159. Joely Walker, "The Age of Lip Fillers—Why We're so Obsessed with the Perfect Pout," *Elle*, July 10, 2018, https://www.elle.com/uk/beauty/body-and-physical-health/longform

/a39422/should-i-get-lip-fillers-lip-plumping-treatment/.

160. Devon Abelman, "Claudia Soare Responds to Anastasia Beverley Hills Subculture Palette Backlash," *Allure*, August 3, 2017, https://www.allure.com/story/anastasia-beverly-hills-subculture-palette-backlash.

161. Faima Baker, "Fenty Beauty Criticised for Not Using Models from Morocco for Moroccan Spice Line," *Metro*, July 27, 2018, https://metro.co.uk/2018/07/27/fenty-beauty-criticised-for-not-using-models-from-morocco-for-moroccan-spice-line-7764521/.

BIBLIOGRAPHY

Abad-Santos, Alex. "Laura Lee, Jeffree Star, and the Racism Scandal Upending the YouTube Beauty Community, Explained." *Vox*, August 31, 2018. https://www.vox.com/2018/8/28/17769996/laura-lee-jeffree-star-racism-subscriber-count

Abelman, Devon. "Claudia Soare Responds to Anastasia Beverley Hills Subculture Palette Backlash." *Allure*, August 3, 2017. https://www.allure.com/story/anastasia-beverly-hills-subculture-palette-backlash.

Adewunmi, Bim. "Kimberlé Crenshaw on Intersectionality: 'I Wanted to Come Up with an Everyday Metaphor that Anyone Could Use.'" *New Statesman,* April 2, 2014. http://www.newstatesman.com/lifestyle/2014/04/kimberl-crenshaw-intersectionality-i-wanted-come-everyday-metaphor-anyone-could.

Agafonov, Mikhael. "Ten Years Ago, 'Umbrella' Turned Rihanna into a Pop Icon." *Dazed*, March 29, 2017. http://www.dazeddigital.com/music/article/35332/1/rihanna-umbrella-10th-anniversary-retrospective.

Aina, Jackie. "Calling ALL Non-Black YouTubers! New Makeup Challenge!." YouTube video, July 26, 2016. https://www.youtube.com/watch?v=3wUc3srYfPI.

Alexander, Ella. "Rihanna Designs." *Vogue*, November 22, 2011. https://www.vogue.co.uk/gallery/rihanna-launches-armani-fashion-collection.

Alexander, Julia. "Shane Dawson Could Use Jake Paul Doc to Address YouTube's Big Issue." *Polygon*, September 25, 2018. https://www.polygon.com/2018/9/25/17902866/shane-dawson-jake-paul-documentary-series-episode-1-david-dobrik-drama-vlog.

Archambault, Alex. "Kat Von D Said She Won't Vaccinate Her Baby—And People Are so Outraged They're Boycotting Her Beauty Line." *Insider*, June 11, 2018. https://www.thisisinsider.com/kat-von-d-not-vaccinating-baby-doctor-says-bad-idea-2018-6.

Arps, Brianna. "Rihanna Fans are Accusing a Beauty Blogger of Copying Fenty Beauty's Foundation Line." *Insider*, October 4, 2017. https://www.thisisinsider.com/rihanna-fenty-beauty-huda-kattan-foundation-2017-10.

Augistin, Camille. "Rihanna's Fenty Beauty to Make Monetary Waves in Saudi Arabia." *Vibe*, April 7, 2018. https://www.vibe.com/2018/04/rihannas-fenty-beauty-launches-in-saudi-arabia.

Baker, Faima. "Fenty Beauty Criticised for Not Using Models from Morocco for Moroccan Spice Line." *Metro*, July 27, 2018. https://metro.co.uk/2018/07/27/fenty-beauty-criticised-for-not-using-models-from-morocco-for-moroccan-spice-line-7764521/.

BallerStatus. "Rihanna Teams Up with Stance for Sock Collection." Accessed March 25, 2019. https://www.ballerstatus.com/2015/07/15/rihanna-teams-up-with-stance-for-sock-collection/.

Barr, Sabrina. "Rihanna's Fenty Beauty Apologises after 'Geisha Chic' Highlighter Sparks Controversy." *The Independent*, April 2, 2019. https://www.independent.co.uk/life-style/fashion/rihanna-fenty-beauty-geisha-chic-highlighter-makeup-remove-apology-a8850526.html.

Bate, Ellie. "Kat Von D Denied Accusations She's a Nazi and an Anti-vaxxer after People Boycotted Her Makeup Line." *Buzzfeed*, March 18, 2019. https://www.buzzfeed.com/eleanorbate/kat-von-d-nazi-anti-vaxxer-accusations-video.

Blaque, Kat. "IS JEFFREE STAR RACIST?" YouTube video, July 29, 2016. https://www.youtube.com/watch?v=7bSE0avpj-A.

Boye, Grace (@n0bleprincess). "Thank You All for Your Support," Instagram photo, December 8, 2017. https://www.instagram.com/p/BcdI77rgXxd/?utm_source=ig_embed.

Bright, Patricia. "OK FENTY BEAUTY . . . YOU HAD TO GO THERE, REALLY? FIRST IMPRESSIONS!." YouTube video, September 9, 2017. https://www.youtube.com/watch?v=NZ-iP-Xxqss.

"Bye Ashy: How to Find Your Right Foundation Shade Using Undertones." Makeup for Melanin Girls. January 2, 2018. https://makeupformelaningirls.com/blogs/community/bye-ashy-how-to-find-your-right-foundation-shade-using-undertones.

Capon, Laura. "Update—A Shane Dawson x Jeffree Star Eyeshadow Palette is Actually Coming, According to Shane's Instagram." *Cosmopolitan*, December 13, 2018. https://www.cosmopolitan.com/uk/beauty-hair/makeup/a23643955/shane-dawson-jeffree-star-eyeshadow-palette/.

Capon, Laura. "The World's Most Pigmented Eyeshadow Palette is FINALLY Launching in the UK." *Cosmopolitan*, July 18, 2018. https://www.cosmopolitan.com/uk/beauty-hair/makeup/a22331747/juvias-place-eyeshadow-palette-uk/.

Cartner-Morley, Jess. "Rihanna: The Pop Star Who Became a Fashion Powerhouse." *The Guardian*, September 15, 2017. https://www.theguardian.com/fashion/2017/sep/15/rihanna-pop-star-fashion-powerhouse-beauty-brand.

Collins, Shawna. "'Dark Shades Don't Sell': Race, Gender, and Cosmetic Advertisements in the Mid-Twentieth Century United States." MA diss., McMaster University, 2018.

"The Company." Harvey Nichols. Accessed March 25, 2019. https://www.harveynichols.com/about/the-company/.

Connell, Alle. "Nyma Tang Tries the Darkest Shade in Makeup for an Important Reason." *Revelist*, July 14, 2017. http://www.revelist.com/bloggers/nyma-tang/8404/nyma-has-a-seriously-amazing-series-on-youtube-called-the-darkest-shade-where-she-tests-out-and-reviews-the-darkest-shade-of-makeup-that-a-brand-or-line-carries/3.

Cooper, Britney. "Intersectionality." *The Oxford Handbook of Feminist Theory*, edited by Lisa Disch and Mary Hawkesworth, 385–407. New York: Oxford University Press, 2016.

Cosey, Alex and Jihee Junn. "Why the Shane Dawson and Jeffree Star YouTube Series is a Big Deal." *The Spinoff*, November 23, 2019. https://thespinoff.co.nz/media/23-11-2019/why-the-shane-dawson-and-jeffree-star-youtube-series-is-a-big-deal/.

Crenshaw, Kimberlé. "Demarganializing the Intersection of Race and Sex: A Black Feminist Critique of Antidiscrimination Doctrine, Feminist Theory and Antiracist Politics." *University of Chicago Legal Forum,* no.1. (1989): 139–167.

Dafoe, Jessica. "Puma Sales Skyrocket Thanks to Kylie Jenner and Rihanna, Kylie Not Backing Down Despite Kanye's Competition." *Inquisitr*, April 30, 2016. https://www.inquisitr.com/3048389/puma-sales-sky-rocket-thanks-to-kylie-jenner-and-rihanna-kylie-not-backing-down-despite-kanyes-competition/#sGEc5imGk1dZLPpK.99.

Dall'Asen, Nicola. "Fenty Is Expanding the Pro Filt'r Foundation Range—Here Are All 10 New Shades." *Revelist*, January 3, 2019. https://www.revelist.com/beauty-news-/new-fenty-foundation-shades/14382.

Decker, Meghan. "This Albino Woman's Review on the Fenty Beauty Shade Range Is Going Viral." Refinery29, September 18, 2017. https://www.refinery29.com/amp/en-us/2017/09/172688/fenty-beauty-foundation-inclusive-tones-albino-photo.

Desmond-Harris, Jenée. "To Understand the Women's March on Washington, You Need to Understand Intersectional Feminism." *Vox,* January 21, 2017. https://www.vox.com/identities/2017/1/17/14267766/womens-march-on-washington-inauguration-trump-feminism-intersectionaltiy-race-class.

"Diamond Ball." Clara Lionel Foundation. Accessed 24 March, 2019. https://web.archive.org/web/20160419215626/http://claralionelfoundation.org/diamond-ball/.

Diaz, Thatiana. "KVD Vegan Beauty Says Its Name No Longer Stands for Kat Von D." Refinery29, January 28, 2020. https://www.refinery29.com/en-us/2020/01/9317417/kvd-vegan-beauty-brand-initials-meaning-rebranding.

"Fenty Beauty." Fenty Beauty. Accessed March 18, 2019. https://www.fentybeauty.com/about-fenty.

"Fenty Beauty FAQ's." Fenty Beauty. Accessed March 18, 2019. https://www.fentybeauty.com/faq.html.

"Fenty Beauty Shipping Information." Fenty Beauty. Accessed March 25, 2019. https://www.fentybeauty.com/shipping-info.html.

Fenty, Robyn Rihanna (@badgalriri). "This is @FentyBeauty. Head to a @sephora, #sephorainJCP or @harveynichols store to get an exclusive behind-the scenes look!." Instagram video, September 1, 2017. https://www.instagram.com/p/BYgX7EAjNF6/?utm_source=ig_embed.

"Fit Me Foundation." Maybelline. Accessed March 25, 2019. https://www.maybelline.com/face-makeup/foundation-makeup/fit-me-matte-poreless-foundation/fair-porcelain.

Friedman, Vanessa. "Puma Explains Its New Creative Director: Rihanna." *New York Times*, December 17, 2014. https://runway.blogs.nytimes.com/2014/12/17/puma-creative-director-rihanna/.

Gawley, Paige. "Shane Dawson and Jeffree Star's 'Conspiracy' Collection Drops and Breaks the Internet." *Entertainment Tonight,* November 1, 2019. https://www.etonline.com/shane-dawson-and-jeffree-stars-conspiracy-collection-drops-and-breaks-the-internet-135489.

Goldstein, Jessica M. "Rihanna is Marketing Her Makeup to Everyone—And It's Paying Off." *Think Progress*, September 14, 2017. https://thinkprogress.org/fenty-beauty-rihanna-caf1fe83a641/.

Greaves, Kayla A. "As Rihanna's Fenty Effect Sets New Standards, Why Do Some Brands Still Refuse to Create Wider Shade Ranges?." *Fashion Magazine*, October 2, 2018. https://fashionmagazine.com/beauty/fenty-effect-40-foundation-shades/.

Hargrove, Channing. "Rihanna's Fenty Line Brings Some Much Needed Inclusivity to the Luxury Space." Refinery29, 22 May, 2019. https://www.refinery29.com/en-gb/2019/05/233437/rihanna-fenty-fashion-line.

Idika, Nicky. "Jeffree Star Just Apologized for His Racist Past but the Internet Isn't Convinced." *Popbuzz*, June 21, 2017. https://www.popbuzz.com/internet/youtubers/jeffree-star-apology/.

"influencer." *Cambridge Dictionary*. Accessed December 22, 2019. https://dictionary.cambridge.org/dictionary/english/influencer.

Izzidien, Ruqaya. "Rihanna's Morroccon Spice Eyeshadow: Shades of Cheap Arab Tokenism." *The New Arab*, July 18, 2018. https://www.alaraby.co.uk/english/comment/2018/7/13/rihannas-moroccan-spice-eyeshadow-shades-of-cheap-arab-tokenism.

Jacques, Renee. "5 Surprising Things You Didn't Know about Anastasia Beverly Hills." *Allure*, December 29, 2015. https://www.allure.com/story/history-of-anastasia-beverly-hills.

Jeffreestar. "Getting Rid of $1,000,000 of Makeup w. Shane Dawson." YouTube video, March 8, 2019. https://www.youtube.com/watch?v=MbtesOrC5t4.

———. "Racism." YouTube video, June 20, 2017. https://www.youtube.com/watch?v=Su6FeI7lHVg.

"jeffree star," YouTube. Accessed March 18, 2019, https://www.youtube.com/user/jeffreestar.

Jones, Lora. "Veganism: Why Is It on the Up?" *BBC*, June 18, 2018. https://www.bbc.co.uk/news/business-44488051.

Jowett, Victoria. "One of These Makeup Looks Cost £500 More Than the Other—Can You Tell Which?" *Cosmopolitan*, July 11, 2017. https://www.cosmopolitan.com/uk/beauty-hair/a10282481/high-end-vs-cheap-makeup-review/.

Leskin, Paige. "The Frenzy Around YouTubers Jeffree Star and Shane Dawson's Makeup Collection Crashed the Website, and People are Freaking Out." *Business Insider*, November 1, 2019. https://www.businessinsider.com/youtube-jeffree-star-shane-dawson-cosmetics-makeup-palette-website-crash-2019-11?r=US&IR=T.

Li, Jason, Amber Thomas, and Divya Manian. "Beauty Brawl—How Inclusive are Beauty Brands Around the World?" *The Pudding*, June, 2018. https://pudding.cool/2018/06/makeup-shades/.

Low, Carver. "Rihanna Partners with Dior to Create Sunglass Collection." *HotNewHipHop*, May 25, 2016. https://www.hotnewhiphop.com/rihanna-partners-with-dior-to-create-sunglass-collection-news.21830.html.

Lugris, Mark. "Jeffree Star and Shane Dawson Are Working on a New Series," *The Talko*, February 25, 2019. https://www.thetalko.com/jeffree-star-shane-dawson-are-working-on-new-series/.

Lukatitis, Natalie. "This Challenge is Putting Unknown Beauty Brands on the Map." *Marie Claire*, October 16, 2017. https://www.marieclaire.co.uk/beauty/make-up/bomb-challenge-440479.

"MAC." Cruelty Free Kitty. Accessed March 18, 2019. https://www.chicagomanualofstyle.org/tools_citationguide/citation-guide-1.html.

MAC "Pro Longwear Nourishing Waterproof Foundation," M.A.C. Make Up For Ever (@makeupforeveroffical). "40 shades is nothing new to us—Since 2015, the #ultraHD foundation released 40 shades for everyone's unique skin tone understanding the difference between red and yellow undertones." Instagram photo, September 25, 2017.https://www.instagram.com/p/BZegQavhi5e/?utm_source=ig_embed.

"Make Up For Ever." Cruelty Free Kitty. Accessed March 18, 2019. https://www.crueltyfreekitty.com/brand/make-up-for-ever/.

"Make Up For Ever—Ultra HD Invisible Cover Foundation." Sephora. Accessed March 25, 2019. https://www.sephora.com/product/ultra-hd-invisible-cover-stick-foundation-P398775.

Mani, Sutheshna. "Rihanna's Charities Prove Rihanna's More than Just a Singer." *Entity*, March 13, 2017. https://www.entitymag.com/rihannas-charities-more-just-singer/.

"Maybelline." Cruelty Free Kitty. Accessed March 18, 2019. https://www.crueltyfreekitty.com/brand/maybelline/.

Mercer, Amira. "How Rihanna's Puma Creeper Became the Year's Must-Have Shoe." *Vanity Fair*, 25 May, 2016. https://www.vanityfair.com/style/2016/05/rihanna-puma-creeper-shoe.

"Mission/Vision of CLF." Clara Lionel Foundation. Accessed 24 March, 2019, https://web.archive.org/web/20160501082735/http://claralionelfoundation.org/about/mission-vision-of-clf/.

MTV. "Rihanna Launches Collection at LFW." MTV. Accessed 25 March, 2019. http://www.mtv.co.uk/rihanna/news/rihanna-launches-collection-at-lfw.

Murphy, Sam. "'Good Girl Gone Bad' Transformed Rihanna from a Popstar to an Icon." *Interns*, June 6, 2017. https://theinterns.net/2017/06/06/good-girl-gone-bad-transformed-rihanna-from-a-popstar-to-an-icon/.

Nicole, Stephanie. "Fenty Beauty Review (#2 Billion & 3) | Demo w/ Wear Check In | Swatches." YouTube video, September 22, 2017. https://www.youtube.com/watch?v=dLj95bKMb_c.

———. "Jeffree Star Beauty Killer Palette, Ice Cold Skin Frost and Brand Review." YouTube video, June 12, 2016. https://www.youtube.com/watch?v=N1qdgArqOSI.

Norvina. "NORVINA Presents: ABH Norvina Palette." YouTube video, July 28, 2018. https://www.youtube.com/watch?v=SD60paoggNo.

Peck, Patrice. "People Love What Rihanna's Makeup Company Did for a Woman Who Thought Her Lips Were 'Too Big' for Red Lipstick.'" *BuzzFeed*, December 4, 2017. https://www.buzzfeed.com/patricepeck/the-fenty-beauty-sisterhood-is-real?utm_term=.lb8O6x8jlj#.iy3qO4RZzZ.

Perry, Monica. "5 Ways to Avoid This Weird but Common Foundation Issue." *Allure*, April 5, 2016. https://www.allure.com/story/dark-skin-foundation-tips.

Peters, Alex. "Jeffree Star dropped by Morphe after years of controversy," *Dazed Beauty*, July 11, 2020, https://www.dazeddigital.com/beauty/head/article/49794/1/jeffree-star-dropped-by-morphe-after-years-of-controversy.

Petter, Olivia. "Prince Charles Names Rihanna a 'Global Style Icon' on Barbados Visit." *The Independent*, March 21, 2019. https://www.independent.co.uk/life-style/prince-charles-rihanna-barbados-visit-bajan-global-style-icon-a8831856.html.

Pham, Jason. "Rihanna Hits Back at Instagrammer Who Criticized How She Runs Fenty Beauty." *Stylecaster*, March 24, 2018. https://stylecaster.com/beauty/rihanna-fenty-beauty-clap-back/.

"PRO FILT'R." Fenty Beauty. Accessed March 25, 2019. https://www.fentybeauty.com/pro-filtr/soft-matte-longwear foundation/FB30006.html?dwvar_FB30006_color=FB0340.

Quinn, Cat. "Rihanna's Fenty Beauty Products Drop Today—And We Tried Them First." Refinery29, September 7, 2017. https://www.refinery29.com/en-us/2017/09/171310/rihanna-fenty-beauty-sephora-new-products-2017.

Reeder, Alyssa. "Anastasia Soare, Founder, Anastasia Beverly Hills." *Into the Gloss*, May 19, 2015. https://intothegloss.com/2015/06/anastasia-soare-founder-anastasia-beverly-hills/.

Reid, Shaheem. "Rihanna Loses Good Girl Image, Thanks to Jay-Z, Justin, Timberland, Ne-Yo." *MTV News*, May 1, 2007. http://www.mtv.com/news/1558496/rihanna-loses-good-girl-image-thanks-to-jay-z-justin-timbaland-ne-yo/.

"Rihanna Launches Fenty Beauty, a Global Makeup Brand, in 17 Countries." Cision PR Newswire. Accessed March 25, 2019. https://www.prnewswire.co.uk/news-releases/rihanna-launches-fenty-beauty-a-global-makeup-brand-in-17-countries-643185393.html.

"Rihanna named Humanitarian of Year." The Harvard Gazette. Accessed 25 March 2019. https://news.harvard.edu/gazette/story/2017/02/rihanna-named-humanitarian-of-year/.

Ritschel, Chelsea. "GIVENCHY CRITICISED FOR FOUNDATION LINE WITH LIMITED SHADE RANGE: 'THIS IS EMBARASSING.'" *The Independent*, February 22, 2019. https://www.independent.co.uk/life-style/givenchy-foundation-makeup-shades-new-color-diversity-dark-skin-a8793066.html.

Robertson, Krystal (@acondria). "@badgalriri #SlayedMyLife 2 Happy . . . what a wonderful day!!!! @fentybeauty #ThankYouAll." Instagram photo, 17 September, 2017. https://www.instagram.com/p/BZIPYk-gBF4/?utm_source=ig_embed&utm_campaign=embed_loading_state_control.

Rodulfo, Kristina. "For New Foundation Ranges, 'Fenty 40' Is the Magic Number." *Elle*, May 31, 2018. https://www.elle.com/beauty/makeup-skin-care/a20967710/makeup-companies-40-foundation-shades-fenty-beauty-influence/.

"shane." YouTube. Accessed March 18, 2019. https://www.youtube.com/user/shane.

Simmons, Shea. "Who Are the Models in the Fenty Beauty Video? The Internet Is Obsessed with the Campaign's Diverse Stars." *Bustle*, September 1, 2017. https://www.bustle.com/p/who-are-the-models-in-the-fenty-beauty-video-the-internet-is-obsessed-with-the-campaigns-diverse-stars-80510.

Singh-Kurtz, Sangeeta. "How Rihanna Forced the Beauty Industry to Acknowledge a World Beyond the Rich and White." *Quartzy*, June 17, 2018. https://qz.com/quartzy/1304635/how-rihanna-forced-the-beauty-industry-to-acknowledge-a-world-beyond-the-rich-and-the-white/.

Soare, Claudia Norvina (@norvina). "What can I say I absolutely love her so much RIVIERA is a getaway in a palette." Instagram photo, February 26, 2019. https://www.instagram.com/p/BuU31wch4Pw/.

Spencer, Tallie. "Rihanna Shows Up and Shows Out in Cheetah Print at Beyonce and Jay-Z's Oscars Afterparty." *Billboard*, February 25, 2019. https://www.billboard.com/articles/columns/hip-hop/8500082/rihanna-oscar-afterparty-beyonce-jayz-cheetah-dress.

"Statistics." The Vegan Society. Accessed March 18, 2019. https://www.vegansociety.com/news/media/statistics.

Steiner, Erica. "YouTuber Laura Lee Dropped from Every Major Sponsorship over Racist Tweet." *Blast*, August 22, 2018. https://theblast.com/laura-lee-dropped-partnerships-ulta-racist-tweet/.

Sung, Morgan. "The Art of the YouTube Apology Video." *Mashable UK*, August 24, 2018. https://mashable.com/article/youtube-apology-video-laura-lee-gabriel-zamora-jeffree-star/?europe=true#hFo4DqNHnSqI.

Symester, Chantelle. "Fenty Beauty Boots Store Locations that Will Stock Rihanna's Make Up Range from TODAY." *The Daily Mirror*, May 9, 2019. https://www.mirror.co.uk/3am/style/3am-fashion-celebrity-beauty/fenty-beauty-boots-store-locations-15019828.

Tang, Nyma. "Fenty Beauty Pro Filt'r Foundation Review|| Nyma Tang #thedarkestshade." YouTube video, 11 September, 2017. https://www.youtube.com/watch?v=hQbeB0YXLhs&t=1s.

Thekatvond. "I am NOT a Nazi. I am NOT Anti-vaxx." YouTube video, March 14, 2019. https://www.youtube.com/watch?v=pc1K_MXe1M4.

Thompson, Avery. "Rihanna Is the New Face of Dior: First Black Spokesperson for the Brand." *Hollywood Life*, March 14, 2015. https://hollywoodlife.com/2015/03/14/rihanna-dior-campaign-first-black-woman/.

Time Staff. "The 25 Best Inventions of 2017." *Time*, November 16, 2017. http://time.com/5023212/best-inventions-of-2017/.

"Top Beauty Influencers." *Forbes*. Accessed March 25, 2019. https://www.forbes.com/top-influencers/beauty/#4f79004a3378.

Turner, Krissy. "I've Been Wearing Fenty Beauty by Rihanna for Three Months, and Here's What I Think." *The Telegraph*, January 10, 2018. https://www.telegraph.co.uk/beauty/make-up/wore-fenty-beauty-rihanna-make-up-every-day-week-happened/.

Von D, Kat (@thekatvond). "So excited to finally announce that @jackiecruz will be the face [and eyes] of our new @katvondbeauty GO BIG OR GO HOME MASCARA!." Instagram photo, March 20, 2019. https://www.instagram.com/p/BvPMT1oFRYP/.

Vox. "How Beauty Brands Failed Women of Color." YouTube video, November 14, 2017. https://www.youtube.com/watch?v=v5e4gwDGrNk.

Walker, Joely. "The Age of Lip Fillers—Why We're so Obsessed with the Perfect Pout." *Elle*, July 10, 2018. https://www.elle.com/uk/beauty/body-and-physical-health/longform/a39422/should-i-get-lip-fillers-lip-plumping-treatment/.

Weatherford, Ashley. "Rihanna's Beauty Line Will Include 40 Foundation Shades." *The Cut*, September 5, 2017. https://www.thecut.com/2017/09/rihanna-fenty-beauty-40-foundation-shades-pro-filtr.html.

"Web 2.0." Techopedia. Accessed March 21, 2019. https://www.techopedia.com/definition/4922/web-20.

"What Is a YouTube Collaboration and How to Make It Work." Vlog Nation. Accessed March 25, 2019. https://www.vlognation.com/how-to-make-youtube-collab/.

"What is Orientalism?" Reclaiming Identity: Dismantling Arab Stereotypes. Accessed March 25, 2019, http://arabstereotypes.org/why-stereotypes/what-orientalism.

Willingham, AJ, and Andrea Diaz. "Netflix Has People (Serenely) Bulldozing Their Closets, and Thrift Stores are Riding the Wave." *CNN*, January 14, 2019. https://edition.cnn.com/2019/01/12/entertainment/marie-kondo-konmari-tidying-up-netflix-trnd/index.html.

Wilson, April. "Feminism and Activism in the 2017 Pepsi Advertisement: Can Anything Be Gained by Them Becoming a Staple of Popular Culture." MA diss., University of Hertfordshire, 2017.

Wischhover, Cheryl. "The Fenty Effect Means Everyone Offers 40 Foundation Shades Now." *Racked*, May 30, 2018. https://www.racked.com/2018/5/30/17409524/fenty-effect-foundation-40-shades.

Yotka, Steff. "Everything You Need to Know about Rihanna's Savage x Fenty Launch." *Vogue*, May 9, 2018. https://www.vogue.com/article/rihanna-savage-x-fenty-lingerie-launch-details .

Young, James O. *Cultural Appropriation and the Arts*. Chichester: Wiley-Blackwell, 2010.

Young, Sarah. "Rihanna Launches Size-Inclusive Savage x Fenty Valentine's Day Collection." *The Independent*, 9 January 2019. https://www.independent.co.uk/life-style/fashion/rihanna-savage-fenty-lingerie-underwear-valentines-day-lookbook-size-inclusive-a8719076.html.

Chapter Three

Microcelebrity, Class, and Participatory Entitlement

The Cases of Jaclyn Hill and Jeffree Star

Anna Barritt

With over 14.9 billion views of beauty-related content,[1] the YouTube beauty community (entailing makeup tutorials, product reviews, themed collaborations, etc.) is one of the most popular YouTube subcultures. It has not only emerged as digital space for sharing interests, but it has disrupted how the cosmetics industry produces, distributes, and markets its products as consumers turn to trusted YouTube influencers for information and advice rather than magazines. During the subculture's exponential growth, some video bloggers (vloggers) who have mastered the discourse of the beauty community have risen through the ranks of YouTube fame and fortune. Two such vloggers who boast millions of subscribers and their own lines of cosmetics or companies are Jaclyn Hill and Jeffree Star. Hill and Star have not only become household names within the beauty community but have also engaged in business ventures that extend their reach to material goods and marketing beyond YouTube. At the same time, they also represent a new era of beauty vloggers who are facing professional challenges as they grapple with the increasing commercialization of YouTube and resulting class tensions.

Of course, though Hill and Star embody the current state of the beauty community, many vloggers came before them. Michelle Phan, known as the "original" beauty vlogger, began a humble career on YouTube in 2007 with minimal resources and went on to build the cosmetics company Ipsy, now worth over $500 million.[2] Ipsy defines itself as a company set out "to democratize beauty, making it accessible and affordable for everyone and fearlessly representing individuality and inclusivity in an industry that was once the total opposite."[3] The theme of democratizing beauty permeates the community and manifests in the belief that anyone can create a channel and reach professional beauty vlogger success. However, as I will explain in this chapter, beauty vloggers' successes do not always follow a trajectory like Phan's, largely due to the competing interests of beauty community participants—whom I will refer to as fans—and corporate entities. Jaclyn Hill and Jeffree Star, who will be the focus of this chapter, are both well known for having started from the bottom in terms of financial resources and industry recognition and now enjoy career success and a wealthy upper-class position. However, fans' perceptions and acceptance of Hill and Star's success are varied and demonstrate the complexity of the increasing commercialization of YouTube's subcultures, specifically as it has manifested in microcelebrity practice and performed class position.

Understanding how beauty vloggers capitalize on the YouTube entrepreneurial ecosystem, and understanding the consequences of reaching that success, requires an analysis of the ways in which vloggers curate an online identity that attracts and sustains a fan base. By maintaining an online public persona intended to be consumed by a targeted digital fan base—a practice known as "microcelebrity"—vloggers construct online identities that are wholly dependent on fans' engagement. Unlike traditional celebrity, microcelebrity entails direct communication with fans and a sense of immediacy and availability. Microcelebrity practitioners, such as the YouTube vloggers discussed in this chapter, differ from mainstream celebrities in that identities are constructed *alongside* fans and those identities are expected to remain authentic, accessible, and relatable. Michelle Phan engaged in microcelebrity practice in its earlier iterations—specifically during the nascent stages of YouTube's partner program, which enabled popular vloggers to monetize channels. Though she documents some of her personal struggles as a YouTube star and her 2016 leave of absence in the video "Why I Left," overall, Phan's microcelebrity practice successfully carried her self-brand from YouTube fame to mainstream fortune. While Phan experienced her own obstacles, her microcelebrity career evaded many of the current complications of the beauty community, namely the oversaturation of beauty vloggers and corporate sponsorship. Now a mentor to other vloggers, Phan reported to *Racked* magazine that beauty gurus are facing unique challenges: "When I started there were probably fewer than five people [doing makeup videos], and now you probably have 50,000 or more globally."[4] The increasing commercialization of YouTube and fans' rejection of corporate influence has complicated the practice of microcelebrity, as we see in the examples of Jaclyn Hill and Jeffree Star and in fans' reactions to the vloggers' professional success and subsequent changing identities.

Specifically, fans notice the change in vloggers' online identities as they are related to socioeconomic status and class position. For Jaclyn Hill, many fans comment on her YouTube videos, celebrate her accomplishments, and praise her as an inspiration for "moving up" from her past class position. Other subscribers, however, lament Hill's changing class identity either as a loss of authenticity or as undeserved success. Contrarily, Jeffree Star, who crafts a more ostentatious online identity than Hill, receives more positive feedback for displays of a newly acquired class position in the form of praise for remaining authentic. This diverse range of fan reactions to vloggers' transcending class position via the YouTube ecosystem thus suggests that there is a complex relationship that ties together microcelebrity, class, and identity—which makes way for a phenomenon I call *participatory entitlement*. In this chapter, I study the most-viewed videos uploaded by Jaclyn Hill and Jeffree Star that document displays of class positions, fans' comments on these videos, and discussion threads from the subreddit[5] "BeautyGuruChatter" to analyze how commercialization has affected the practice of microcelebrity as well as fans' perception of class and identity within the beauty community.

MICROCELEBRITY, CLASS, AND YOUTUBE BEAUTY VLOGGERS

The success of YouTube, in general, is predicated on its function as a site of participatory culture—a coin termed by media theorist Henry Jenkins that describes a culture "in which fans and other consumers are invited to actively participate in the creation and circulation of new content."[6] The nascent stages of the social media platform allowed for digital subcultures to coalesce around shared interests and values, such as the beauty community. Michelle Phan is one such example of an early beauty vlogger who engaged in the participatory nature of the site and found professional success in business ventures first within and eventually outside of YouTube's boundaries. If Phan's Cinderella-like story seems to have helped her reach the top, what accounts for the differences in Jaclyn Hill and Jeffree Star's professional endeavors and fans' reactions to them? One explanation might lie in YouTube's growing pains in recent years, which seem to have changed its purpose and function as a participatory site—namely, the tension between public interests and commercial interests.[7] This tension is complicated by what Jean Burgess and Joshua Green describe as YouTube's "double function as both a 'top-down' platform for the distribution of popular culture and a 'bottom-up' platform for vernacular creativity."[8] Though this tension has always been present, as Burgess and Green argue that YouTube has never been completely free of commercialization, it has become more evident within the beauty community because of its ability to influence consumer buying trends.[9] I argue that the changing nature of microcelebrity and vloggers' ability to transcend class position through YouTube's ecosystem highlight these tensions and offer valuable insights for the future of YouTube and Web 2.0[10] at large.

Microcelebrity practice has increased alongside what Graeme Turner calls the "demotic turn," which is the increasing visibility of "ordinary people" establishing themselves as a consumable brand or form of media. First defined by Theresa Senft, microcelebrity is "the commitment to deploying and maintaining one's online identity as if it were a branded good, with the expectation that others do the same."[11] Since Senft's labeling of microcelebrity practice amid research on webcam culture in the early 2000s, scholars have expanded and complicated the term to account for changes in technology and brand culture. Senft herself has since considered the complicated role of identity for microcelebrity, specifically how the internet has shifted from a medium for research to a medium for socialization and creating and selling goods, which has subsequently changed how users identify themselves.[12] Catalyzed by the internet's own identity crisis, microcelebrity no longer exists solely as a practice intended to build community around a shared online identity; it has become a practice of self-branding that practitioners may exploit as an avenue to make money and thus transcend class position. Alice Marwick has further refined the term, emphasizing two of its key attributes: authenticity and strategic intimacy. According to Marwick, a sense of authenticity is what fans believe separates bloggers and vloggers (both microcelebrity practitioners) from mainstream celebrities.[13] Because microcelebrity practitioners employ strategic intimacy, fans perceive them as authentic and relatable. The perception of microcelebrities as authentic is further complicated, however, by late capitalism and the notion of class.

June Deery and Andrea Press have brought to the forefront the discussion of class as an object of scholarly inquiry, especially as it impacts and is impacted by media. They define class as "one's position within a social structure of unequal access to available resources (material, social, political)."[14] In past decades, class has not been theorized as frequently or as critically as other sites of identity construction, such as race, sexuality, ability, or gender; even more, when theorized, class is largely considered only in its relation to these other identifying categories. However, Deery and Press find that recent political events in the United States and United Kingdom, combined with the media's role in shaping and representing class, have spurred a renewed interest in class as an object of study. They argue that in addition to establishing stratifications for positions of class, scholars should consider how class operates, what effects it produces, and how class is perceived by outside observers.[15] These points of interrogation are especially relevant for analyzing the impact of class and microcelebrity within the beauty community—specifically, the outside observer's perspective of class as the participatory function of YouTube necessitates audience engagement and buy-in. A vlogger's performance of his or her class position not only shapes a viewer's perspective of and relatability to the vlogger, but also shapes the audience's perception of the class that she or he now represents.

METHODOLOGY

This chapter contributes to the conversation of YouTube's function as a site of participatory culture that is increasingly influenced by commercialization by looking at how class and microcelebrity have impacted communal identity within the beauty vlogger subculture, specifically as it is demonstrated in the microcelebrity practices and class positions performed by Jaclyn Hill and Jeffree Star. To do so, I look at the most-viewed YouTube videos of Hill and Star and analyze how they perform their class position through microcelebrity practices. In addition to being categorized as the vloggers' most popular uploads (having the most views),[16] videos were selected for analysis based on their adherence to tropes within the beauty community, namely the makeup tutorial (vlogger instructs viewers how to achieve certain looks), the "full face" video (vlogger applies makeup with themed products), and the closet/beauty room tour (vlogger displays his or her walk-in closet or the room devoted to filming YouTube videos). Though this chapter analyzes Hill and Star's microcelebrity practice and class performances in these videos, I primarily focus my analysis on the comment threads on these videos posted by fans in order to gauge how the beauty community makes sense of class position and the influence of commercialization. While the selected comments do not represent *all* fans' perceptions of Jaclyn Hill and Jeffree Star, I aggregate reactions expressed in the comments based on commonalities that I observe across comment threads. Selected comments are grouped into themes and are not chronological. Because comment sections are often monitored, I also analyze two discussion forums on the subreddit "BeautyGuruChatter" for a clearer picture of how fans perceive the vloggers' changing class position and fluctuating identity. By analyzing these cases, I hope to illuminate some of the consequences of the commercialization of YouTube and its impact on the beauty community specifically, which is further complicated by microcelebrity practices and fan perceptions of class positioning.

JACLYN HILL AND THE CLOSET TOUR

Jaclyn Hill joined YouTube in 2011 and has since accumulated over five million subscribers and upwards of 450 million views.[17] She has also developed product lines with the cosmetics companies BECCA and Morphe, including the Morphe Jaclyn Hill Eyeshadow Palette which is inscribed with this message: "This palette is dedicated to all my loving subscribers XO Jaclyn." As evidenced by this dedication, Hill's specific microcelebrity practice has always maintained a sense of strategic intimacy with her subscriber fan base, such as asking for feedback for content they want to see from her and thanking subscribers for their continued support. Since microcelebrities are expected to share personal information with their fan base, openness and intimacy are required for fans to remain engaged.[18] Building on Marwick's emphasis on strategic intimacy as a variable of microcelebrity, Tobias Raun argues that as part of microcelebrity, intimacy serves as a form of a YouTuber's affective labor. This affective labor is an integral component of fans' perceptions of the YouTuber's authenticity, and "when intimacy is perceived as an essential part of the attraction of micro-celebrities, intimacy also becomes a form of cultural, social and economic capital."[19] Thus, as a microcelebrity practitioner, Jaclyn Hill frequently employs strategic intimacy not only to appear authentic and relatable to her audience but to give fans what they ask for—to commodify herself. One example of Hill's use of strategic intimacy is the 2018 "Closet Tour" video.

While a subscriber fan base is evidence enough that a YouTuber has reached internet fame and fortune, a specific trope within the beauty community that signifies success is the beauty-room tour or closet tour. Jaclyn Hill's closet tour is one of Hill's most popular uploads with over five million views. It is also emblematic of Hill's self-presentation of her success as a vlogger—and her subsequent wealth and new class position—and the beauty community's perception of that success. I will first discuss how Hill engages in strategic intimacy in this upload, which we see in the following excerpt of the formal introduction to the video: "Welcome back to my channel! I am so excited to film this video—also a little bit nervous but that's okay I'm gonna get over it. At this time, this is the most requested video on my channel, which is my closet tour. Without further ado, let's just get started." In this quote, Hill reveals both her feelings of discomfort about displaying a personal, behind-the-scenes picture of her life—the kind of openness and transparency that Marwick frames as necessary microcelebrity practice—and her attunement to the demands of her fan base by uploading requested content, thus performing affective labor and reinforcing her online identity as a form of capital.

Hill further employs strategic intimacy when discussing a pair of expensive shoes that she was gifted from the company Morphe after her recent product line launch: "This shoe here is one of the most special pairs in my closet. . . . They're so beautiful I felt like Cinderella . . . I'm gonna be honest I loved them so much that I came home and I bought my bitch-ass the same pair in rose gold because you know what? I felt like I deserved it so I did it." In this quote, Hill's transparency in her discussion of the luxury items in her closet further illustrates the use of strategic intimacy that she displays to her fan base, which is usually veiled in a sense of sarcasm about her "bougie" lifestyle.[20] When Hill does discuss her affinity for expensive items, she often qualifies her preferences with terms such as "my bitch-ass" as a form of self-deprecation or humor, a discursive trope that long-term subscribers are usually familiar with. Hill's blending of self-deprecating humor with a more serious display of her upper-class position resembles a larger trope within the beauty community that Aditi Bhatia calls "interdiscursive performance," which includes "colloquial talk to curate an authentic and real self; jargon and formal instructional talk to curate an expert self; and promotional talk to brand their YouTuber self in the construction of identity online."[21] Many of Hill's makeup tutorials and product reviews display this interdiscursive performance as she interchanges informal humor about her personal life with industry-specific jargon about cosmetics products, especially ones she has helped develop. In this scenario, though, Hill's interplay of self-deprecating humor and more serious discussion of luxury shoes, clothes, and accessories aligns with her regular microcelebrity practice. Hill also emphasizes her brand of sarcasm and self-deprecation by filming a satirical intro and outro to the closet tour. While seemingly overtly sarcastic, the intro and outro appear to be received positively only by her long-term subscribers who are more familiar with her discursive practices.

Feigning a diva-esque attitude and dressed in a bathrobe with a butler serving her champagne, Hill begins the closet tour video with this narration before beginning the more formal introduction: "Hey guys. I hope that you just enjoyed that small little tidbit of what it's like to live my everyday life. I just wake up to puppies and champagne and diamonds and there's no hard work ever involved in what I do. No seriously. Thank you so much for joining me today." By indicating that the introduction is not serious, Hill satirizes the image of her life as never-ending luxury devoid of all hard work, an image that many users express to believe as truth. This satirical component of the closet tour upload, and the larger perception of Hill's class position, in general, leads to three primary reactions to the closet tour expressed in the comment section of the video. First, as we see in the following comments, fans regard Hill as a hard worker who *earned* her success and serves as an inspirational figure for fans. Fans also express an understanding of the satirical intro and outro:

> Comment 1: This is the GOALS. To have worked so hard to own all of these beautiful items, and yet still be so humble. I can confidently say that I KNOW that if someone came and took all of Jaclyn Hill's belongings from her, she wouldn't give a damn. Yes, she loves her clothes and shoes and sparkle. But I know for a fact that material things is not #1 on her

> priority list. Jaclyn if you're reading this, I love YOU. You are absolutely wonderful. I want to be just like you someday

> Comment 2: this is the girl who used to skip lunches just because she didn't have enough money . . . look where she is right now. OmyGod Jaclyn you're such an inspiration! I love the endiinggg

> Comment 3: For those who don't understand the intro or outro: it's satire. Jaclyn has always been nervous about filming/posting a video like this because of the backlash it might receive. Just remember that growing up she didn't have a lot of money. Like the stories she said when she worked at Mac, she was sleeping in her car and sometimes couldn't even afford to eat. She's worked really hard for her money. She has a lot of material things but she's still humble inside. Just take this into consideration.

As demonstrated in these comments, fans who celebrate Hill's professional success—success that is illustrated by her ability to purchase luxury items—tend to consider themselves insiders who are not only familiar with Hill's sarcasm but are also able to recall her early YouTube videos in which Hill expressed financial hardship. Because of this apparent insider knowledge, fans express a nuanced understanding of how Hill has been able to transcend her class position, as well as a belief that she *deserves* the resulting professional and financial success. For these fans, Hill's identity has not necessarily changed, as they believe she has retained her humility and work ethic even if she is now wealthy. While her *class position* has changed, fans who claim to know her best believe that her *identity* has not.

Another set of fans situates, Hill's display of her new class position as over the top and her professional success as undeserved:

> Comment 4: Honest feedback? I enjoy your tutorials but you try way too hard when it comes to anything else. I understand you've put your hard work in to get where you are but this is so unattractive. Let's be honest, you're bragging and loving every minute of it. You know what is attractive? Successful women who stay humble after they make it. Seems to me you care way too much about material possession, but what do I know?

> Comment 5: It's disgusting. Too many things. Too many poor people who have nothing. I hate Communism but when a person is mega rich, they should just open their hearts and give. Maybe she does give, I don't know . . . this is just over the top.

> Comment 6: every amount of respect i had for u is no longer existent girl. i can guarantee i work harder than u for minimum wage . . . and i'm blessed every month to pay my bills.

In these comments, fans primarily express a sense of disapproval of Hill's microcelebrity practices, especially the display of her material possessions. Comment 4 acknowledges that Hill does work hard but that her display of her wealth is unnecessary, whereas comment 6 illuminates the belief that Hill does *not* work hard and therefore does *not* deserve her wealth. What is missing from these comments is a reference to Hill's earlier videos and/or earlier perceived online identities, suggesting that commenters who remark on Hill's microcelebrity practice on this particular video with this negative reaction have not followed her channel for a long period of time. Comment 5 acknowledges that this user does not know for sure if Hill "gives back," to which other fans quickly respond that Hill does provide elaborate giveaways for her fans during the holidays. Comment 5 also admits that the fan is not intimately familiar with Hill as a microcelebrity and is not in tune with her deployments of strategic intimacy. This gap in fan knowledge poses the question: Do all beauty community participants qualify as Hill's targeted fan base and intended co-constructors of her microcelebrity practice? These fans appear to be assessing Hill's worthiness of success based on her perceived identity within one isolated video rather than as a changing identity over time. Though this adverse reaction to the closet tour suggests a tension between the upper-class position of Hill and the assumed lower-class position of these fans, a third reaction emerges from the closet-tour comment section.

A third group of fans lament what they judge to be the loss of Hill's authenticity. Considering that authenticity is a key component of microcelebrity practice, according to Alice Marwick, a loss of authenticity directly impacts a vlogger's success and engagement with his or her targeted fan base:

> Comment 7: Remember when Jaclyn Hill said something similar to: I'll never do a closet tour, I'm not that kind of girl—touch hypocritical, you think? Money changes everything
>
> Comment 8: I thought you said you would never do a closet tour cause you don't like being ostentatious? You just dragged yourself down trying to talk bad about others.

From these comments, we see users who display a working knowledge of Hill's earlier videos, like the first grouping of fan reactions, specifically regarding Hill's past declaration of her distaste of the closet-tour trope within the beauty community. Though Hill indicates that she was nervous to film a closet tour, as explained in the formal introduction to the video, she chose to film the video in order to fulfill fans' requests—thus engaging in strategic intimacy. However, comment 7 and comment 8 exemplify a subset of fans who find this action to be a betrayal of Hill's identity as a vlogger who does not adhere to such tropes, a betrayal that comment 7 attributes to wealth—or, in other words, to her new class position. As demonstrated in these three groupings, fan reactions to Hill's performance of class position, linked to her specific microcelebrity practice, varies widely. These reactions depend on how fans perceive Hill's online identity, largely influenced by how intimately and for how long the fan has followed the vlogger. In addition to these three primary reactions, two additional themes seem to influence fans who exhibit a long-term relationship with Hill's microcelebrity practice, namely a sense of nostalgia and a sense of loyalty as a "true subscriber."

JACLYN HILL, NOSTALGIA, AND LOYALTY

Jaclyn Hill's most popular video at the time this analysis was conducted is "Smokey Cat Eye Tutorial," which was posted in 2012 and has since been viewed over fifteen million times. On the surface, the most obvious difference between this makeup tutorial and the 2018 closet tour is the setting in which each is filmed and the filming quality itself. In this video, Hill is sitting in a dimly lit room with a TV in the background and a rack of clothes hanging to the side. The camera quality also appears grainier. In the closet tour—though a different genre of video—the closet is bright, organized, and appears to be filmed by a professional videographer. Though one of Hill's earliest videos, current fans still view the 2012 makeup tutorial and leave comments, which generally fall into two themes that help to clarify the varied reactions expressed in the closet-tour comment section: nostalgia and loyalty. As seen in the following comments, fans long for the perceived past identity of the Jaclyn Hill microcelebrity of 2012:

> Comment 9: I miss this Jaclyn . . . she was genuine, funny, fun to watch. Now it's just . . . money, money, money.
>
> Comment 10: What happened to THIS Jaclyn?!?!
>
> Comment 11: I miss these types of tutorials :/
>
> Comment 12: Uh it's so nice not to hear her say "coupon code" in her video

These comments, all posted in 2017 and 2018, suggest that fans who have followed Jaclyn since her career beginnings do not see her past identity represented in her current identity. Comment 9 attributes this dissonance to money, which is representative of the influence of commercialization on class position. In 2012, Hill's microcelebrity practice seems to have entailed a public persona that focused more on the application of makeup than on reviews of makeup products, which many users now associate with money and commercialization. These fans' musings on the "old Jaclyn" evokes a sense of nostalgia rather than disapproval, like that expressed from fans who accused Hill's closet tour video of shallow materialism. Will Kurlinkus defines notalgia as "pride and longing for lost or threatened personally or culturally experienced pasts."[22] For these fans, their nostalgia resides in pride and longing for a more personable and "authentic" Jaclyn Hill identity, unaffected by commercialization. Fans acknowledge that Hill's online identity has, in fact, changed, and, as comment 9 implies, it has changed due to her new class position. However, the second theme of loyalty that emerges from the current-day comments on the 2012 tutorial video complicates fans' perception of Hill's online identity.

On the same tutorial, fans who claim loyalty to Jaclyn Hill, regardless of her commercial ties, post comments such as the following:

> Comment 13: Jaclyn gurlll your TRUE fans are always happy with what you do! You could do 50 straight videos of morphe products and I can promise you that I would never be mad! I can't believe people have the audacity to complain when you are taking time out of your day to try to please us. . . . Anyways you're beautiful and inspire me and so many others in a million ways! Keep doing you boo!

> Comment 14: this video is 3 years old and Jaclyn hasn't changed one bit! Only thing that has is her setup, so improved, so proud to see her have made it so far

> Comment 15: Jaclyn Hill from 2012 to Jaclyn Hill 2016. This video shows how young and talented she is to where she is now! I love going through older videos

As demonstrated in these comments, some fans who have engaged with Hill's microcelebrity practices from the beginning of her YouTube career do not appear to feel betrayed by Hill's fluctuating online identity—or, fans do not perceive Hill's identity to have changed at all. As comment 13 suggests, fans who celebrate Hill's success, whether it is related to commercialization or not, are "true" subscribers, perhaps subscribers who are in opposition to fans who watch Hill's videos only occasionally. The tension between fans who identify as "true subscribers" who celebrate her success and fans who believe that Hill's identity has been adversely affected by commercialization is further explained in the "BeautyGuruChatter" subreddit discussion forum in response to the following question about Jaclyn Hill:

> Discussion question 1: Over the last couple of months there has been a huge shift in this sub's views and opinions on Jaclyn. Admittedly I am not

> a fan, but just a few months ago I would get downvoted for making comments that are now made on almost every post about her recently. I'm genuinely curious as to what caused the shift. Is it all the Morphe hawking? Is it just her?

Many Reddit users reference rumored events or conversations circulating within other social media platforms about Hill's business dealings and her recent divorce from Jon Hill. The following response, however, demonstrates a common theme among this subreddit and several other YouTube comment sections:

> Discussion response 1: Her talking so much about being on food stamps when they were younger, and then turning around and claiming that a high schooler can afford a $60 foundation or claiming that her Nordstrom back to school look is affordable. You'd think if she did used to be on food stamps, she'd retain some idea of what financial struggle truly means.

This Reddit user echoes a theory that Jung Eun Lee and Brandi Watkins discuss called "social comparison theory." They argue that "in the luxury brand context, through upward social comparison, viewers perceive higher value for luxury brands after watching the vlog, which, increases the desire to purchase luxury products."[23] Though Lee and Watkins situate this phenomenon as a marketing tool for small luxury brands, its manifestation within this context causes a rift for Jaclyn Hill's microcelebrity practice. The above discussion response embodies one of the primary causes I find for fans' negative reactions that gives rise to feelings of longing or betrayal and the loss of Hill's authenticity: Hill builds her *ethos* by relying on past struggles within her former class position while failing to relate persuasively to current fans who may now occupy that same class position. In this specific scenario, the Reddit user notes Jaclyn Hill's promotion of luxury items, which may entice a viewer to want to buy the item. However, the promotion of luxury items creates distance between her class position and viewers' class positions by referencing products that many fans would not be able to afford. By drawing on the *ethos* of class hardship without performing class hardship, Hill causes a rupture between her online identity and her fans, thus impacting Hill's microcelebrity practice.

The tension between Hill's class position and many beauty community participants' class positions is further aggravated by a phenomenon that I call participatory entitlement: fans' belief that they are, in part, responsible for a microcelebrity's professional success. I argue that participatory entitlement can engender either positive or negative reactions to a microcelebrity's success, depending on how the fan perceives his or her part in supporting the vlogger. For example, the comments in which fans believe that Jaclyn Hill's identity has not changed and that she serves as an inspiration demonstrate a *positive* experience of participatory entitlement. This experience leads them to share in her success and her ascension to an upper-class position, which further leads them to believe that they have helped her reach that class position and that they could one day do the same. Contrarily, the comments in which fans believe Hill's achievements are undeserved or that her identity has changed for the worse demonstrate a *negative* experience of participatory entitlement. This experience leaves them feeling either betrayed by her change in identity or unappreciated because their own work in helping Hill build her brand is not recognized—loyalty and recognition that they feel they are owed.

The tension of negative reactions arising from participatory entitlement is due largely to the perpetuation of the belief that YouTube still functions purely as a site of participatory culture. Jeanne Morreale argues that faith in YouTube's function as a democratic site of participatory culture perpetuates the myth that hard work can allow for *anyone*—even amateurs—to reach fame and fortune. The problem with this myth, Morreale finds, is that "few of those who post content on YouTube are able to make a living, and real wealth remains concentrated elsewhere."[24] Fans who experience participatory entitlement, either negatively or positively, exemplify the continued belief of this myth as demonstrated in the picture of Jaclyn Hill as either (1) evidence of how one can transcend class position via YouTube or as (2) a traitor to the perceived democratic nature of YouTube by prioritizing commercial interests over participants' interests. As Morreale concludes, though, real wealth exists outside YouTube—as demonstrated in the introductory example of Michelle Phan who phased out her beauty vlogger channel and moved to more traditional commercial avenues. Why, then, does Jaclyn Hill appear to receive more negative feedback for her own attempts at branching out to commercialized endeavors?[25]

Michelle Phan's business empire generates significantly more revenue than her original beauty vlogger channel, and Stuart Cunningham and David Craig find that "Phan has gone beyond relating to and managing her community and she has consistently mentored others into the business."[26] Since real wealth comes only tangentially from YouTube, Phan diversified her professional endeavors and transitioned out of YouTube professionalism and to the more traditional beauty industry—thus averting the class tensions that Jaclyn Hill is currently experiencing. Phan's lingering presence within the YouTube beauty community projects an identity of "giving back" as indicated by other beauty vloggers, such as Zoella or Bethany Mota, who acknowledge the opportunities that Phan has made for them.[27] Since Jaclyn Hill still appears to be "taking in" money from YouTube, as fans indicate she promotes the brand Morphe in her videos ad nauseam, fans react more negatively toward

Hill, illustrating a negative experience of participatory entitlement due to the feeling of helping Hill succeed without being compensated. Anne Jerslev finds that in the case of fellow beauty vlogger Zoella, a vlogger's attempts to seek either corporate sponsorship or mainstream celebrity can cause adverse reactions from fans. In Jerslev's study, she reports that "when Zoella was accused of diminishing the trustworthiness and authenticity on which she had branded herself on YouTube, she immediately scaled down the temporality of plenty that was part of her brand."[28] In the case of Zoella, much like Phan, a close attention to an established brand of microcelebrity determines if and how a vlogger can successfully expand his or her career outside of a traditional YouTube channel. The case of Jaclyn Hill exemplifies some of the negative consequences of commercialization due to fans' sense of participatory entitlement. The case of Jeffree Star, however, serves as another example of how commercialization of YouTube impacts fans' perception of identity and class position, although with a different experience of participatory entitlement.

JEFFREE STAR AND PARTICIPATORY ENTITLEMENT

If numbers are the primary indicator of success, Jeffree Star is arguably more successful than Jaclyn Hill. Boasting over eleven million YouTube subscribers and his own company—Jeffree Star Cosmetics—Star has surpassed Jaclyn Hill in terms of financial gain and industry influence. Like Hill, Star also came from a lower-socioeconomic status and often speaks of incredible hardship, abuse, and trauma during his upbringing. Star also overtly preferences high-end, expensive cosmetics, displays his very expensive cars, and plugs his own cosmetics company in videos without qualifying phrases and with less self-deprecating humor than Jaclyn Hill. However, fans' reactions to Star's luxury image reveals a less negative opinion than that of Jaclyn Hill. If Jeffree Star flaunts a more overt upper-class position than Jaclyn Hill, why do fans react more positively? I argue that the primary difference between fans' perceptions of Hill and Star, other than sexuality and gender, lies in fans' sense of participatory entitlement for the vloggers' wealth and ability to transcend class position.[29]

As of 2019, Star's most popular upload is the 2018 video "Full Face of Brands That Hate Me," with over twenty million views. In this video, having been highly requested much like Jaclyn Hill's closet tour, Star applies makeup products from companies he no longer likes or has never liked, providing candid commentary of his personal opinions and events that transpired between him and these companies. In the introduction, Star acknowledges his subscribers' requests—thus practicing microcelebrity—and also reminds viewers of his upper-class position as seen in the following extract: "I know

I've never done a beauty room tour, which will come later this year—I think I promise I hope—but I have like three beauty rooms, okay?" Within this microcelebrity practice, Star adheres to his online identity as a wealthy vlogger who enjoys a luxurious lifestyle—including having three separate rooms devoted to makeup products and filming YouTube videos. Star flaunts his class position, and fans react mostly positively, as seen in the following comments on "Full Face of Brands That Hate Me," in which fans praise Star for his authenticity:[30]

> Comment 16: I adore your brand and your honesty about products!! Thank you for being so fantastic at product reviews
>
> Comment 17: It is great how unapologetic you are about how you feel . . . with everything being so PC and sensitive lately . . . this is refreshing . . . I have a new respect for you <3
>
> Comment 18: Only Jeffree has the guts and audacity to make a video like this! Love you babe xx

Openness and transparency, which Alice Marwick associates with successful microcelebrity practice, appear, in this video, to be Star's strongest microcelebrity strategy. In this case, fans perceive Star to be an authentic beauty vlogger because he is honest and unapologetic, suggesting that vloggers who are less transparent about either their personal feelings and experiences or about their relationships with brands are, therefore, inauthentic. Fans' perceptions of Star's authenticity is further exemplified in a multi-part series featuring Jeffree Star but hosted and uploaded by fellow YouTuber Shane Dawson.[31]

In "The Secret World of Jeffree Star," with Star's permission and participation, Shane Dawson exposes many never-before-seen parts of Star's life, such as his several businesses and commercial warehouses that run successfully outside of YouTube. Because Star has not filmed a closet tour or beauty-room tour, as Star expresses in the video "Full Face of Brands That Hate Me," this series serves as the best example of Star's most overt display of class position due to Shane Dawson's filming of the interior of Star's California mansion and expansive warehouses. Like Jaclyn Hill's closet tour, many fans responded to this display of class position as an inspiration, but, interestingly, many fans comment on their perception of Star as humble. Despite Star's ostentatious displays of class position, fans perceive him as down to earth:

> Comment 19: jeffree is so rich yet so humble . . . i love him

> Comment 20: I've never been in to make-up or fashion or anything, but I can appreciate when a celebrity is actually pretty nice and chill and funny. Jeffery Star is known for being totally over the top, but from what little I've seen of him, he seems like a guy who's just being himself and is lucky enough to be able to make so much bank off of that.

As indicated in comment 19, fans do not tend to perceive Star's success as undeserved, unlike the common perception of Jaclyn Hill's success as undeserved even though Hill's wealth is considerably less than Star's. This particular fan regards Star's success as *lucky*. I argue that fans react more positively to Star's online identity and authenticity largely because of how they perceive the way Star came to his wealth, which is not directly or exclusively from YouTube. As Shane Dawson exposes, most of Star's wealth comes from business ventures not related to the beauty industry. As a result, fans do not negatively experience participatory entitlement, as they do not feel responsible for creating his wealth and aiding him in transcending his former lower-class position. This sentiment is echoed in the BeautyGuruChatter discussion forum about Jeffree Star entitled "Jeffree Star stans—why do you love him so? (a genuine question)":

> Discussion question 2: Before anyone gets super defensive and irrational, please let me explain: of all people, I am someone who understands the beauty of second—nay third, or even fourth—chances and I realized today that I've made a sweeping statement about my hatred for this person whom I've 1 never met and 2 haven't followed recently, let alone from the beginning or anywhere in between, and 3 haven't researched at all. I would honestly like to hear from you, people who accept his past as genuinely in the past,[32] and why you feel he is deserving of your stanship.[33] I am completely open-minded. I don't want to be someone who makes decisions like who to hate based on a few facts that I am not even fully researched on.

Though this discussion question is referencing fans' ability to forgive Star for past controversies on YouTube and other social media platforms, many Reddit users' responses to this discussion forum reference Star's class position, such as in the following response:

> Discussion response 2: Since he's so rich money really isn't a concern for him when it comes to youtube as I imagine he only does it for fun and as a hobby while running all of his other businesses on the side. Sort of like those housewives with rich husbands who start up their own small little businesses like a clothing store just for funsies. Because of this, he doesn't need to cherry pick positives and sometimes lie to stay on PR lists

> like every other beauty guru and instead delivers the truth, and also doesn't need to be fake with anyone else because he has everything he wants so he wouldn't have anything to gain from being fake-nice and making friends to climb the social ladder.

Despite the clear distance between Star's class position and that of most beauty community participants, fans regard Star as authentic, primarily because he does not *need* YouTube to sustain his career, thus precluding fans from feeling responsible for his success. Like Michelle Phan, Star finds wealth through mainstream commercialization rather than primarily through a YouTube channel—which results in more positive fan perceptions of Star's newly acquired class position.

CONCLUSION

This chapter has analyzed the cases of Jeffree Star and Jaclyn Hill to understand how the commercialization of YouTube has impacted microcelebrity strategies and class position within the beauty community, both in how vloggers perform microcelebrity and in how beauty community participants perceive vloggers' identities. While many variables influence beauty community participants' perceptions of vloggers' transitioning through social classes, I have argued that the primary difference between the cases of Jeffree Star and Jaclyn Hill lies in fans' sense of their own involvement in and responsibility for vloggers' success, wealth, and class positioning—a phenomenon I call participatory entitlement. Because Jeffree Star does not appear to depend on YouTube as heavily for his professional success—thus precluding fans from negatively experiencing participatory entitlement—fans tend to perceive his microcelebrity practices and identity as authentic despite the distance between Star's class position and his fans' class positions. Because Jaclyn Hill built her career primarily through YouTube alongside her long-term fans, and is now pursuing commercial interests, fans tend to react negatively toward her microcelebrity practices—operating under the belief that either Hill's identity has changed due to her class position or that Hill's display of her upper-class position is undeserved or exploitative. As commercialization continues to infiltrate YouTube, thus slowly disintegrating the participatory culture of the social media platform, further research is needed to better understand how this phenomenon is changing the nature of microcelebrity and thus impacting participants' perception of online identity and class position.

NOTES

1. "Beauty on YouTube," Pixability, accessed November 26, 2018, https://www.pixability.com/industry-insights/beauty-youtube-2015/.
2. Natalia Robehmed. "How Michelle Phan Built a $500 Million Company," *Forbes*, October 5, 2015, https://www.forbes.com/sites/natalierobehmed/2015/10/05/how-michelle-phan-built-a-500-million-company/#5c67d7b8c4a2.
3. "About Us," Ipsy, accessed December 8, 2018, https://www.ipsy.com/about.
4. Cheryl Wischover, "The Rebirth of YouTube Beauty Pioneer Michelle Phan," *Racked*, April 10, 2017, https://www.racked.com/2017/4/10/15185246/michelle-phan-giving-up-youtube-em-cosmetics.
5. A subreddit is an online community devoted to a niche topic of interest that is hosted by the social media platform Reddit.
6. Henry Jenkins, *Convergence Culture: Where Old and New Media Collide* (New York: New York University Press, 2013), 290.
7. Jean Burgess and Joshua Green, *YouTube: Online Video and Participatory Culture* (Cambridge: Polity Press, 2009), vii.
8. Burgess and Green, *YouTube*, 6.
9. Burgess and Green, *YouTube*, 90.
10. First introduced by Tim O'Reilly, Web 2.0 refers to the internet as a digital space that emphasizes participatory culture, user-generated content, and a "reorganization of the relations between producers and their audiences in a maturing Internet market" (Jenkins et al. 49).
11. Theresa M. Senft, "Microcelebrity and the Branded Self," in *A Companion to New Media Dynamics*, eds. John Hartley, Jean Burgess, and Axel Bruns (West Sussex: Wiley-Blackwell, 2013), 346.
12. Senft, "Microcelebrity," 349.
13. Alice Marwick, "You May Know Me from YouTube: (Micro)-Celebrity in Social Media," in *A Companion to Celebrity*, eds. P. David Marshall and Sean Redmond (West Sussex: Wiley-Blackwell, 2015), 16.
14. June Deery and Andrea Press, "Introduction: Studying Media and Class," in *Media and Class, TV, Film, and Digital Culture*, eds. June Deery and Andrea Press (New York: Routledge, 2017), 3.
15. Deery and Press, "Introduction," 3–5.
16. Videos were selected by their total number of views in the spring of 2019.
17. As of spring 2019.
18. Alice Marwick, *Status Update: Celebrity, Publicity, and Branding in the Social Media Age* (New Haven: Yale University Press, 2013), 117.
19. Tobias Raun, Jane Arthurs, Sophia Drakopoulou, and Alessandro Gandini, "Capitalizing Intimacy: New Subcultural Forms of Micro-celebrity Strategies and Affective Labour on YouTube," *Convergence: The International Journal of Research into New Media Technologies* 24, no. 1 (2018): 108.
20. A slang term that Hill frequently expresses. Short for the French word "bourgeoisie" referencing anything or anyone perceived as upscale or high-class.
21. Aditi Bhatia, "Interdiscursive Performance in Digital Professions: The Case of YouTube Tutorials," *Journal of Pragmatics* 124 (2018): 108.
22. William C. Kurlinkus, *Nostalgic Design: Rhetoric, Memory, and Democratizing Technology* (Pittsburgh: University of Pittsburgh Press, 2018), 6.
23. Jung Eun Lee and Brandi Watkins, "YouTube Vloggers' Influence on Consumer Luxury Brand Perceptions and Intentions," *Journal of Business Research* 69, no. 12 (2016): 5755.
24. Joanne Morreale, "From Homemade to Store Bought: Annoying Orange and the Professionalization of YouTube," *Journal of Consumer Culture* 14, no. 1 (2014): 125.
25. In fall 2019, after this analysis was completed, Jaclyn Hill launched her brand Jaclyn Cosmetics. The launch was considered a failure due to major quality control issues with the products, resulting in all purchases being refunded. Hill received major criticism for her poor business handlings and took a leave of absence from social media. Hill has since returned to social media, admitted her failures and promised to learn from her mistakes, and successfully

launched a new line of products under her brand name. Though the timing of this event precluded inclusion in my analysis, it warrants further research on the YouTube beauty community and its relationship with the beauty industry and with consumers.

26. Stuart Cunningham and David Craig, "Being 'Really Real' on YouTube: Authenticity, Community and Brand Culture in Social Media Entertainment," *Media International Australia* 164, no. 1 (2017): 77.

27. Cunningham and Craig, "Being 'Really Real,'" 77.

28. Anne Jerslev, "In the Time of the Microcelebrity: Celebrification and the YouTuber Zoella," *International Journal of Communication* 10 (2016): 5247.

29. While other important variables impact fans' perceptions of a vlogger's identity, such as gender and sexuality, this analysis limits its scope to class in order to more thoroughly investigate class as a site of identity construction.

30. It is important to note that Star does receive many negative comments about his gender and sexuality, which is outside the scope of this analysis.

31. Dawson did not typically post videos related to the beauty community prior to this series with Star. He has since published several videos containing beauty content and has also released a line of makeup products in collaboration with Star.

32. Among other controversies, Jeffree Star has been accused of making many racist remarks in earlier videos during his time as a MySpace music artist.

33. A "stan" is a slang term for an excessively fanatic supporter of a celebrity, microcelebrity, fictional character, etc. The word is assumed to be a blend of "stalker" and "fan."

BIBLIOGRAPHY

Bhatia, Aditi. "Interdiscursive Performance in Digital Professions: The Case of YouTube Tutorials." *Journal of Pragmatics* 124 (2018): 106–20.

Burgess, Jean, and Joshua Green. *YouTube: Online Video and Participatory Culture*. Cambridge: Polity Press, 2009.

Cunningham, Stuart, and David Craig. "Being 'Really Real' on YouTube: Authenticity, Community and Brand Culture in Social Media Entertainment." *Media International Australia* 164, no. 1 (2017): 71–81.

Dawson, Shane. "The Secret World of Jeffree Star." YouTube Video, 29:50. August 2, 2018, https://www.youtube.com/watch?v=xUf2-jGqQw&list=PLDs0tNoNYTz05R0xo7PCVc-RgL2fsJnGg.

Deery, June, and Andrea Press. "Introduction: Studying Media and Class," in *Media and Class: TV, Film, and Digital Culture*, edited by June Deery and Andrea Press, 1–17. New York: Routledge, 2017.

Hill, Jaclyn. "CLOSET TOUR." YouTube Video, 21:33. February 11, 2018, .youtube.com/watch?v=9G4iSJBf6QQ.

Hill, Jaclyn. "Smokey Cat Eye Tutorial." YouTube Video, 11:06. August 11, 2012, https://www.youtube.com/watch?v=Y4fur_12EEc .

Ipsy. "About Us." Accessed December 8, 2018. https://www.ipsy.com/about.

Jenkins, Henry. *Convergence Culture: Where Old and New Media Collide*. New York: New York University Press, 2006.

Jenkins, Henry, Sam Ford, and Joshua Green. *Spreadable Media: Creating Value and Meaning in a Networked Culture*. New York: New York University Press, 2013.

Jerslev, Anne. "In the Time of the Microcelebrity: Celebrification and the YouTuber Zoella." *International Journal of Communication* 10 (2016): 5233–51.

kknope. "What changed your mind about Jaclyn Hill?" Reddit. Accessed November 23, 2018. https://www.reddit.com/r/BeautyGuruChatter/comments/9b2vye/what_changed_your_mind_about_jaclyn_hill/.

Kurlinkus, William C. *Nostalgic Design: Rhetoric, Memory, and Democratizing Technology*. Pittsburgh: University of Pittsburgh Press, 2018.

Lee, Jung Eun, and Brandi Watkins. "YouTube Vloggers' Influence on Consumer Luxury Brand Perceptions and Intentions." *Journal of Business Research* 69, no. 12 (2016): 5753–60.

Marwick, Alice. *Status Update: Celebrity, Publicity, and Branding in the Social Media Age*. New Haven: Yale University Press, 2013.

Marwick, Alice. "You May Know Me from YouTube: (Micro)-Celebrity in Social Media." In *A Companion to Celebrity*, edited by P. David Marshall and Sean Redmond, 333–50. West Sussex: Wiley-Blackwell, 2015.

Morreale, Joanne. "From Homemade to Store Bought: Annoying Orange and the Professionalization of YouTube." *Journal of Consumer Culture* 14, no. 1 (2014): 113–28.

Phan, Michelle. "Why I Left." YouTube Video, 11:11. June 1, 2017, https://www.youtube.com/watch?v=UuGpm01SPcA.

Pixability. "Beauty on YouTube." Accessed November 26, 2018. https://www.pixability.com/industry-insights/beauty-youtube-2015/.

Raun, Tobias, Jane Arthurs, Sophia Drakopoulou, and Alessandro Gandini. "Capitalizing Intimacy: New Subcultural Forms of Micro-celebrity Strategies and Affective Labour on YouTube." *Convergence: The International Journal of Research into New Media Technologies* 24, no. 1 (2018): 99–113.

Robehmed, Natalie. "How Michelle Phan Built a $500 Million Company." *Forbes,* October 5, 2015. https://www.forbes.com/sites/natalierobehmed/2015/10/05/how-michelle-phan-built-a-500-million-company/#5c67d7b8c4a2. Accessed 1 December 2018.

SatinUnicorn. "Jeffree Star stans—why do you love him so? (a genuine question)." Reddit. Accessed November 27, 2018. https://www.reddit.com/r/BeautyGuruChatter/comments/9kutnw/jeffree_star_stans_why_do_you_love_him_so_a/.

Senft, Theresa M. *Camgirls: Celebrity and Community in the Age of Social Networks*. New York: Peter Lang, 2008.

Senft, Theresa M. "Microcelebrity and the Branded Self." In *A Companion to New Media Dynamics*, edited by John Hartley, Jean Burgess, and Axel Bruns, 346–54. West Sussex: Wiley-Blackwell, 2013.

Star, Jeffree. "FULL FACE OF BRANDS THAT HATE ME." YouTube Video, 30:19. July 17, 2018, https://www.youtube.com/watch?v=9G4iSJBf6QQ.

Turner, Graeme. *Ordinary People and the Media: The Demotic Turn*. London: Sage Publications Ltd., 2010.

Wischhover, Cheryl. "The Rebirth of YouTube Beauty Pioneer Michelle Phan." *Racked*, April 10, 2017. https://www.racked.com/2017/4/10/15185246/michelle-phan-giving-up-youtube-em-cosmetics.

Chapter Four

Subscribe to My Empire

Jeffree Star and Self-Branding on YouTube

Alexandra Hauke and Florian Zitzelsberger

On December 20, 2017, *The Guardian* published an online quiz testing readers on their knowledge of social media events, news, and scandals of the past year. While several of the questions require the readers' regular frequentation of networks such as Twitter, YouTube, and Instagram in order to be able to choose the correct answer, one question in particular stands out among the others for its blunt opening statement: "'Influencers' are people who don't do anything but have lots of followers and are able to make a living by shilling brands."[1] The author's controversial declaration, in turn, raises questions about the role, significance, and overall conceptualization of the so-called social media influencer (SMI)[2] who "works to generate a form of 'celebrity' capital by [. . .] crafting an authentic 'personal brand' via social networks."[3] With over six million subscribers on the video-sharing platform YouTube, makeup artist Jeffree Star has become one of the most significant SMIs ever since he posted his first tutorial in 2015. As such, his efforts as one of the first male beauty gurus to establish both a career on the internet and a cosmetics company offline have shaped the disputed yet undeniably successful brand that is *Jeffree Star.*[4] His company, Jeffree Star Cosmetics, founded in 2014, continues to revolutionize the makeup industry through the creation and distribution of cruelty-free and vegan makeup products, with bestsellers such as his Skin Frost™ highlighters, the Androgyny Eyeshadow Palette, and, especially, his Velour Liquid Lipsticks. With an estimated net worth of five million US dollars in 2017, Jeffree has undoubtedly built an empire around his brand and successfully established himself as a celebrity in makeup communities both on and off YouTube. In this chapter, we focus on the narrative, medial, and cultural economics through which Jeffree Star engages in processes of self-branding. Through close readings of his 2017 makeup campaigns and their reveals on YouTube,[5] we highlight how Jeffree uses the platform's participatory features and its possibilities for self-making and self-representation. We argue that Jeffree Star transcends both "traditional" and more recent understandings of celebrity because of the conflation of his makeup brand, Jeffree Star Cosmetics, and his performance of an allegedly authentic and relatable, yet ultimately exclusive and unattainable, self as brand. For this purpose, the following section maps out a theoretical trajectory toward Jeffree's unique stardom.

Without question, stars like Jeffree appeal to a plethora of audiences across a variety of media platforms, but why are consumers so invested in the public presences and private lives of SMIs? The increase in online productions since the early 2010s within the realm of lifestyle—including health, fashion, and especially beauty—promotes a surge of interest in these spheres also by consumers: the mutual enthusiasm for popular formats such as the makeup tutorial, which celebrates the democratic experience of (re)creating a specific look, continues to generate a seemingly exponential number of new followers on the side of beauty gurus as the producers of tutorials and reviews. This constant increase in supporters is symptomatic of the SMIs' popularity as twenty-first-century celebrities whose status within both online and offline communities has developed from "Internet fame" to "proper fame."[6] While more established notions of the celebrity are typically associated with stars who are "produced *by* the media industries,"[7] such as actors or musicians, we question whether such conceptualizations can still sufficiently grasp the celebrity phenomenon in the Digital Age—particularly with regard to prominent SMIs like Jeffree Star. Participatory platforms such as YouTube allow beauty gurus *as* SMIs to create their own star image *through* the online networks they are invested in; as such, their brand is autopoietically sustained by digital self-reproduction, a performative act[8] that contributes to a comprehensive reframing of earlier ideas of the celebrity.

Richard Dyer asserts that the appeal of celebrities lies in their ability to "articulate the business of being an individual."[9] This approach not only implies that stars can lend themselves to companies in order to sell products but also that the star persona itself may be marketed—that is, the "human brand can become synonymous with the [material] brand and hence with the product, service or firm."[10] On top of that, when stars strategically exploit the appeal of their personae for business purposes, individual and business can merge into a brand of their own. In this context, Jeffree Star refashions more conventional business models by embodying his own brand—by both producing and marketing *his* products—instead of simply standing in as the face of another company. The ways in which a brand such as *Jeffree Star* is shaped is not just a question of economics, however; it rather consists "of *everything* that is publicly available about stars."[11] Within the frame of social media networks such as YouTube, Twitter, and Instagram, this is especially relevant, as information about and content by SMIs is always readily available and can be accessed easily and quickly via smartphones. The discursive manifestations of celebrities as brands are thus becoming progressively more pronounced, as SMIs, especially beauty gurus, are figuratively made into celebrities in pockets by consumers. Unlike film stars, for example, SMIs like Jeffree thereby accompany their followers in everyday activities; they uphold the "impression of exclusive, 'intimate' exchange"[12] when it comes to sharing their morning and nighttime routines, or revealing the secrets of their makeup looks, which results in the ambiguous status of SMIs as paradoxically both public and private figures.[13]

In this sense, because social media is such a "consumer-centric space,"[14] YouTube, in particular, relies heavily on the establishment of the *celebrity as brand* because they, after all, become the consumed product. Beauty gurus are no exception in this narrative; however, their practices of branding digress from those of athletes, for example, "for whom a strong public image [is] expected"[15] from the beginning. The difference lies in their initial status as "'ordinary' people" who advertise their online identities to achieve star status and, accordingly, exploit "the marketing possibilities of contemporary convergent technologies"[16] in an attempt to appeal to and capitalize on consumers. This approach goes back to the frameworks of reality television, in which everyday people are used as bait for the establishment of the respective program's critical acclaim through the relatability of the performer and their relationship with the viewer—a process that ultimately projects the show's popularity onto the individual and transforms them into a celebrity.[17] In 2004, when Jeffree Star was still unknown, he already invested in his lifelong interest in makeup by working at the MAC Cosmetics counter as a makeup artist, partially fulfilling his teenage dream: "I discovered makeup at the age of 13 and have been obsessed with it ever since. I used to copy looks from fashion ads in my mother's *Cosmopolitan* magazines and steal her eye shadows."[18] Jeffree's evolution from an ordinary makeup consumer to a professional cosmetics producer, made possible by his devoted online following, highlights that the "increased powers of self-determination are now in the hands of media consumers."[19] The possibility of establishing *oneself* as a celebrity through the employment of (social) media has been denoted by Graeme Turner as the demotic turn,[20] a decisive socio-cultural development of the twenty-first century which can and must necessarily be applied to SMIs and their methods of self-(re)production and -marketing. The aforementioned notions of celebrity are adapted at this point to fit the constraints of YouTube as an inherently self-marketed space that continues to grow with its stars and viewers. While we call for a reconceptualization of the star image as a whole because of the idiosyncrasies SMIs add to this very notion, we argue that celebrities on YouTube continue to inhabit a special position within the realm of stardom: that of the microcelebrity. First introduced by Theresa M. Senft in 2001 and developed further by Khamis et al.,[21] the microcelebrity is intrinsically linked to the idea that "anyone can be famous and hence become ostensibly successful"[22] and thus to the need for self-branding online through which this success is ultimately made possible. In line with this, it is insufficient to perceive the SMI and the "self-brander [. . .] before it"[23] as mutually exclusive since self-branding is constitutive of the establishment of YouTubers *as* microcelebrities. As such, the demotic turn from ordinary person to microcelebrity is celebrated and "validates the celetoid commercially inasmuch as he/she experiences celebrity not despite their ordinariness, but *because* of it, since it is a precondition for eligibility"[24] as a beauty guru on YouTube. This suitability additionally stipulates the imperative of authenticity;[25] that is, becoming a microcelebrity is not only dependent on one's ordinariness but also on the validity of one's unique, sincere, and consistent identity, which is strategically created and infinitely adaptable within the online network. What makes microcelebrities "micro," therefore, is the framing of their profession and personae online and the consumer's engagement in this digital projection of authenticity and individualism. When the celebrity becomes micro through the demotic turn, the self becomes a brand and thus the "emotional labour"[26] of identity construction is transformed through the online medium into the business of self-promotion and -mediation.

Considering that YouTube is a "social space,"[27] it does not suffice to look at it as a medium facilitating this turn: "there needs to be a social contract between participants and a sense that their actions have consequence within the community"[28] in order to provide a democratic experience online. Following this assertion, participation cannot solely be regarded as consumption because "audiences and communities [require] different modes of address,"[29] that is, communication demands that both sender and addressee partake equally in the conversation as opposed to unilateral performances. Within the frame of makeup tutorials, participation moves beyond mere spectatorship because it also offers the viewer the opportunity to engage offline in the same beauty routines as the gurus. As such, the makeup community transcends the limits of YouTube as a medium. While all media can be considered loci of discourses about stars, it is social media platforms, in particular, that also provide audiences with the possibilities of validation, for example, in the form of dis/likes or comments,[30] thus maintaining a direct feedback culture and continuously shaping and adding to the public perception of the microcelebrity's brand. This participatory practice also opens up a space for creative (re)production on the side of the viewer, that is, former consumers can "tak[e] on the role of producer"[31] by sharing the results of their experiences online. Jeffree Star's videos promise consumers, who use his products to recreate the makeup looks he presents on screen, the unique exclusivity of actually becoming like Jeffree, part of his brand, and thus "Jeffree-Star-approved." Jeffree acknowledges their efforts on Instagram, for example, where his official account jeffreestarcosmetics frequently reposts photographs by followers who have purchased and applied his makeup products, thus dipping into the capitalization of *Jeffree Star* and eventually becoming part of the Star family.

This active interplay between audience engagement and recognition by the microcelebrity constitutes another variant of the demotic turn: by publicly commenting on the respective follower's application of his products or realization of his makeup looks, Jeffree offers his "ordinary" subscribers their fifteen minutes of fame, thus transforming them into temporary stars within the community until the next photo is reposted. Such an incentive motivates other subscribers to become part of this tradition as well; their commitment to the labor necessary for an undertaking of this kind hints at the twenty-first-century "trend [of] putting consumers to work—turning them into prosumers."[32] Processes of transforming the consumer into a producer reinforce the type of social contract SMIs like Jeffree establish with their followers at the moment of subscription: a silent, unwritten agreement between two parties with the promise of bilateral benefit. Because the prosumer must necessarily invest financially in the respective products to uphold their end of the bargain, thereby strengthening "prosumer capitalism" through "unpaid rather than paid labor,"[33] Jeffree is able to maximize both his popularity and monetary gain. Exploiting the social contract in this way authenticates the process of self-branding as a socioeconomic modus operandi and manipulates Jeffree's viewers into coming back to his channel: ultimately, both Jeffree and his followers are caught in a loop of prosumption that promises both sides the status of microcelebrity. In the latter case, however, their fame is reduced to the illusive fifteen minutes in the spotlight, while the former continues to enjoy the commercial benefits of self-branding both on and off YouTube.

These preliminary theoretical reflections on the practices of (self-)branding and the establishment of (micro)celebrities as brands have demonstrated that an analysis of YouTubers—one of the major and arguably most heterogeneous groups among SMIs—and "traditional" celebrities allows a predominantly conclusive subsumption of their positions within either of the aforementioned categories. However, Jeffree Star as a pioneer in the digital spheres of the self-marketed makeup industry reveals the fault lines of such binary understandings. While Marwick, for example, claims that microcelebrity "is a state of being famous to a niche group of people,"[34] the ever-growing popularity of YouTube and its content creators evinces that the medium has moved far beyond its initial niche status. Specifically, the online makeup community and Jeffree Star, as one of its biggest contributors, expedite this development: Jeffree's construction of a seemingly authentic and deliberately ambiguous identity as part of his brand translates to a hybrid conceptualization of his status as *Star*, promoting both a continuous oscillation between and transcendence of the notions of the microcelebrity and the "traditional" celebrity. Thus, Jeffree Star occupies an entirely new position within and beyond contemporary (social) media landscapes, reflected, above all, in his self-selected last name, which signifies the realization of his lifelong dream—becoming a star and thereby exceeding the implications of self-branding.

The subsequent sections are dedicated to an analysis of *Jeffree Star* as brand. We scrutinize how Jeffree as an SMI and beauty guru uses YouTube as a medium to construct a self-image that appeals to the YouTube makeup community through its ordinariness and relatability. These videos nonetheless exhibit his exclusiveness, both in terms of his personality and his commercial status, inasmuch as Jeffree's persona and his official brand, Jeffree Star Cosmetics, converge and generate the self-fashioned brand *Jeffree Star*. We argue that this is made possible through the audience's investment in his character, his videos, and his products; Jeffree thus continuously reinvents himself by strategically exploiting the mechanics, politics, and aesthetics of self-branding on YouTube. Ultimately, we want to show how his online presence as a brand and the performance thereof—as exemplified in his three promotional videos of 2017, in which he introduces the individual makeup products included in the Chrome Summer Collection, the Star Family Collection, and the Holiday Glitter Collection—are both symptomatic of and result in a reconceptualization of the (micro)celebrity which sets the course for his sui generis *Star*dom.

As we initially argued, *Jeffree Star* consists of abstract discourses surrounding Jeffree Star which enter the public spheres of the internet and, subsequently, the economic market through the demotic turn. Upon first glance, the image that constitutes *Jeffree Star* as a brand may be reduced to aspects of sexuality and gender, focusing on the transgressive and subversive attitudes of the makeup guru who captivates his audience due to his androgynous and often female-inspired looks as well as his skillful use of makeup—a fascination paralleled by the increasing public interest in drag queens and their growing presence in popular culture. As such, the image ascribed to Jeffree is one which challenges heteronormativity in accordance with binary-coded expressions of gender. For example, his relationship with the allegedly straight Nathan Schwandt seems to defy the heterosexual matrix as a "permanent and incontestable structure of culture."[35] It is important to note, however, that the majority of the discourses that shape our perception of *Jeffree Star* are perpetuated by Jeffree Star himself: the question is, therefore, not how *Jeffree Star* relates to normative categorizations of gender and sexuality but how Jeffree uses YouTube to publicly redraft these notions to fit his brand. Sexuality and gender become mere vehicles for self-branding and, in this sense, emphasize Jeffree's relatability while maintaining the exclusive status of *Jeffree Star*. In other words, his brand resonates deeply with consumers, especially those of a younger demographic, because it shows that Jeffree sees no need to follow these prescribed norms and instead continues to be unapologetically himself.[36] With his YouTube channel, Jeffree works against the pressures of hetero- and cisnormativity by creating an inclusive space for "anyone on earth,"[37] especially for people who are, like him, "all down for being a weirdo"[38] and feel like they cannot find their place offline. His videos, at the same time, represent the frame within which *Jeffree Star* as a brand materializes and which is employed to make the (micro)celebrity not only accessible to a large audience but also readily consumable inside and beyond the digital spheres. In this sense, Jeffree uses YouTube to market the products of Jeffree Star Cosmetics by screening his construction of an authentic identity, which signifies "the ability to both become *and* sell yourself."[39] However, even if his views do not translate directly into product sales, Jeffree Star still profits from his audience: the sole act of watching without engaging in other forms of participation, such as commenting, accumulates monetary gain through the branded identity, the basic purpose of *Jeffree Star*. With each new video or makeup product released, the brand is thus reshaped, emphasizing different aspects of Jeffree Star that facilitate the commercialization of that persona; although *Jeffree Star* as a whole relies on the construction of a *consistent* online identity, the brand is adapted to the cause.

While his reveals of the Summer Chrome Collection and the Holiday Glitter Collection on his YouTube channel feature only Jeffree and his products in a face-to-face conversation with the camera, his video about the Star Family Collection impresses with an elaborate opening sequence that resembles the style of music videos and a documentary-like part that establishes the main themes of the video and the collection: Jeffree's relationship with Nathan as well as their family and unique lifestyles.[40] Everything in this video appears to be on brand: from Jeffree's custom-made pink-and-white Rolls Royce and luxurious mansion to details like his makeup and even his boyfriend's clothing, virtually everything screams *Jeffree Star*. About five minutes in, Jeffree reveals the idea behind the Star Family Collection: "six brand new liquid lipsticks that represent me, him [Nathan], and the dogs."[41] More than any other reveal video, "The Star Family Collection" shows how the personae of Jeffree and Nathan—and their dogs, for that matter—become part of Jeffree's brand. The announced products are not only named after family members but also adhere to their individual character profiles; for example, the color of the lipstick named Delicious is modelled after their dog of the same name. The representation of the respective family members as products is authenticated through narrated backstories of their private histories and supported by a visual collage of puppy photographs that appeal to the audience on a commercial as well as an affective level. In this sense, the video has "switched from a language of strategic self-branding in order to consolidate an income, to a very specific appeal to authenticity."[42]

"The Star Family Collection" thus contributes to an understanding of the brand as a whole and becomes part of a palimpsestuous layering of meaning which implies the existence of *Jeffree Star* as an architext, a body of characteristics "from which emerges each singular text"[43] about the brand. Indeed, upon closer inspection one will realize that the three videos share numerous idiosyncrasies in terms of video structure, editing, and language which determine Jeffree's self-branding processes and ensure the consumers' recognition of and familiarity with *Jeffree Star.* Ritualistic phrases like "welcome back to my channel" create a sense of intimacy with the viewer while simultaneously spelling out the clear hierarchy between Jeffree as producer and his audience as consumers who are repeatedly invited to witness the exclusiveness embodied and created by *Jeffree Star*. His videos imagine Jeffree as a businessman who is in charge of every step, from the development and production, to the marketing and distribution of his makeup. In the "Holiday 2017 Collection" video, for example, Jeffree reminds his audience of the difficulties that occur during the production process: "getting glitter that does not feel gritty or like sandpaper was very difficult so *I've been working on this for months* and it's finally here, it feels so smooth"[44]—positing himself as the singular developer behind Jeffree Star Cosmetics. We need not forget that this corporate identity is carefully crafted, however, and that Jeffree's strong presence as the head of his company and the embodiment of *his* brand therefore obscures the blue-collar labor put into the production of his products. The fact that he imposes a strong filter upon the fabrication of his makeup nevertheless does not carry weight because his audience solely relates to, and is most interested in, the finished good and not how it came about. Jeffree only ever lifts the veil in order to show that the laboratory is "where [he] spend[s] a lot of [his] time creating"[45] or to provide information relevant to his audience in terms of consumption, for example, by repeatedly explaining that his lip scrubs are "infused with aloe vera, [. . .] are also edible, [and] have vitamin E in them."[46] Despite the fact that *Jeffree Star* is seemingly articulated differently in his various videos, the brand relies on these recurring structures and elements to performatively constitute itself: it is thus reinforced by a reciprocal conjunction of Jeffree Star as a person and his company Jeffree Star Cosmetics, both of which converge in his videos. That is to say, Jeffree's lifestyle as makeup producer and SMI is made possible by his brand, which attracts an audience that ensures his existence as a (micro)celebrity. As long as his efforts in terms of both social and economic endeavors pay off, his brand continues to grow in turn. The mechanisms of self-branding at work here disclose a circular logic: while we heretofore maintained that the demotic turn facilitates the transformation of individual into brand, this is only partly true in the case of Jeffree Star because, as shown above, the brand also fashions and constitutes the individual to a great extent. As Jeffree himself claims, "the brand is literally [his] entire life,"[47] which is why both Jeffree Star and *Jeffree Star* engage in a loop of perpetual self-branding and therefore underlie inverse processes of constant re-actualization.

This prolonged regeneration of the layers of the palimpsest that is *Jeffree Star* is first and foremost made possible by YouTube's opportunity for audience participation, that is, the beauty guru's perpetuation of the notions of microcelebrity that emerge through the continuous give and take of feedback culture, which is primarily sustained through comments. In the "Holiday 2017 Collection," for example, consumers are expected to "sound off in the comment section below and let [Jeffree] know what [their] favorite shade [of lipstick] is,"[48] whereby Jeffree seemingly validates the viewer's preference without actively replying to these comments as a next move. In "The Star Family Collection," Jeffree takes his expectations of his viewers even a step further: he teases that he "may even have a few secret pieces of merch dropping"[49] at some point, never revealing in the video what these include or when they will be made public. His subscribers are left with the promise of new products, a conscious marketing decision on behalf of the producer with the hope of reeling consumers back in to look for signs of these exclusive items. In both cases, Jeffree feigns bilateral partnership—an alleged quid pro quo agreement in which producer and consumer encourage each other with the result of mutual benefit. However, the way the consumer is left without a reply comment in the former case reinforces not communication with the star/Star, but with other consumers instead. As such, the comment sections below Jeffree's videos display an abundance of discussions among many subscribers about the shades, formulae, and packaging choices of his makeup products as well as opinions about Jeffree Star as a person. By "expanding the potentials for participation," YouTube as an interactive platform thus allows viewers of all origins as well as political and sexual orientations to engage in feedback culture in a way that "represents the greatest opportunity for cultural diversity."[50] While this participatory commitment builds upon the idea of democracy, which "entails a political community in which there is some form of *political equality*,"[51] fosters kinship among viewers, and provides for active exchange within and beyond the Jeffree Star fandom, the comment sections push the previously established social contract between producer and consumer even further toward asymmetry: Jeffree's empire allows for no "[r]ule by the people."[52] It is clear in these instances that Jeffree thus occupies the exclusive star position while his followers simply consume him and his products, thereby boosting his commercial status and his brand. Coming back to the aforementioned examples, the consumer cannot be sure when or if the merchandise is ever brought forward; subscribing to Jeffree's channel or other social media platforms is required in order to be informed of these and other new products upon their release. From this follows that the brand *Jeffree Star* and Jeffree himself as its on-screen extension ultimately perpetuate a self-image that professes to be directed toward and to rely on the audience: in the "Holiday 2017 Collection," for instance, Jeffree claims that he has "been getting so many requests to do a dark teal"[53] shade of liquid lipstick. His compliance with these demands suggests to the audience that Jeffree is entirely invested in fulfilling their wishes and making them happy. By supposedly giving the people what they want, he manipulates them into buying his products, ultimately transforming consumers into offline sales. In this way, Jeffree's influence as a beauty guru and skills as a marketing representative and makeup producer transcends YouTube as a medium and enters off-screen realms. His image and brand are thus kept intact: he remains the sole beneficiary of this unequal exchange while his consumers are shaped into the ultimate commodity of his brand.

The consumer's interest in and support of *Jeffree Star* are continuously guaranteed through the relatability of Jeffree's persona. His strategic exploitation of his ordinariness validates the significance and functions of the demotic turn: by emphasizing that his viewers already "know [he is] such a sucker for candy and sweets and sugar" or proclaiming that, "this summer," he and his viewers are "gonna relax"[54] together, Jeffree creates the illusion of an intimate friendship with his audience. When he expresses his wish that his viewers "could taste [the liquid lipsticks] through this screen,"[55] however, he self-referentially exposes the distance between them by alluding to the very technology that continues to make his brand a (virtual) reality: the screen. Be it through a smartphone, tablet, laptop, or TV, the relationship between Jeffree and his followers necessarily remains cut off. While views, comments, and purchases signify active participation in his brand, the intimate connection Jeffree invokes when he claims, for instance, "I know so many of you are a fan of [the liquid lipsticks],"[56] succumbs to the limits of the medium and the disproportionate numbers of followers to a single star. Jeffree's appeal to the audience's affective side when suggesting that "*we* all know and love these Skin Frosts,"[57] articulates a sense of community that connects the star and the fan through their mutual appreciation of a material good. In this sense, despite Jeffree's continuous signposting of his and his audience's shared ordinariness, it remains clear that this form of relatability only exists because of their similar proclivities for his products: the (micro)celebrity's only real interest is the audience's interest in his brand, not the audience itself. Ultimately, this alleged intimate relationship serves as a form of "viral advertising"[58] for Jeffree's products, as the popularization of Jeffree's down-to-earth persona directly translates into the promotion and commercialization of his products and thus of his brand.

This endeavor is further supported by his boyfriend Nathan, whose online recognition stems from a more fathomable case of relatability: a former petshop employee, Nathan rose to fame through skateboard stunts on Instagram and occasional appearances in Jeffree's videos. While his Instagram account sports 850,000 followers as of 2017, most websites credit him with nothing more than the status of "Jeffree Star's boyfriend." However, as "The Star Family Collection" shows, Nathan has largely graduated from his position as bystander and has advanced to an active participator in *Jeffree Star*: he claims that "*we* [he and Jeffree] live and breathe makeup," that he had "fun [playing] around with the colors" in Jeffree's makeup lab, and that "*we* just wanted to make something really special for [. . .] the fans [because] you guys know so much about *our* lives, so *we* just wanted to give you a little piece of it."[59] His implications of their conjoined work ethic in the creation of the collection underlines Nathan's involvement in practices that were previously reserved for Jeffree alone; by sharing Jeffree's production and decision-making processes, "one of the key sites of the articulation of the concept of participation,"[60] and narrating his experiences online, the audience is able to live vicariously through Nathan, a persona representing, even more than Jeffree himself, the type of relatable ordinariness the viewer enjoys on YouTube. His glamorous life by association supports the fact that anyone "can craft a public presentation of self that is ostensibly a reflection of their 'reality.'"[61] In the end, Nathan's role in the perpetuation of the brand *Jeffree Star* encompasses much more than that of boyfriend and confidante: through him, Jeffree is not only able to create yet another link to his audience but also to exploit this very connection by boosting his self-image as a loveable partner and successful businessman who can bring anyone to fame. From this ability follows that Jeffree Star's audience is given the opportunity to identify and crave a connection with both Jeffree and Nathan, whose idiosyncrasies appeal to viewers through the promise of both personal ordinariness and productive exclusivity. As such, *Jeffree Star* experiences the kind of "visibility and efficacy [. . .] clearly indebted to communication capabilities distinct to the early twenty-first century, and a cultural milieu increasingly primed for self-promotion and triumphant individualism."[62] The audience's appreciation of this distinctiveness and participation in the processes of self-branding subsequently play into the emergence of consumers as *pro*sumers, who "can no longer be seen as merely inhabiting the restricted domain of privatized consumption"[63] but rather as re-creators of Jeffree's exclusive looks and thus reproducers of *Jeffree Star* as a whole. Thereby, both Jeffree and the prosumer-audience draw on *Jeffree Star* as architext to tell the same story in different ways: they participate in the reiterative practices of (self-)branding through which the ordinary person becomes the (micro)celebrity. As a consequence, Jeffree Star is able to use the synergy between him and his audience to (re)create and (re)circulate his brand and *Star*dom.

Following Richard Dyer's assertion that "images have to be made,"[64] processes of branding raise the question of where these images originate from and who creates them. In this sense, it has become clear that branding is a matter of framing: while "traditional" celebrities continue to depend on extrinsic means of marketing their personae—such as actors who are commissioned by companies for the commercialization of a product—microcelebrities "fashion their own autonomously authored brand."[65] This is made possible through the demotic turn, which itself serves as a basis for the increasing urgency of self-branding on YouTube. This necessity is directly linked to audience participation, which can only be sustained once SMIs have accumulated a following in the first place by relying on the appeal of their ordinariness and relatability. Social media platforms such as YouTube form parts of an "infinite canvas"[66] which offers unlimited possibilities for self-branding, that is, updating and expanding a palimpsest of the discourses constituting the brand through ongoing reiteration and reactualization. Where once microcelebrities were only celebrated by a small number of people, through the ever-growing popularity and importance of social media they are now being "[fed] back into the mainstream media":[67] YouTube is on the verge of replacing more traditional forms of entertainment, exemplified by the audience's tendency to consume online videos instead of home television.[68] If, therefore, the "microcelebrity changes the game of celebrity,"[69] Jeffree Star, in turn, challenges the notion of microcelebrity through the perpetuation of his seemingly private identity in public discourse. The emanating attraction of his brand lies in the careful construction of authenticity—the selective presentation of his ordinariness and relatability, on the one hand, and his economic success, on the other—which reverberates with the audience and prompts participation. However, as we have demonstrated, the underlying social contract between Jeffree and his subscribers culminates in an asymmetrical relationship; thereby, Jeffree's empire is strategically maintained through the monetization of the views his videos generate and, by extension, his followers. Developing this thought further, it shows that the audience's investment in *Jeffree Star* is not limited to the consumption of his videos; if a follower wants to become part of the Star family, financial investment in Jeffree's makeup products becomes a requirement. This capitalization of his viewers transforms them into commodities, while their acts of consuming Jeffree Star through *Jeffree Star* make him a commodity in turn. The herein implied processes of self-branding on and through the participatory features of YouTube illustrate that a distinction between Jeffree as person, the Jeffree Star persona, and *Jeffree Star* as brand is no longer possible. From this follows that neither "traditional" notions of celebrity nor features of microcelebrity adequately frame Jeffree's status as *Star* as a result of the embodiment of his own brand: Jeffree Star occupies a position that ceases to be "micro" because his efforts transcend the boundaries of You-Tube as a medium through the possibilities of self-branding.

NOTES

1. Sam Wolfson, "The Social Media Quiz of 2017," *The Guardian*, December 20, 2017, https://www.theguardian.com/media/2017/dec/20/the-social-media-quiz-of-2017.

2. A brief remark on terminology: We use the terms "star" and "celebrity" interchangeably without implying any hierarchies between them. "Microcelebrity" as a phenomenon of the Digital Age will be discussed in relation to these concepts and developed with a focus on the social media influencer, which we will refer to as "SMI," an abbreviation suggested by Khamis et al.

3. Alison Hearn and Stephanie Schoenhoff, "From Celebrity to Influencer: Tracing the Diffusion to Celebrity Value accross the Data Stream," in *A Companion to Celebrity*, ed. P. David Marshall and Sean Redmond (West Sussex: Wiley-Blackwell, 2016): 194.

4. In order to be able to distinguish between Jeffree Star as person and the brand based on his online identity, we use *Jeffree Star* to indicate the latter.

5. This chapter's engagement with a closed-off corpus, namely reveal videos published on Jeffree Star's YouTube channel in 2017, leads to an exclusion of primary data preceding and succeeding the selected time frame. While we do not examine Jeffree's more recent collections (Blood Sugar, Thirsty, Blue Blood, Alien, Jawbreaker, etc.), collaborations (Morphe, Conspiracy, etc.), and YouTuber Shane Dawson's two docuseries about him, these examples, nevertheless, speak to and are illustrated by our deliberations. The sheer expansiveness of Jeffree's cosmetics empire demonstrates his brand's vigor in shaping, managing, and sustaining itself through perpetual acts of self-reproduction. Viewers might expect cases such as Jeffree's break-up with his boyfriend Nathan Schwandt in early 2020 to pose a threat to the stability of the Star foundation; however, the additional online attention and media publicity afforded to Jeffree's channel and persona in these instances open up even more possibilities for (re)furnishing the brand. Neil M. Alperstein echoes this idea: "Along with acquiring facts or information about a celebrity, we may also acquire a relationship history, as we watch the celebrity's career rise, waver or fall, and perhaps applaud them as they get up again, all of which is part of the American narrative—never give up or try again" [Neil M. Alperstein, *Celebrity and Mediated Social Connections: Fans, Friends and Followers in the Digital Age* (Cham: Palgrave Macmillan, 2019), 97].

6. Susie Khamis, Lawrence Ang, and Raymond Welling, "Self-branding, 'Micro-celebrity' and the Rise of Social Media Influencers," *Celebrity Studies* 8, no. 2 (2017): 203.

7. Richard Dyer, *Heavenly Bodies: Film Stars and Society* (London and New York: Routledge, 2004), 4 (emphasis added).

8. We are drawing on Judith Butler's notion of performativity, which she describes as the "reiterative and citational practice by which discourse produces the effects that it names" [Judith Butler, *Bodies that Matter: On the Discursive Limits of "Sex"* (London and New York: Routledge, 2011), xii.]. While Butler's approach is focused, first and foremost, on gender, an aspect which will also be considered in our case study of Jeffree Star, performativity can also be used to explain the processes of self-branding (e.g., the construction of a self-image through citation) at play on YouTube.

9. Dyer, *Heavenly Bodies*, 16.

10. Khamis, Ang, and Welling, "Self-branding," 193.

11. Dyer, *Heavenly Bodies*, 2 (emphasis added).

12. Crystal Abidin, "Communicative Intimacies: Influencers and Perceived Interconnectedness," *ada: A Journal of Gender, New Media and Technology* 8 (2015): n. p., accessed January 27, 2018, http://adanewmedia.org/2015/11/issue8-abidin/.

13. See also Mingyi Hou, "Social Media Celebrity and the Institutionalization of YouTube," *Convergence: The International Journal of Research into New Media Technologies* 25, no. 3 (2018): 534–553. Hou provides a detailed literature review and state of the art regarding the

study of social media celebrity as well as quantitative data samples examining beauty vloggers through the lens of digital ethnography.

14. Khamis, Ang, and Welling, "Self-branding," 194.

15. Ibid., 195.

16. Ibid.

17. Graeme Turner, "The Mass Production of Celebrity: 'Celetoids,' Reality TV and the 'Demotic Turn,'" *International Journal of Cultural Studies* 9, no. 2 (2006): passim.

18. "About Me," jeffreestarcosmetics.com, accessed January 27, 2018, https://jeffreestar cosmetics.com/.

19. Graeme Turner, *Understanding Celebrity* (London: SAGE Publications, 2004), 83.

20. Ibid.

21. See also Hearn and Schoenhoff, "From Celebrity to Influencer," and Alice E. Marwick and danah boyd, "I Tweet Honestly, I Tweet Passionately: Twitter Users, Context Collapse, and the Imagined Audience," *New Media and Society* 13, no. 1 (2010).

22. Khamis, Ang, and Welling, "Self-branding," 194.

23. Hearn and Schoenhoff, "From Celebrity to Influencer," 194.

24. Khamis, Ang, and Welling, "Self-branding," 197 (emphasis added).

25. Roman Marek, *Understanding YouTube: Über die Faszination eines Mediums* (Bielefeld: transcript, 2013), 22.

26. Alice E. Marwick, *Status Update: Celebrity, Publicity, and Branding in the Social Media Age* (New Haven and London: Yale University Press, 2013), 196.

27. Michael Strangelove, *Watching YouTube: Extraordinary Videos by Ordinary People* (Toronto: University of Toronto Press, 2010), 4.

28. Henry Jenkins, *Convergence Culture: Where Old and New Media Collide* (New York and London: New York University Press, 2006), 228.

29. Theresa M. Senft, "Micro Celebrity and the Branded Self," in *A Companion to New Media Dynamics*, ed. John Hartley, Jean Burgess, and Axel Bruns (West Sussex: Wiley-Blackwell, 2013): 350.

30. Carpentier goes one step further and argues that, when defined in contradistinction to access and interaction, participation arises as a "political [. . .] process where the actors involved in decision-making processes are positioned towards each other through power relationships that are (to an extent) egalitarian." [Nico Carpentier, "The Concept of Participation: If They Have Access and Interact, Do They Really Participate?" *Revista Fronteiras—Estudos Midiáticos* 14, no. 2 (2012): 175.]

31. Strangelove, *Watching YouTube*, 163.

32. George Ritzer and Nathan Jurgeson, "Production, Consumption, Prosumption: The Nature of Capitalism in the Age of the Digital 'Prosumer,'" *Journal of Consumer Culture* 10, no. 1 (2010): 18.

33. Ibid., 14.

34. Marwick, *Status Update*, 114.

35. Butler, *Bodies that Matter*, xxviii.

36. For example, when asked about his sexuality and gender identity on fellow YouTuber Shane Dawson's podcast *Shane and Friends*, he states: "I get asked that a lot, I always say I'm just Jeffree." ["Jeffree Star—Shane and Friends Ep. 117," soundcloud.com, accessed January 26, 2018, https://soundcloud.com/shaneandfriends/episode-117-jeffree-star.]

37. "Holiday 2017 Collection and Skin Frost Palette Reveal | Jeffree Star Cosmetics," YouTube Video, 27:03, posted by "jeffreestar," November 12, 2017, https://www.youtube.com /watch?v=9fNvbeBLwGc.

38. "The Chrome Summer Collection: Reveal and Swatches | Jeffree Star Cosmetics," YouTube Video, 18:44, posted by "jeffreestar," June 9, 2017, https://www.youtube.com/watch ?v=LVRZdANny3M.

39. Tom van Nuenen, "Here I Am: Authenticity and Self-branding on Travel Blogs," *Tourist Studies* 16, no. 2 (2016): 208 (original emphasis).

40. The opening passage is accompanied by CØDE feat. Joseph Feinstein's song "We're Invincible." While a film crew follows Jeffree and Nathan around their self-proclaimed Barbie House, the lyrics remind the viewer that the two "are bored of regularities," hinting at their

exclusive status as Stars "living all the dreams." The video is no longer informed by the self-made vlog-style known by regular watchers of YouTube content, but rather features camera techniques found in reality television shows such as *MTV Cribs*. The evoked effect of authenticity is, again, enforced by the lyrics of the song, which suggest that Jeffree's American Dream has become "pure reality."

41. "The Star Family Collection: Reveal and Swatches | Jeffree Star Cosmetics," YouTube Video, 28:43, posted by "jeffreestar," October 9, 2017, https://www.youtube.com/watch?v=4HZv5HzFfGk.

42. Van Nuenen, "Here I Am," 193.

43. Gérard Genette, *Palimpsests: Literature in the Second Degree*, trans. Channa Newman and Claude Doubinsky (Lincoln and London: University of Nebraska Press, 1997), 1. Genette uses the word "palimpsest" to describe phenomena of textual transcendence.

44. "Holiday 2017 Collection and Skin Frost Palette Reveal" (emphasis added).

45. "The Star Family Collection: Reveal and Swatches."

46. "The Chrome Summer Collection."

47. "The Star Family Collection: Reveal and Swatches."

48. "Holiday 2017 Collection and Skin Frost Palette Reveal."

49. "The Star Family Collection: Reveal and Swatches."

50. Jenkins, *Convergence Culture*, 257.

51. David Held, *Models of Democracy* (California: Stanford University Press, 2006), 1 (original emphasis).

52. Ibid.

53. "Holiday 2017 Collection and Skin Frost Palette Reveal."

54. "The Chrome Summer Collection."

55. Ibid.

56. .bid.

57. "Holiday 2017 Collection and Skin Frost Palette Reveal" (emphasis added).

58. Marek, *Understanding YouTube*, 19.

59. "The Star Family Collection: Reveal and Swatches" (emphases added).

60. Carpentier, "The Concept of Participation," 165.

61. Hearn and Schoenhoff, "From Celebrity to Influencer," 202.

62. Khamis, Ang, and Welling, "Self-branding," 205.

63. Strangelove, *Watching YouTube*, 163.

64. Dyer, *Heavenly Bodies*, 4.

65. Khamis, Ang, and Welling, "Self-branding," 198.

66. Scott McCloud, *Reinventing Comics* (New York: HarperCollins, 2000), 222.

67. Jenkins, *Convergence Culture*, 257.

68. Ever since the introduction of YouTube Red—which requires paid monthly subscriptions—YouTube is no longer an exclusively free broadcasting platform. Instead, it offers, like other streaming services such as Netflix, movies and serialized formats on demand, which are developing into new modes of watching TV, accessible at home and/or on the go.

69. Senft, "Micro Celebrity and the Branded Self," 350.

BIBLIOGRAPHY

Abidin, Crystal. "Communicative Intimacies: Influencers and Perceived Interconnectedness." *ada: A Journal of Gender, New Media and Technology* 8 (2015): n. p., accessed January 27, 2018, http://adanewmedia.org/2015/11/issue8-abidin/.

Alperstein, Neil M. *Celebrity and Mediated Social Connections: Fans, Friends and Followers in the Digital Age*. Cham: Palgrave Macmillan, 2019.

Butler, Judith. *Bodies that Matter: On the Discursive Limits of "Sex."* London and New York: Routledge, 2011.

Carpentier, Nico. "The Concept of Participation: If They Have Access and Interact, Do They Really Participate?" *Revista Fronteiras—Estudos Midiáticos* 14, no. 2 (2012): 164–177.

"The Chrome Summer Collection: Reveal and Swatches | Jeffree Star Cosmetics." YouTube Video, 18:44. Posted by "jeffreestar," June 9, 2017, https://www.youtube.com/watch?v=LVRZdANny3M.

Dyer, Richard. *Heavenly Bodies: Film Stars and Society*. London and New York: Routledge, 2004.

Genette, Gérard. *Palimpsests: Literature in the Second Degree*. Translated by Channa Newman and Claude Doubinsky. Lincoln and London: University of Nebraska Press, 1997.

Hearn, Alison, and Stephanie Schoenhoff. "From Celebrity to Influencer: Tracing the Diffusion to Celebrity Value across the Data Stream." In *A Companion to Celebrity*, edited by P. David Marshall and Sean Redmond, 194–212. West Sussex: Wiley-Blackwell, 2016.

Held, David. *Models of Democracy*. California: Stanford University Press, 2006.

"Holiday 2017 Collection and Skin Frost Palette Reveal | Jeffree Star Cosmetics." YouTube Video, 27:03. Posted by "jeffreestar," November 12, 2017, https://www.youtube.com/watch?v=9fNvbeBLwGc.

Hou, Mingyi. "Social Media Celebrity and the Institutionalization of YouTube." *Convergence: The International Journal of Research into New Media Technologies* 25, no. 3 (2018): 534–553.

jeffreestarcosmetics.com. "About Me." Accessed January 27, 2018. https://jeffreestarcosmetics.com/.

Jenkins, Henry. *Convergence Culture: Where Old and New Media Collide*. New York and London: New York University Press, 2006.

Khamis, Susie, Lawrence Ang, and Raymond Welling. "Self-branding, 'Micro-celebrity' and the Rise of Social Media Influencers." *Celebrity Studies* 8, no. 2 (2017): 191–208.

Marek, Roman. *Understanding YouTube: Über die Faszination eines Mediums*. Bielefeld: transcript, 2013.

Marwick, Alice E. *Status Update: Celebrity, Publicity, and Branding in the Social Media Age*. New Haven and London: Yale University Press, 2013.

Marwick, Alice E., and danah boyd. "I Tweet Honestly, I Tweet Passionately: Twitter Users, Context Collapse, and the Imagined Audience." *New Media and Society* 13, no. 1 (2010): 114–133.

McCloud, Scott. *Reinventing Comics*. New York: HarperCollins, 2000.

Ritzer, George, and Nathan Jurgeson. "Production, Consumption, Prosumption: The Nature of Capitalism in the Age of the Digital 'Prosumer.'" *Journal of Consumer Culture* 10, no. 1 (2010): 13–36.

Senft, Theresa M. "Micro Celebrity and the Branded Self." In *A Companion to New Media Dynamics*, edited by John Hartley, Jean Burgess and Axel Bruns, 346–354. West Sussex: Wiley-Blackwell, 2013.

soundcloud.com. "Jeffree Star—Shane and Friends Ep. 117." Accessed January 26, 2018. https://soundcloud.com/shaneandfriends/episode-117-jeffree-star.

"The Star Family Collection: Reveal and Swatches | Jeffree Star Cosmetics." YouTube Video, 28:43. Posted by "jeffreestar," October 9, 2017, https://www.youtube.com/watch?v=4HZv5HzFfGk.

Strangelove, Michael. *Watching YouTube: Extraordinary Videos by Ordinary People*.
Toronto: University of Toronto Press, 2010.

Turner, Graeme. "The Mass Production of Celebrity: 'Celetoids,' Reality TV and the 'Demotic Turn.'" *International Journal of Cultural Studies* 9, no. 2 (2006): 153–165.

———. *Understanding Celebrity*. London: SAGE Publications, 2004.

Van Nuenen, Tom. "Here I Am: Authenticity and Self-branding on Travel Blogs." *Tourist Studies* 16, no. 2 (2016): 192–212.

Wolfson, Sam. "The Social Media Quiz of 2017." *The Guardian*, December 20, 2017. https://www.theguardian.com/media/2017/dec/20/the-social-media-quiz-of-2017.

Part II

Makeup (Vlogging) as Empowerment

Chapter Five

The Ladies' Dressing Rooms

Cosmetic "Trickery" from Tertullian's Eve to Kandee Johnson's Barbie

Elizabeth Johnston Ambrose

On the Kandee Johnson YouTube channel, the popular "Barbie Doll Make-Up Transformation"[1] tutorial opens to a split screen. To the right is a framed still of Barbie's face, to the left a framed still of celebrity makeup artist Kandee Johnson's face transformed into Barbie. Lest her extraordinary artistry confuse viewers, Johnson has labeled each "Barbie" and "Kandee" respectively. Johnson's tutorial then begins with Kandee-as-Barbie standing in front of a pink, tinsel-laden backdrop. Filmed from the shoulders up, she stiffly waves her right arm at the elbow: "Hi Guys! It's Kandee. This is my official Barbie wave because she can't move her fingers." As if to further prove that she is actually Kandee and not Barbie, Kandee spreads her fingers. She says she's going to show viewers how to do a "super fun Barbie look" distinct from an "old Barbie video" she did "forever ago" because now her "camera is better" and "this [Barbie] is a totally different look." The view quickly shifts to a series of shots of Kandee with the same Barbie makeup but in different wigs: "Brunette Barbie," "Redhead Barbie," "80s Barbie" complete with lace gloves, and a braided "Anna from *Frozen*." Returning to Kandee as iconic blonde Barbie, she points enthusiastically to the bottom of the screen, encouraging viewers to participate by "comment[ing] below who should I do next." Flashing thumbs up, she also tells viewers to "subscribe if you haven't already because you don't know who I'll turn into next." A thirteen minute and five second tutorial follows in which Kandee demonstrates how she transforms her face into that of Barbie. In other tutorials, Kandee shows off her artistic trickery by transforming herself into celebrities real and mythical, including Angelina Jolie, Disney's Pocahontas, and Cleopatra, among others. She also has a popular video turning herself into Barbie's boyfriend Ken as well as several other videos where she turns into men: Donald Trump, Tony Stark, Willie Robertson from *Duck Dynasty*, even a generic comic book man.

Of course, Kandee Johnson is only one of many such talented artists who shapeshift. So convincing are their transformations that one might be tempted to consider these tutorials to be a kind of technology of social disruption. After all, Judith Butler has famously argued that "[g]ender is the repeated stylization of the body, a set of repeated acts within a highly rigid regulatory frame that congeal over time to produce the appearance of substance, of a natural sort of being."[2] For Butler, there is no natural self, just a series of culturally inscribed rituals people perform, which collectively construct their identities; "Gender identity," she says, "is performatively constituted."[3] Do these tutorials, which walk viewers step-by-step through the transformative process, work to expose the constitutive acts of identity?

I would argue that the potential "liberatory" performance of cosmetic vloggers remains inextricably bound up with historic, deeply misogynistic ideas that reduce women's subjectivity to their bodies, then shames those bodies in their "natural" state; further, these tutorials exploit their viewers' desire for agency by promising them they can unlock their own natural beauty via material consumption. The cosmetic artist, who styles herself as both a visual and linguistic illusionist, is in the business of constructing an essentialized identity. It's true that as she narrates and performs her "transformation" for viewers, she makes visible the various tools and effort on which the illusion of ideal femininity depends; however, at the same time she supports and sustains the belief in an identity with "an ontological status apart from the various acts which constitute its reality."[4] That is, the vlogger's transformation depends on a chronology of subjectivity with a beginning—a moment pre-cosmetics or a point of origin constructed for the viewers as "real" or "natural." Moreover, that body—in its real, natural, and "undressed" state—is defined by the YouTube makeup artist as a site of deficiency, lacking beauty and, therefore, in need of material transformation explicitly tied to the consumption of beauty products.

BEAUTY VLOGGERS, AUTHENTICITY, AND "NATURAL" BODIES

Kandee Johnson, whose net worth was estimated at around four million dollars in 2018[5] is one of a slew of video bloggers (vloggers) who has built a massive following on social media sites and, in doing so, garnered lucrative commercial sponsorships and brand partnerships. Interestingly, the top earning makeup vloggers are men, a gender disparity that mirrors the larger economic wage gap. These vloggers include Jeffree Star, a makeup artist who reportedly made eighteen million dollars in 2018,[6] CoverGirl's first CoverBoy James Charles, and Maybelline's first male ambassador Manny Gutierrez. Other popular female makeup vloggers include Bethany Mota, Zoe "Zoella" Elizabeth Sugg, Rachel Levin, Nikkie de Jager, Eva Gutowski, Marzia Bisognin, Carli Bybel, Mindy McKnight, and Michelle Phan.

Kandee Johnson routinely appears on the list of *Forbes*' annual Top Beauty Influencers, having started her vlogging career in 2008 by conducting a "glaminar" beauty seminar. In 2020, she boasts over 1.8 million followers on Instagram, 770,000 followers on Twitter, and close to a million followers on Facebook. Her YouTube channel has received more than 3.9 million subscriptions and upwards of 453 million views. Her Barbie video described above is her most watched video, with almost thirty-five million views on YouTube and over 130,000 views on Instagram. Her next highest, at nearly six million YouTube views, is her "Angelina Jolie Makeover Transformation Tutorial."[7]

In the beauty industry, vloggers like Johnson are called "influencers," people who wield the power of social media to initiate and shift consumer trends among young people. Byron Donics, founder, president, and chief executive officer of HTI Collection, a health and beauty marketing company, explains, "The blogger has now taken the place of the beauty editor and the beauty consultant."[8] Between 2013 and 2015, YouTube users went from uploading half a million beauty videos a month to 1.5 million beauty videos a month. In 2015, viewers "watched more than 600 million hours of beauty videos."[9] A lot of the attraction to beauty vloggers has to do with their beauty advice being perceived as genuine, that is as coming from a "real" person. This attraction is due to the fact that millennials have grown increasingly skeptical of traditional marketing approaches. A 2017 study by the McCarthy Group found that while 84 percent don't trust traditional advertising, 85 percent watch YouTube on a regular basis, and 58 percent of respondents said they would watch ads which feature a "digital personality."[10] Gender theorist Emma Maquire (2015) explains, "The self-brand of a YouTuber relies on the absence (or at least the appearance of the absence) of commercial or corporate interference. The YouTube vlogger's appeal stems from the seeming authenticity and apparently real personality expressed through such self-marketing platforms as Instagram, Facebook, and Twitter."[11] Mingyi Hou concurs, noting that the vloggers often identify themselves as explicitly divorced from commercial influence or a desire to be a celebrity: "[V]loggers claim efforts not to achieve the *best* of something, but to be *oneself*. Both vloggers and viewers are very cautious about making personal judgments on beauty and fashion styles. Some vloggers refuse the role as a makeup expert, and they simply share how they do it and what is suitable for them."[12] That "seeming authenticity" is a powerful tool for replacing the increasingly illusive brand loyalty marketers covet. Thus, we sit at an interesting cultural moment wherein the same viewers seeking "authenticity" are also fully comfortable with, even seek out and embrace, the tutelage of someone engaged in endless performance.

Of course, some argue that YouTube has provided a space within which girls can empower themselves by expressing their "true" selves. Samara Anarbaeva (2016), for example, claims that YouTube vloggers appeal to "a community of women who are thirsty for self-expression and meaning-making. . . . One way young women feel safe and in control of their channels on YouTube is by posting about beauty products without feeling the pressure from a male-dominated society or being called superficial. Women from all over the world come together on YouTube to create global beauty and Do-It-Yourself (DIY) talk."[13] In other words, one of the appeals of the YouTube makeup tutorial is female-driven community. The YouTube makeup tutorial, then, appears to young girls as an avenue to independent self-construction. Hou continues, "[T]he new media empowers those who can create online content; thus, it becomes women's new tool for means of power. The YouTube audience is not the typical audience who is used to interpreting stories from a male-dominated perspective. In the beauty community of women on YouTube, women produce and share their own stories, edit their own histories, and have the freedom to construct their own meanings. Hence, their ability to create their own stories makes them powerful, not weak."[14] "Join the Kandee family," Johnson says at the end of each of her videos, holding out her arms in a mock embrace to give "huge hugs" to her followers: "You are more beautiful than you know. I love you." If, historically, women have learned to self-objectify and, in so doing, to surrender agency and authenticity, the space provided by YouTube might seem a space for inclusive, gynocentric self-expression, free from the supervision of the heterosexual male gaze.

However, any authenticity, liberation from male control, or space for inclusive community is undercut by the fact that, in the end, the vloggers are selling a product, and that product depends on convincing viewers that they are, first, rooted in a fixed body, and, second, that the "fixed" body in its "natural" state is fundamentally flawed.

ANTI-COSMETIC RHETORIC AND FEMALE "TRICKERY" IN HISTORY, FROM ANTIQUITY TO MODERNITY

"Kandee Johnson is basically a sorceress," gushes one *Popsugar* article about the popular beauty guru.[15] While the *Popsugar* article celebrates Johnson's beauty tricks and hacks, the reference to witchcraft is especially interesting given historic anti-cosmetic rhetoric that has aligned the use of make-up with witchcraft[16] and devil worshipping.[17] Folklore, fairy tales, mythology, and urban legends are rife with examples of desirable women who seduce men only to be exposed as grotesque hags who have sold their souls to the devil in exchange for beauty.

However, it is with the early modern period—with the advent of print technology, increased literacy, and the emergence of both a literary and global marketplace—that cosmetic use explodes into mass consumption and, along with it, even more widespread misogyny. Philosophers like Michel Foucault (1976)[18] and literary critics like Ian Watt (1957)[19] and Nancy Armstrong (1990)[20] have also argued that it is from the early modern period that we derive our contemporary notions of gendered subjectivity, in particular the gendered public/private divide and idealized femininity. Thus, it's helpful to consider contemporary makeup tutorials within the context of historic discourses about women and "female trickery," as well as within the early modern impulse to expose, that is, "undress" these sorceresses threatening the "Angel in the House" ideal.

Much of the early modern rhetoric about women derives from early Christian rhetoric, which figures the female body as, at best, an inferior version of men's bodies, and, at worst, hellbent on destroying mankind. Consider, for example, the misogynist language of third-century theologian Tertullian as he shames women who decorate their bodies and faces:

> And do you not know that you are (each) an Eve? The sentence of God on this sex of yours lives in this age: the guilt must of necessity live too. *You* are the devil's gateway: *you* are the unsealer of that (forbidden) tree: *you* are the first deserter of the divine law: *you* are she who persuaded him whom the devil was not valiant enough to attack. *You* destroyed so easily God's image, man. On account of *your* desert—that is, death—even the Son of God had to die. And do you think about adorning yourself over and above your tunics of skins?[21]

Tertullian goes on to speculate that if Eve had access to the fashionable clothes, accessories, and mirrors that third-century women do, she would have compounded her sin with vanity:

> Come, now; if from the beginning of the world the Milesians sheared sheep, and the Serians spun trees, and the Tyrians dyed, and the Phrygians embroidered with the needle, and the Babylonians with the loom, and pearls gleamed, and onyx-stones flashed; if gold itself also had already issued, with the cupidity (which accompanies it), from the ground; if the mirror, too, already had license to lie so largely, Eve, expelled from paradise, (Eve) already dead, would also have coveted *these* things, I imagine![22]

The desire for adornment, to make oneself attractive via material goods and to use that deceptive ("lying") attractiveness to ensnare men, is thus constructed as an evil motivation inherent in women.

Fast forward fourteen hundred years to the early modern period, and we see the grip these anxieties still possess on the cultural imagination. When we first meet Eve in John Milton's canonical epic poem *Paradise Lost* (1667), she has just woken after being created by God from Adam's rib. Adam is not around, and, while searching for her better half, she encounters a mirror of sorts, a body of water. She later recounts to Adam how she was hardly able to tear herself away from her own lovely reflection:

> . . . There I had fixed
> Mine eyes till now, and pined with vain desire,
> Had not a voice thus warned me: "What thou seest,
> What there thou seest, fair creature, is thyself;
> With thee it came and goes. But follow me,
> And I will bring thee where no shadow stays
> Thy coming, and thy soft embraces, he
> Whose image thou art, him thou shalt enjoy
> Inseparably thine, to him shalt bear
> Multitudes like thyself, and thence be called
> Mother of human race."[23]

In his imagining of the first woman, Milton takes a page from Tertullian, depicting Eve as fixated on her own beauty and saved only from her own narcissism by God's intervention. It is also significant that the authoritative and disembodied voice of God defines Eve's reflection in the water as an insubstantial "shadow."[24]

Imagine, then, how cosmetic use could be seen as both further evidence of women's vanity as well as a disavowal of God's divine planning. In *Cosmetics in Shakespearean and Renaissance Drama*, Farah Karim-Cooper (2016) explains that arguments against cosmetics in Christian rhetoric speak to "three main concerns: an anxiety of transformation, an anxiety that God's workmanship is being altered, and an anxiety about recognizability."[25] We can see this anxiety surfacing in Alexander Brome's 1661 poem, "To a Painted Lady." The speaker begs his female addressees, "Leave these deluding tricks and shows"[26] and ends his poem with the ultimatum, "Give me the pure or none."[27] Cosmetic use is thus explicitly tied to the destruction of women's most important marketable commodity: their virtue.

A less religious-based concern with "painting" amid the nascent early-modern global market and the widespread marketing and availability of cosmetics concerns how cosmetics might be used to destabilize the social hierarchy. In "Inventing Whiteness: Cosmetics, Race, and Women in Early Modern England" (2011), Kimberly Poitevin explains that one of the concerns was that cosmetics possessed the potential to upend racial categories:

"[S]ince the most sought after cosmetics in the period were foreign products from Asia, Africa, or the Americas, and since cosmetics were applied directly to the skin (a porous bodily boundary), women who used these products encoded anxieties about race-mingling and cross-cultural contact on their skins."[28] White skin was discursively constructed as the standard of beauty, but cosmetics could be used to lighten skin, blurring racial categories. As a result, a "flood of anti-cosmetic discourses . . . sought not only to strip women of these modes of self-representation, but also to recuperate 'natural' skin color as a reliable racial marker and to begin constructing race as a category that was no longer fluid, but unchanging and essential."[29] A woman of color might be able to paint herself "white" and thus commit the unauthorized transgression of racial and ethnic boundaries.

Similarly, anti-cosmetic rhetoric occurred around themes of class migration. Since being pale was a mark of the leisure time associated with wealth, women began painting blue veins on their skin to emphasize their paleness. One writer complained about the effect of this deception on potential male suitors: "[W]e are not able to know a Lady from a Landresse, we cannot distinguish between those women that be of honor, from those that are but base in parentage, whose best bringing up hath been in washing, in starching, in scraping of trenches."[30] Another cautioned men that "a deformed quean, a crooked carcass, a maukin, a witch, a rotten post, a hedgestake may be so set out and tricked up, that it shall make as fair a show, as much enamour as the rest: many a silly fellow is taken."[31] As these quotations suggest, a woman wearing cosmetics can upend not only class but gender hierarchies too. The latter quotation's use of the word "taken" is especially revealing of these anxieties. To be "taken" is to be deceived. But the painted lady has done more than simply lie because to be "taken" also means to steal or possess. By marrying up, she has "taken" the social ranking that does not belong to her. Further, in tricking her lover, she has destabilized male authority and "taken" a husband in the same way a man who marries is said to have "taken a wife." Cosmetics, then, give women unauthorized and dangerous power.

Obvious is a palpable fear about women's power to emasculate men. The result is the masculinist impulse to strip women of their cosmetic charms, to reveal them in their "natural" state, which is *not* a resplendent image of God's handiwork but something inherently loathsome. One of the most misogynistic texts of the Renaissance is Joseph Swetnam's *The Arraignment of Lewd, Idle, Froward, and Unconstant Women* (1615). "Painted pots," he warns men, "commonly hold the deadly poison."[32] Chapter 2 opens with the premise that "the beauty of Women has been the bane of many a man, for it has overcome valiant and strong men, eloquent and subtle men." Swetnam goes on to say, "[C]ommonly women are the most part of the forenoon painting themselves, and frizzling their hairs, and prying in their glass like Apes to prank up themselves in their gaudies."[33] He goes on to instruct his readers to disregard the outer appearance of women: "For take away their painted clothes, and then they look like ragged walls; take away their ruffs, and they look ruggedly; their coifs and stomachers, and they are simple to behold; their hair untrussed, and they look wildly."[34] Women in their natural state are as beastly as the hungry eagles he compares them to: "ragged," "rugged," and "wild."[35]

The impulse to "undress" women to reveal them in their natural, wild state takes off in the eighteenth-century "dressing room" satires in which male observers who have gained access to women's cosmetic routines describe them for readers. As Tita Chico notes in *Designing Women: The Dressing Room in Eighteenth-Century Literature* (2005), starting in the late seventeenth century, the dressing room, the architectural space within which women apply their public faces, becomes a site of anxiety about female consumerism as well as women's privacy and, therein, the potential for escape from the scrutinizing male gaze. Chico points to Pope's *The Art of Beauty: a Poem* (1719), in which she says cosmetics are figured as "'a specious Art' that enables women to dissemble and exert power over 'Conquests,' whether imaginary or not."[36] She also refers to Richard Steele's magazine, *Spectator,* which, in issue forty-one, coins the term "picts" to define women who paint their faces with makeup: "A 'Pict' is a body of parts, a construction ready to come apart at any moment. A 'Pict' is also clearly a picture, an art object, though explicitly an inferior one."[37] A "Pict," then, is not a "real" woman but a copy of a woman, and it is the job of the male voyeur to expose the copy and to point others back to the original who is, more often than not, without value, grotesque, and wholly undeserving of male desire. Perhaps the most famous of these dressing room satires is Jonathan Swift's canonical poem "The Lady's Dressing Room" (1732). In the poem, worth quoting from at length, the narrator describes a man named Strephon who visits the bedchamber of his beloved Celia while she is away. In so doing, he learns the tricks by which "gaudy tulips [are] raised from dung."[38] As he investigates her room, he begins to enumerate the "inventory" of deceit, deconstructing her counterfeit identity find by find. At first it is her clothes he examines, finding on them evidence of sweat. The speaker of the poem revels in Strephon's discovery:

> And first a dirty Smock appear'd,
> Beneath the Arm-pits well besmear'd.
> Strephon, the Rogue, display'd it wide,
> And turn'd it round on every Side.
> On such a Point few Words are best,
> And Strephon bids us guess the rest;
> But swears how damnably the Men lie,
> In calling Celia sweet and cleanly.[39]

Strephon, in a position of privilege in so far as he sees what his peers cannot, begins to bemoan that he believed other men who found Celia beautiful. But his horror only grows as he moves from an examination of her clothes to an inspection of her cosmetics, laying them out as a doctor might lay out surgical instruments before a surgery:

> Now listen while he next produces,
> The various Combs for various Uses,
> Fill'd up with Dirt so closely fixt,
> No Brush could force a way betwixt.
> A Paste of Composition rare,
> Sweat, Dandriff, Powder, Lead and Hair;
> A Forehead Cloth with Oyl upon't
> To smooth the Wrinkles on her Front;
> Here Allum Flower to stop the Steams,
> Exhal'd from sour unsavoury Streams,
> There Night-gloves made of Tripsy's Hide,
> Bequeath'd by Tripsy when she dy'd,
> With Puppy Water, Beauty's Help
> Distill'd from Tripsy's darling Whelp;
> Here Gallypots and Vials plac'd,
> Some fill'd with washes, some with Paste,
> Some with Pomatum, Paints and Slops,
> And Ointments good for scabby Chops.[40]

Having first stripped her of her clothes, the narrator has now stripped Celia of her body. If the sweat on her dress was evidence that a body existed beneath her clothes, that body is missing. In its place is a litany of commodities: vials and ointments, paints, and slops.

Where has the body gone? It has disappeared, the only evidences that it might have existed—its secretions and excrement—collected in jars as if shelved in a witch's cabinet:

> Hard by a filthy Bason stands,
> Fowl'd with the Scouring of her Hands;
> The Bason takes whatever comes
> The Scrapings of her Teeth and Gums,
> A nasty Compound of all Hues,
> For here she spits, and here she spues.
> But oh! it turn'd poor Strephon's Bowels,
> When he beheld and smelt the Towels,
> Begumm'd, bematter'd, and beslim'd
> With Dirt, and Sweat, and Ear-Wax grim'd.
> No Object Strephon's Eye escapes . . .[41]

There is no subjectivity; she is all body, a sum of her own gruesome parts. The poem famously culminates in Strephon's discovery of Celia's full chamber pot; he rushes from the room, disavowing all women, forever "blind/To all the charms of Female kind."[42] Importantly, the narrator of the poem *has not* given up women despite knowing about their deceits. Instead, the poem ends with the narrator wishing Strephon could just "stop his nose."[43] Then, the narrator says, Strephon would know what the speaker knows and instead

> . . . bless his ravisht Sight to see
> Such Order from Confusion sprung,
> Such gaudy Tulips rais'd from Dung.[44]

However, this closing is not really a generous acceptance of Celia in her natural use, nor is it an advertisement for cosmetics to help women make "order" of their natural "confusion"; instead, by narrating Strephon's deconstruction of his beloved Celia, the speaker of the poem makes sure readers see and remember what Strephon sees and remembers: Celia's equation with feces. The impulse of the poem is not to embrace Celia's fluid identity but, rather, to root her in the waste of her own embodied materiality.

Swift repeats the theme of dismembering a woman by removing her cosmetics in "A Beautiful Young Nymph Going to Bed" (1734).[45] The speaker is a voyeur watching the beautiful prostitute Corinna undress. She removes her wig, her fake eye, her eyebrows made of mouse fur (a common beauty accessory), and her false teeth, among other accessories, until, in the final stanza, we see her in her "natural" form:

> The nymph, tho' in this mangled plight,
> Must ev'ry morn her limbs unite.
> But how shall I describe her arts
> To recollect the scattered parts?
> Or shew the anguish, toil, and pain,
> Of gath'ring up herself again?[46] (lines 65–70)

Like "The Lady's Dressing Room," the speaker revels in tearing apart the woman who otherwise exerts power over men.[47] She is violently "mangled" and "scattered" and must exert much effort to "unite" herself again.

Because the eighteenth century is also the dawn of the early feminist movement, these dressing room satires receive plenty of pushback from women writers. Lady Mary Wortley Montague has a biting response poem, "The Reasons that Induced Dr S to Write a Poem Call'd the Lady's Dressing Room" (1734),[48] in which she accuses Swift's misogyny as stemming from anxieties about his own impotence. However, perhaps the best defense of women's cosmetic use can be found in Eliza Haywood's "Fantomina" (1726);[49] the amatory fiction piece often read as a cautionary tale narrates the story of a young woman of aristocratic birth who falls in love with a rake named Beauplaisir. Acknowledging that most men are quick to lose interest in women after they've had sex with them, the main character manages to retain Beauplaisir's interest by disguising herself as new women every few weeks—a prostitute named "Fantomina," a servant girl named "Celia," a widow named "Widow Bloomer," and a mysterious, veiled figure who signs her letters to Beauplaisir, "Incognita." Via the use of cosmetics, changes in dress, and various accents, she tricks her wayward lover over and over again; every time he grows tired of one identity, she disposes of that identity and re-creates another. If the impulse of Swift's poem, and of anti-cosmetic rhetoric, in general, is to trap women in their materiality, Haywood's story reveals how little the "real" identities of women matter to men anyway. This gives her a vantage point from which to criticize societal expectations for both men and women. As Juliette Merritt argues in *Beyond Spectacle: Eliza Haywood's Female Spectators* (2004), the protagonist "can now use her position as observer to become a theorist of masculinity; Beauplasir stands exposed before her, his duplicity fully revealed."[50] Moreover, the protagonist successfully evades his desire to possess or confine her since "a woman so obviously disembodied, split between mind and body, cannot easily be consumed."[51] In her final ruse, Fantomina covers her face and body entirely, refusing to allow Beauplaisir to see her, and adopts the name Incognita, refusing to be known and, thereby, possessed by her lover. The protagonist continues to enjoy sex with her lover (whose name in French means "good pleasure") and is found out only when her own very real body betrays her; she becomes pregnant, tries to disguise her pregnancy, goes into labor at a ball, and is forced to admit to both Beauplaisir and her mother what she has been up to. Beauplaisir is aghast, having never suspected the ruse, and the story ends with the protagonist in a convent.

Fantomina appears, prior to the discovery of her pregnancy, to have claimed agency. However, as Merritt recognizes, the repertoire of identity the protagonist can assume is confined to the sexual stereotypes of the day, that is, within a sexual economy that nevertheless situates women's value as an object of men's desire. At the end of the day, if subjectivity is defined by agency, the protagonist's choices are always already determined for her. To act as somebody, she must turn herself into a nobody. She is, like Eve, an image of an image, at the end of the story, literally generating an infant image of herself who, at the end of the story, disappears entirely. We never learn what happens to her daughter after the protagonist is sent to a convent. In fact, we never learn Fantomina's real name. She is as much a shadow as Milton's Eve, as dismembered as Swift's Celia.

Given that our ideas about gender derive from early modern constructions of the body, it makes sense that when we turn to contemporary discourses about women and cosmetic use we see similar vocabulary and images.

BARBIE AND THE PLASTIC BODY

Barbie is undoubtedly Eve's secular counterpart, an icon for modern, late capitalist society. As such, Barbie has long served as a sort of vexed cultural barometer for feminists trying to determine whether she represents oppressive or liberatory potential. Given that Kandee Johnson's transformation into Barbie is her most popular video, it's useful to think about the iconic doll and society's relationship to that doll as a symbol for how identity is understood in the twentieth and twenty-first centuries.

In *Barbie Culture* (1999), Mary F. Rogers employs Jean Baudrillard's theories about simulacrum and similitude to identify Barbie's body as one of many "humanoid facsimiles" desired more than a "real" body.[52] In her discussion of rising trends in plastic surgery, she calls Barbie "an icon of an emergent, consumerist 'somatics'—a technology of the body driven by the idea that our bodies can be whatever we like if we devote enough money and attention to them."[53] According to Rogers, by the end of the twentieth century the millennial body had become "an aerobic instrument, a surgical object, a dietary experiment, a fleshy clay capable of endless remodeling."[54] Rogers also depends on earlier theories of plasticity discussed in Susan Bordo's now canonical book *Unbearable Weight* (1995), in which Bordo says of plastic surgery trends, "Gradually and surely, . . . technology . . . has generated an industry and an ideology fueled by fantasies of rearranging, transforming, and correcting, an ideology of limitless improvement and change, defying the historicity, the mortality, and, indeed, the very materiality of the body. In place of that materiality, we now have what I will call cultural plastic."[55]

Nearly a decade after Bordo and Rogers, Kim Toffoletti, author of *Cyborgs and Barbie Dolls: Feminism, Popular Culture and the Post-human Body* (2007), also reads Barbie within Baudrillard's theories about simulacra: "[H]er exaggerated styling and the relentless proliferation of her form in media and popular culture characterize her as an 'unbound signifier' that prompts us to consider whether there can be any definitive truth to the term 'woman' at all."[56] Barbie's plastic body, she says, "is an object of potentially endless transformation," and its plasticity "dissolves the opposition between the real and what it represents."[57] For Toffoletti, the cyborg/posthuman/plastic Barbie is liberatory:

> [Barbie] invalidates a notion of the material body as the limit point of subjectivity. . . . Conceiving of the subject in terms of transformation can help us to decode that mindset that writes the plastic body as a technology of control and containment, or as fixed in the real. It can serve as a strategy to hack into the phallogocentric codes that structure ideals of femininity, and scramble interpretations of embodiment that reinscribe an unchanging and essentialized myth of woman as tied to nature.[58]

In other words, she claims that Barbie is a phantom identity resisting consumption.

However, these descriptions of Barbie's plasticity don't sound all that different from discussions of the painted female body in the early modern dressing room literature I've discussed above. A *phantom* Barbie has little more opportunity to scramble gender or beauty ideals than a Fantomina. There is no "liberatory potential" inherent in conceiving of the body as plastic, as an unbound signifier, a consumerist somatic, or a proliferation of "do-able" bodies. Haywood's protagonist, although seeming in control of her own self-simulation, can only choose from the prescriptive repertoire of an oppressive sexual economy within which her value is solely defined in relation to male desire.

Of course, Haywood's protagonist chose from only four models of femininity (a prostitute, a working-class girl, a widow, and the mysterious, veiled Incognita); today's young women have many more choices. Since Mattel debuted a new line of Barbie dolls in 2016, consumers can choose from Original, Tall, Petite, or Curvy versions that come in seven skin tones, thirty hair colors, twenty-four hair styles, and twenty-two eye colors.

Indeed, it would seem that celebrating the "natural" body is trending. For example, social media sites that find investors for inventors—like Kickstarter—have helped to launch off-brands like the Makie dolls, which can be customized with 3D technology to come with scars and hearing aids, and the Lammily doll, which comes with stick-on pimples and cellulite. Dove, of course, has been running their popular and financially lucrative "Real Beauty" campaign since 2004, featuring hashtags like #BeautyBias and #Womengettold which encourage women to share their stories of feeling excluded from mainstream media's definition of what it means to be beautiful. However, the popularity of YouTube makeup tutorials with tags like "The Power of Makeup: Ugly Betty Inspired Story" (over 43 million views), "From Bum to Baddie" (3.4 million views), and "Impressive Makeup Transformations [Pure Magic]" (9.6 million views), not to mention the ubiquity of television shows like *Extreme Makeover*, attest to the view that a sense of empowerment comes not from embracing one's "natural" self but from transforming oneself to look as close as possible to a monolithic view of beauty defined by Eurocentric standards.

Dana Berkowitz draws on symbolic interactionism theory in her book *Botox Nation: Changing the Face of America* (2016) to consider how the plastic body is understood in contemporary culture. Rejecting the notion of a "natural body" as illusory, Berkowitz reiterates that "the body is a subject that individuals experience, create, and negotiate . . . [P]eople do not merely have bodies, but *do* bodies."[59] "Humans," she agrees, "cultivate their bodies in ways that meaningfully construct and demonstrate their selves and social identities."[60] At the same time, however, Berkowitz argues that power relations embedded in social institutions and cultural discourses shape the way we both talk about and govern these bodies.[61] She acknowledges that the late-capitalist construction of the modern individual as an autonomous subject responsible for her own reality makes it difficult for people to distinguish between what she chooses and what has been chosen for her. This is because the self-expression increasingly performed through and on the body is inseparable from commodity capitalism. The bodies we choose to "do" are bodies we "buy" via the cosmetic purchases we make and the biomedical technologies we invest in. Therefore, if anything, the liberatory potential of the plastic or malleable body is even more delimited in the twenty-first century than it was in the eighteenth century, when options to buy were fewer and technologies to "do" the body were more rudimentary.[62] Indeed, the makeup vlogger's primary purpose is not to show viewers how to "do" bodies or looks but to sell them the cosmetics and brushes they're using to "do" these bodies. "Doing" is secondary to "buying," and a body can't be done unless one has already purchased the requisite, name-brand (often quite costly) instruments.

"THE THINGS I WENT THROUGH TO MAKE THIS VIDEO": THE DISCOURSE OF EFFORT

It's also interesting to think back on the language of effort that Jonathan Swift uses to describe Corrina's and Celia's cosmetic routine when listening to the way contemporary makeup vloggers describe their own process of transformation. A frequent feature of the YouTube tutorial is its emphasis on how much concerted *work* it takes to create the illusion. A quick Google search for "face contouring" produces innumerable images of the female face carved up into shaded regions labeled with words like "highlighter," "blush," and "contouring." These images literally and visibly inscribe the body with signs of illusion, reinforcing the narrative of a fixed subjectivity that always already exists beneath its various performances. In other words, rather than being released from a point of origin, the point of origin—the "natural" face—is always the starting point for the tutorial.

This discursive and visual grammar of effort functions as a sort of confession, reinforcing the idea that the made-up face is unnatural. The makeup vlogger, by "starting over" with each video—beginning with a "natural" face—assuages anxieties that her intent is to deceive.

In contrast, the sort of anti-cosmetic virulence we hear in early modern rhetoric is reserved for those understood as actually intending to deceive. For example, Ukrainian model/actor/singer Valeria Lukyanova, Russian models Angelica Kenova and Yulia Kriger, and, most recently, German Paris Herns, have made headlines for spending excessive amounts of money on surgeries to turn their bodies into living Barbie dolls via breast enhancement, rib removal, and cosmetic surgeries to their noses and lips, and so forth. However, rather than being read as desirable bodies, their efforts are largely pathologized in mainstream culture. The difference is that the "playfulness" associated with the use of makeup and non-biomedical cosmetic technologies derives, in part, from their impermanence. Those using these technologies are not perceived as intent on "hacking" phallocentric codes; instead, they are understood as merely engaged in a type of innocuous role-playing, the temporariness of which assures others that beneath the performance their "real" or "natural" subjectivity remains intact.

Consider, for example, vlogger Jenna Marbles's tutorial on how to create fake freckles entitled "Making Fake Freckles ~* WORK*~ For Me,"[63] which has nearly seven million views as of February 2020. Ironically, freckles in the early modern period were a marker of the working class who would have labored in the sun. As noted above, historically, women have lightened their skin to hide freckles and tans; however, in the late twentieth and early twenty-first centuries, freckles, like tans, have become a mark of leisure time spent relaxing in the sun (or under the bulbs of a tanning bed). In fact, Marbles says she is too busy working to tan naturally, so she needs to "fake" freckles. Her rhetoric as she fumbles through various attempts to make her fake freckles look real demonstrates how difficult this trickery is while at the same time underscoring how inept she is at her attempts. "Sometimes I think you just watch me to see me fail," she says to her viewers as she dots her face with Henna. "I'm not particularly gifted," she reiterates, and then adds that "if a dummy dumb dumb can get it done, maybe they [her viewers] can, too."

As noted earlier, humility is a defining characteristic of the most popular cosmetic tutorials. Take, for instance, YouTube celebrity Zoella, who, in videos like "My Everyday Winter Makeup"[64] (1.3 million views), is quick to distinguish showing viewers how to do a "look" from doing a "tutorial" "because all I do is ramble," she explains. She also seems uncertain as she tries different ways to do her makeup. "I don't know if that's bad," she says of using a lot of the same brushes. Like Marbles, she is quick to differentiate herself from the "pros." These "makeovers," then, are not inherently dangerous (and, therefore, not a threat to the status quo) because the intent is never to deceive. It's also common practice for the vlogger to edit text into the video later, pointing out parts of the video that are unprofessional (for example, in her Cleopatra video described below, Johnson has superimposed the words "crazy spider hair" in big, bold letters to draw attention to unruly hair slipping from her headband). These admissions of error again reinforce that the intent is not to deceive, but that this is all just in fun.

In fact, it was Ms. Marbles's ironic "How to Trick People into Thinking You're Good Looking"[65] that launched her into internet fame in 2010 with 5.3 million views in the first week and that has now been viewed over sixty-nine million times. As she tells the story, she uploaded the video on a whim before heading to her job as a go-go dancer; of course, the "accidental" nature of her fame only adds to her perceived authenticity. In the "How to Trick People" video, she tells her viewers that if they were born ugly like her, they can take some simple steps to trick people into thinking they're pretty. She then walks viewers through her beauty routine, emphasizing the fakeness of her looks while at the same time implicitly criticizing a monolithic view of beauty and a culture which rewards women for their looks more than for their intellect (she pretends to weep over her MBA diploma before she heads out for her gig as a go-go dancer). However, if she's confessing to "tricking" people, then she's never really intending to "trick" people. Her confession is a joke that everyone is already in on. She's not, it should be noted, taking out her teeth or removing a glass eye. Her "trickery" then, is constructed, and, thereby, perceived as benign.

"YOU HAVE TO LOVE YOURSELF WITHOUT A FULL FACE ON": THE DISCOURSE OF DISEMBODIMENT

There is another interesting parallel to eighteenth-century dressing room satires. Linguistically, the vloggers reveal that they experience a disembodiment when doing "makeovers." When Kandee Johnson turns herself into Angelina Jolie, for instance, her face becomes not her own but something separate from herself. She doesn't say "my nose," but "*the* nose," not "my cheekbones," but "*my Angelina* cheekbones," and not "shadowing in my eyes," but "shadowing in *her* eyes."[66] Johnson appears to be creating a picture, her face a blank, shadowy palette.

Indeed, it's important that viewers see she *is* copying a picture. She's not becoming Angelina Jolie. She's not even copying Angelina Jolie. She's copying Angelina-Jolie-who-is-performing-Angelina-Jolie-in-a-particular-moment. When Johnson transforms herself into a beautiful celebrity, she makes clear to her viewers that she's using a picture of the celebrity as a base—and that a picture, like all photos, is a representation filtered through a professional lens, in the hands of a professional camera person, under professional lights, of a person who knows how to model within that context. Therefore, Johnson narrates how she uses the shadows that are on the image of Angelina Jolie to create her own Johnson-as-Angelina-Jolie image.

Consider also Kandee Johnson's Cleopatra tutorial,[67] viewed more than 930,000 times. When most people today imagine Cleopatra, they think of Elizabeth-Taylor-as-Cleopatra—even those who have never seen the 1963 film. This comes as no surprise since the media proliferation of Elizabeth Taylor's Cleopatra has all but entirely consumed any historic reference to Cleopatra. Interestingly, when Johnson's video begins, roaring '20s music is playing and she pops up onscreen looking very much like Elizabeth Taylor's

Cleopatra but talking with a stereotypical 1920s flapper accent, no doubt because the beaded headdress she's wearing was referred to as a Cleopatra headdress. "People ask me all the time, Cleopatra, what's your favorite dance move?" she says in a nasally voice, then begins to sing the Bangles' "Walk like an Egyptian" while bobbing her head and her hands side to side. "It's Kandeeee," she says, stopping to clarify in case viewers are confused. She goes on to say she'll award a matching Cleopatra headdress to the best version of this look to any viewer. "Happy Cleopatra-ing," she says, turning Cleopatra the subject into Cleopatra the verb; this "verbing" of Cleopatra is a perfect example of "doing" the body. Later in the video, she does clarify that "our" eye (which we all "own" since it doesn't belong to her) in the video is "from The Cleopatra with Elizabeth Taylor." At one point, she describes her makeup as "Egypsy," and turquoise text appears over the screen admitting, "yes I said 'Egypsy' . . . I mad [sic] it up . . . like Egypt . . . but add an 'y' on the end . . . ha ha ha." Of course, she can make up words, just as she is making up "Cleopatra." In this virtual, plastic world of floating signifiers, everything is made up. Even the country "Egypt" is detached from any real referent.

Another interesting thing happens in this same Cleopatra video. Johnson notes that she has a scar on her bottom lip and pulls the camera close to see it (though it's difficult to see); she also says that her teeth used to be chipped from the accident that caused the scar but that they were "sanded down" and fixed. "That's what the bump is in my lip. I know. I've just been too scared to get it fixed," she says. Again, the language is confessional, pointing out her flaws. Text appears over her image while she talks: "Scars are beautiful . . . it would be boring to be plain and perfect! Ha ha ha." However, this text is undercut by what she implies in her confession: that her appearance is "broken" in some way and, but for her fear, she'd fix it. This is not the language of empowerment, though it may appeal to viewers as the language of authenticity.

Being open about one's imperfections appeals to viewers, even as those viewers rush to buy the products that will resolve those imperfections. "Just be who you as you really are" is the mantra of YouTube celebrity James Charles. In a 2019 *Glamour* interview he explains that his use of cosmetics isn't an attempt to "fix" himself but an expression of the multiple aspects of his selfhood:

> I have 3 faces, maybe 4. It's the no makeup and just moisturiser which is my everyday moment. I'll have a phase where I'll do just do fake freckles and brows when I'm going out to a dinner with friends or maybe when I wanna feel cute when I go to the mall! Then it's this face minus eyeshadow which is my typical red carpet go to glam or there's a full glam look with a full look and eyeshadow . . . I tell people you don't need makeup to be beautiful! I wear makeup as an art form and to express myself, but you will never see me walk

> out the house in the morning with a full face of makeup because it doesn't change my confidence—I'm very adamant that you are beautiful with or without. It's important to love yourself no matter what and be proud of who you are. At the end of the day you have to just love yourself without a full face on.[68]

These sentiments undoubtedly appeal to young viewers. Like Johnson's, Suggs's, and Marbles's emphasis on self-expression, Charles's mantra about "loving yourself without a full face on" would seem to encourage viewers to eschew restrictive beauty norms. Charles, a male beauty vlogger, is certainly eschewing gender norms related to masculinity, but I am skeptical of the authenticity of these mantras given that their discourse is also so inextricably linked to consumer culture and given their persistent use of the language of disembodiment. After all, the underlying message here is that one's face is not fully one's face without cosmetics on it.

When we look back at history, we see a consistent effort to anchor women to their bodies and to inscribe those bodies as inherently sinful and even monstrous—even at their most natural. Anti-cosmetic rhetoric, which increased in response to the availability and commercialism of cosmetic technologies in the early modern period, looked nostalgically back to Eve as the most authentic version of women; but that rhetoric is undercut by a symbolic system that writes Eve as twice-removed from God (a copy of a copy) and as "the destroyer of God's image, man." Moving forward in history to a more secular society, Eve's replacement, Barbie, has reached a similar iconic status. Her plasticity perfectly captures an ideological framework within which female bodies are understood as malleable, but that flexibility is not their own with which to play. Instead, the plastic Barbie body at its base is always a signifier of value defined by the male heterosexual gaze and commodity capitalism. Barbie is also a symbol of what Baudrillard has called hyperreality: a sign that refers only to other signs, eradicating substance and subjectivity.

When Kandee Johnson or other bloggers "do" Barbie or Cleopatra or Angelina Jolie or countless other iconic images of beautiful women, this "expression" of identity is one based on floating signifiers. Thus, while the beauty vlogger performs and makes visible what Butler would call the constitutive acts of gender, she is not scrambling them since they are always, already imagined as scattered.

NOTES

1. Kandee Johnson, "Barbie Doll MakeUp Transformation," YouTube Video, 13:05, October 30, 2014, https://www.youtube.com/watch?v=H_IfRNp0ncU.
2. Judith Butler, *Gender Trouble* (New York: Routledge, 2006), 25.

3. Ibid, 25.
4. Ibid, 136.
5. Brooke Carter, "Kandee Johnson Net Worth 2018," *Gazette Review*, January 15, 2018, https://gazettereview.com/2018/01/kandee-johnson-net-worth/.
6. Natalie Robehmed and Madeline Berg, "Highest-Paid YouTube Marketers 2018," *Forbes*, December 3, 2018, https://www.forbes.com/sites/natalierobehmed/2018/12/03/highest-paid-youtube-stars-2018-markiplier-jake-paul-pewdiepie-and-more/#2dac8873909a.
7. Kandee Johnson. "Angelina Jolie Makup Transformation Tutorial," November 8, 2014, Video, 14:58, https://www.youtube.com/watch?v=GDcQJ32zmvg&t=7s.
8. Qtd. in Amber Alston, "Beauty the $445 Billion Beast," *License Global*, September 23, 2018, www.licenseglobal.com/resource/beauty-445-billion-beast-0.
9. Maria Del Russo and Mi-Anne Chan, "Death of the Beauty Counter: How Social Media Is Changing the Industry," *Cosmetics*, April 11, 2016, http://cosmeticsmag.com/headlines/2016/4/death-of-the-beauty-counter-how-social-media-is-changing-the-industry.
10. Andrew Arnold, "Millennials Hate Ads but 58 percent of Them Wouldn't Mind If It's from Their Favorite Digital Stars," *Forbes*, January 21, 2018, http://www.zgenmedia.com/millennials-hate-ads-but-58-of-them-wouldnt-mind-if-its-from-their-favorite-digital-stars/.
11. Emma Macquire, *Girls, Autobiography, Media: Gender and Self-Mediation in Digital Economies* (London: Palgrave Macmillan, 2018), 89.
12. Mingyi Hou, "Social Media Celebrity and the Institutionalization of YouTube," *Convergence: The International Journal of Research into New Media Techologies*, January 3, 2018, https://doi.org/10.1177/1354856517750368.
13. Samara M. Anarbaeva, "YouTubing Difference: Performing Identity in Video Communities," *Journal for Virtual Worlds Research*, 9, no. 2 (2016): 3, doi:10.4101/jvwr.v9i2.7193.
14. Ibid, 5.
15. Emily Orofino, "See 1 Makeup Artist Transform into 4 Kardashians in 2 Minutes," *Popsugar: Beauty*, July 21, 2015, https://www.popsugar.com/beauty/Kandee-Johnson-Kardashian-Transformation-37932971?fb_comment_id=968268613223806_1288390474544950
16. Many scholarly articles refer to a supposed 1770 Bill of Parliament stating that "[a]ll women of whatever age, rank, profession, or degree, whether virgin maid or widow, that shall from and after such Act impose upon, seduce, and betray into matrimony any of His Majesty's subjects by means of scent, paints, cosmetics, washes, artificial teeth, false hair, Spanish wool, ironstays, hoops, high-heeled shoes, or bolstered hips, shall incur the penalty of the law now in force against witchcraft and like misdemeanors, and that the marriage upon conviction shall stand null and void." First cited in an 1877 article in *Scientific American Supplement* the claim has been disproven. However, the fact that so many people believed such a bill might be passed (it's cited in innumerable articles) suggests how enduring the popularity of the conceptual link between cosmetic use and witchery is. See *Scientific American: Supplement*, Vol. 3. (New York: Munn & Co. Publishers, Jan.–June 1877), 1031.
17. Interestingly, there is a thirty-nine-page *Gurugossip* thread titled "Kandee Is Dancing with the Devil," which demonstrates hate-filled rhetoric about Johnson, with criticism ranging from her artistic skills to her personal life. "Kandee Is Dancing with the Devil," *Gurugossip*, April 2019, https://gurugossiper.com/viewtopic.php?t=29525&start=800.
18. *The History of Sexuality* (New York: Random House, 1978).
19. *The Rise of the Novel*, (Berkeley: University of California Press, 1957).
20. *Desire and Domestic Fiction*, (London: Oxford University Press, 1990).
21. *De Cultu Feminarum*, Trans. Thelwall, 1869, Part 1; bk. 1, ch.1, http://www.tertullian.org/works/de_cultu_feminarum.htm.
22. Ibid, Part 1; bk. 1, ch. 1.
23. John Milton, *Paradise Lost* (Rpt. New York: Penguin, 2003), lines 466–476.
24. Ibid, line 472.
25. Farah Karim-Cooper, "'This alters no thy beauty': Face-Paint, Gender and Race in Richard Brome's *The English Moor*," *Early Theatre* 10, no. 2 (July 2007): 140.
26. "To a Painted Lady," *Songs and Other Poems* (London: 1664), line 1, https://quod.lib.umich.edu/e/eebo/A29623.0001.001?view=toc.
27. Ibid, line 24.

28. Kimberly Poitevin, "Inventing Whiteness: Cosmetics, Race, and Women in Early Modern England," *Journal for Early Modern Cultural Studies*, 11, no. 1 (Spring/Summer 2011): 64.
29. Ibid, 64.
30. Qtd in Poitevin, 82.
31. Qtd. in Poitevin, 82.
32. Joseph Swetnam. *The Arraignment of Lewd, Idle, Froward, and Unconstant Women* (1615), Ch. 1. https://pages.uoregon.edu/dluebke/WesternCiv102/SwetnamArraignment1615.htm.
33. Ibid, Ch. 2.
34. Ibid, Ch. 2.
35. Ibid, Ch. 2.
36. *Designing Women: The Dressing Room in Eighteenth-Century English Literature and Culture,* (Lewisburg, PA: Bucknell University Press, 2005), 113.
37. Ibid, 113.
38. Jonathan Swift, "The Lady's Dressing Room," in *Poetry Foundation* (1732; rpt. 2020), line 144 https://www.poetryfoundation.org/poems/50579/the-ladys-dressing-room.
39. Ibid, lines 11–18.
40. Ibid, lines 19–36.
41. Ibid, lines 37–47.
42. Ibid, lines 129–130.
43. Ibid, line 136.
44. Ibid., lines 141–44.
45. "A Beautiful Young Nymph Going to Bed," in *Poetry Foundation*, (1731; rpt. 2020) https://www.poetryfoundation.org/poems/50580/a-beautiful-young-nymph-going-to-bed
46. Ibid, lines 65–70.
47. Because I have brought up Barbie as the contemporary female ideal, it's important as an aside here to note the oft recounted stories of boys' committing violence against the plastic doll, tearing her limb from limb. The masculinist impulse to commit violence against women's bodies when those bodies are seen as "misbehaving" occurs against both plastic bodies and human bodies.
48. Lady Mary Wortley Montagu, "The Reasons that Induced Dr. Swift to Write a Poem Called 'The Lady's Dressing Room," *Essays and Poems and Simplicity, A Comedy*, Eds. Robert Halsband and Isobel Grundy. (Oxford: Clarendon P, 1977), 273–276.
49. *Fantomina*, eEd. Jack Lynch (Rpt, Newark: Rutgers, 1725), Accessed February 11 2020, https://andromeda.rutgers.edu/~jlynch/Texts/fantomina.html.
50. Juliette Merritt, *Beyond Spectacle: Eliza Haywood's Female Spectators* (Toronto: University of Toronto, 2004), 61.
51. Ibid, 64.
52. Mary Rogers, *Barbie Culture* (Portland, ME: SAGE Cultural Icon Series, 1999), 125.
53. Ibid., 112.
54. Ibid, 112.
55. Susan Bordo, *Unbearable Weight: Feminism, Western Culture, and the Body* (Berkeley: University of California Press, 1995) 335.
56. Kim Toffoletti, *Cyborgs and Barbie Dolls: Feminism, Popular Culture and the Posthuman Body* (New York: Tauris, 2007), 69.
57. Ibid., 71.
58. Ibid, 79.
59. *Botox Nation: Changing the Face of America* (New York: NYU Press, 2017), 7.
60. Ibid, 8.
61. Ibid, 9.
62. See Joan Jacobs Brumber's *The Body Project* (New York: Vintage, 1997) for a fantastic overview of how American girls, because of commodity capitalism, have increasingly viewed their bodies as projects, things to be fixed via the purchase of beauty products. In her research, Brumberg examines the diaries of girls from the Victorian period through the 20th century.
63. JennaMarbles, "Making Fake Freckles ~* WORK*~ For Me," YouTube Video, January 31, 2019, 14: 48, https://www.youtube.com/watch?v=I_v8zPpId_A.

64. Zoella, "My Everyday Winter Makeup," YouTube Video, January 29, 2018, 15:11, https://www.youtube.com/watch?v=vn3EiuUVjBk.

65. JennaMarbles, "How to Trick People into Thinking You're Good Looking," YouTube Video, July 9, 2010, 2:36, https://www.youtube.com/watch?v=OYpwAtnywTk.

66. Kandee Johnson, "Angelina Jolie Makup Transformation Tutorial," YouTube Video, November 8, 2014, 14:58, https://www.youtube.com/watch?v=GDcQJ32zmvg&t=7s.

67. Kandee Johnson, "Cleopatra Costume Make-up," YouTube Video, September 25, 2009, 15:17, https://www.youtube.com/watch?v=hfBYSsmk3DA&t=747s.

68. Josh Smith, "700 Million Views, 4 Faces and 1 Empowering Coming Out Story: Why James Charles Is THE Male Beauty Icon of Today," *Glamour*, February 4, 2019, https://www.glamourmagazine.co.uk/article/james-charles-beauty-tutorial.

BIBLIOGRAPHY

Alston, Amber. "Beauty the $445 Billion Beast." *License Global*, September 23, 2018, www.licenseglobal.com/resource/beauty-445-billion-beast-0.

Anarbaeva, Samara M. "YouTubing Difference: Performing Identity in Video Communities." *Journal for Virtual Worlds Research*, vol. 9, no. 2, 2016, doi:10.4101/jvwr.v9i2.7193.

"Angelina Jolie Makup Transformation Tutorial." *KandeeJohnson.* November 8, 2014. Video, 14:58, https://www.youtube.com/watch?v=GDcQJ32zmvg&t=7s.

Armstrong, Nancy. *Desire and Domestic Fiction*. Oxford University Press, 1990.

Arnold, Andrew. "Millennials Hate Ads but 58 percent of Them Wouldn't Mind If It's from Their Favorite Digital Stars." *Forbes* January 21, 2018.

Banet-Wieser, Sara. "Branding the Post-Feminist Self: Girls' Video Productions and YouTube." *Mediated Girlhoods: New Explorations of Girls' Media Culture*. Edited by Mary Celeste Kearney. New York: Peter Lang, pp. 277–294.

"Barbie Doll MakeUp Transformation." *Kandee Johnson*. October 30, 2014. Video, 13:05. https://www.youtube.com/watch?v=H_IfRNp0ncU.

Baudrillard, Jean. *Simulacra and Simulation*. University of Michican Press, 1994.

Berkowitz, Dana. *Botox Nation: Changing the Face of America*. New York University, 2017.

Bordo, Susan. *Unbearable Weight: Feminism, Western Culture, and the Body*. University of California Press, 1995.

Brome, Alexander. "To a Painted Lady." *Songs and Other Poems*. London: 1664. *Early English Books*. https://quod.lib.umich.edu/e/eebo/A29623.0001.001?view=toc.

Brumber, Joan Jacobs. *The Body Project: An Intimate History of American Girls*. Vintage Books, 1997.

Butler, Judith. *Gender Trouble*. Routledge, 2006.

Carter, Brooke. "Kandee Johnson Net Worth 2018." *Gazette Review*. January 15, 2018. https://gazettereview.com/2018/01/kandee-johnson-net-worth/.

Chico, Tita. *Designing Women: The Dressing Room in Eighteenth-Century English Literature and Culture*. Bucknell Studies 18th C. Bucknell University Press, 2005.

"Cleopatra Costume Make-up." *Kandee Johnson*. September 25, 2009. Video, 15:17. https://www.youtube.com/watch?v=hfBYSsmk3DA&t=747s.

Farah Karim-Cooper. *Cosmetics in Shakespearean and Renaissance Drama*. Edinburgh: Edinburgh University Press, 2006.

———. "'This alters no thy beauty': Face-Paint, Gender and Race in Richard Brome's *The English Moor*," *Early Theatre* 10.2 (July 2007): 140+.

Foucault, Michel. *The History of Sexuality*. Random House, 1978.

"From Bum to Baddie." *Simplynessa15*. August 7, 2017. Video, 25:06. https://www.youtube.com/watch?v=FAA3pdABuQw&t=1321s.

Harris, Anita. *Future Girl: Young Women in the 21st Century*. NY Routledge, 2003.

Haywood, Eliza. *Fantomina*. Ed. Jack Lynch, Rutgers. https://andromeda.rutgers.edu/~jlynch/Texts/fantomina.html.

Hou, Mingyi. "Social Media Celebrity and the Institutionalization of YouTube." *Convergence: The International Journal of Research into New Media Techologies*. January 3, 2018. https:

//doi.org/10.1177/1354856517750368.

"How to Trick People into Thinking You're Good Looking," *JennaMarbles*. July 9, 2010. Video, 2:36, https://www.youtube.com/watch?v=OYpwAtnywTk.

"Impressive Makeup Transformations [Pure Magic]." *Amazing Transformations Lux*. June 6, 2016. Video, 4:01. https://www.youtube.com/watch?v=jThtfQjKllU.

"Kandee Is Dancing with the Devil." *Gurugossip*, April 23, 1016. https://gurugossiper.com/viewtopic.php?f=62&t=29525.

Maquire, Emma. *Girls, Autobiography, Media: Gender and Self-Mediation in Digital Economies*. Palgrave Macmillan, 2018.

"Making Fake Freckles ~* WORK*~ For Me." *JennaMarbles* January 31, 2019. Video, 14: 48. https://www.youtube.com/watch?v=I_v8zPpId_A.

Merritt, Juliette. *Beyond Spectacle: Eliza Haywood's Female Spectators*. University of Toronto, 2004.

Milton, John. *Paradise Lost*. Rpt. Penguin, 2003.

Montagu, Lady Mary Wortley. "The Reasons that Induced Dr. Swift to Write a Poem Called 'The Lady's Dressing Room." *Essays and Poems and Simplicity, A Comedy*. Eds. Robert Halsband and Isobel Grundy. Oxford: Clarendon Press, 1977, 273–276. Print.

"My Everyday Winter Makeup." *Zoella*. January 29, 2018. Video, 15:11. https://www.youtube.com/watch?v=vn3EiuUVjBk.

Newis-Smith, Josh. "700 Million Views, 4 Faces and 1 Empowering Coming Out Story: Why James Charles is THE Male Beauty Icon of Today." *Glamour*, February 4, 2019. https://www.glamourmagazine.co.uk/article/james-charles-beauty-tutorial?utm_medium=Social&utm_source=Facebook&fbclid=IwAR1yBQVpeFIa0W7rBtewwGV3a8SFW zXrNsXwVM0Z5xsr42-dONR24-tNXGE#Echobox=1549299589.

Orofino, Emily. "See 1 Makeup Artist Transform into 4 Kardashians in 2 Minutes." *Popsugar: Beauty*. 21 July 2015. https://www.popsugar.com/beauty/Kandee-Johnson-Kardashian-Transformation-37932971?fb_comment_id=968268613223806_1288390474544950.

Poitevin, Kimberly. "Inventing Whiteness: Cosmetics, Race, and Women in Early Modern England." *Journal for Early Modern Cultural Studies*, 11. 1 (Spring/Summer 2011), pp. 59–89.

"The Power of Make-up (Ugly Betty Inspired Story)." *Dope2111*. January 21, 2003. https://www.youtube.com/watch?v=KWFWoHr89Tk.

Robehmed, Natalie, and Madeline Berg. "Highest-Paid YouTube Marketers 2018." *Forbes* 3 December 2018. https://www.forbes.com/sites/natalierobehmed/2018/12/03/highest-paid-youtube-stars-2018-markiplier-jake-paul-pewdiepie-and-more/#2dac8873909a.

Rogers, Mary. *Barbie Culture,* SAGE Cultural Icon Series, 1999.

Russo, Maria Del, and Mi-Anne Chan. "Death of the Beauty Counter: How Social Media Is Changing the Industry." *Cosmetics*. April 11, 2016. Accessed March 8, 2019. http://cosmeticsmag.com/headlines/2016/4/death-of-the-beauty-counter-how-social-media-is-changing-the-industry.

Schott, Julie. "How to Finally Master Contouring in 4 Easy Steps." *ELLE*, 5 November 2018. www.elle.com/beauty/news/a28308/how-to-contour-pro/.

Scientific American: Supplement, Vol. 3. Munn & Co. Publishers, New York. January–June 1877.

Senft, Theresa. *Camgirls: Celebrity and Community in the Age of Social Media*. Peter Lang, 2008.

Smith, Josh. "700 Million Views, 4 Faces and 1 Empowering Coming Out Story: Why James Charles Is THE Male Beauty Icon of Today." *Glamour*, February 4, 2019. https://www.glamourmagazine.co.uk/article/james-charles-beauty-tutorial.

Swetnam, Joseph. *The Arraignment of Lewd, Idle, Froward, and Unconstant Women* (1615). https://pages.uoregon.edu/dluebke/WesternCiv102/SwetnamArraignment1615.htm.

———. "A Beautiful Young Nymph Going to Bed." *Poetry Foundation*. https://www.poetryfoundation.org/poems/50580/a-beautiful-young-nymph-going-to-bed.

Swift, Jonathan. "The Lady's Dressing Room." *Poetry Foundation*. https://www.poetryfoundation.org/poems/50579/the-ladys-dressing-room.

"Ten Most Popular Beauty Gurus on YouTube." *Filmora*, January 11, 2019. https://filmora.wondershare.com/vlogger/most-popular-beauty-gurus-on-youtube.html.

Tertullian. *De Cultu Feminarum*. Trans. Thelwall, 1869. http://www.tertullian.org/works/de_cultu_feminarum.htm.

Toffoletti, Kim. *Cyborgs and Barbie Dolls: Feminism, Popular Culture and the Post-human Body*. Tauris, 2007.

"Top Influences: Beauty." *Forbes Online*. 2019, https://www.forbes.com/top-influencers/beauty/#51136a753378.

Watt, Ian. *The Rise of the Novel*. University of California Press, 1957.

Chapter Six

The Pigments of Patriarchy and Femme Trans Exclusion in the History of the "All Natural" Makeup Movement

Laken Brooks

People have used makeup since the ancient Egyptians first adorned their eyes with mesdemet.[1] For our ancestors, beauty items provided practical and expressive benefits; creams protected people's skin and eyes from the sun, and makeup styles indicated both class and religion. Over time, makeup built on ideals of femininity to conceal imperfections or highlight idealized features. In the twentieth century, women faced increasing pressure to wear makeup from the burgeoning beauty industry; therefore, many Second Wave feminists disavowed makeup as a tool of patriarchal subjugation and encouraged their peers to embrace their "natural" feminine beauty. Generations later, makeup continues to evoke debate and incredible profit margins. In almost a godlike way, people become the artisans of their own faces. In subtle strokes, makeup-wearers bring out or hide certain features of their faces to control how they want to be physically perceived. This autonomy over our physical appearance is one of the driving appeals for transgender and gender-nonconforming makeup wearers who can finally shape their faces to better express their gender identities; nonetheless, many cisgender men and women have pushed back against full-face makeup trends by preaching "natural beauty" and establishing makeup users as untrustworthy or dishonest. Therefore, the "all natural"[2] movement both defines and polices cisgender femininity while excluding transfeminine self-expression.

While beauty may seem limited to the quotidian of pop culture, academics have long studied the politics and hegemonic structures that exist behind makeup; nonetheless, many of these analyses adhere to typical gender binaries. Mary Wollstonecraft[3] lamented the beauty norms that limited young girls' opportunities to participate in more thoughtful or active pastimes: "personal beauty, woman's glory! The limbs and faculties are cramped with worse than Chinese bands, and the sedentary life which they are condemned to live, whilst boys frolic in the open air, weakens the muscles and relaxes the nerves." Wollstonecraft describes beauty norms as a tool to perpetuate female "weakness" and ostracize girls from boys. Sandra Bartky also dissects female beauty norms.[4] Bartky describes the artifice of makeup as such: "woman's body is an ornamented surface . . . since a properly made-up face is, if not a card of entree, at least a badge of acceptability in most social and professional contexts" because "the woman who chooses not to wear cosmetics at all faces sanctions." However, historical and cultural analysis demonstrate that makeup, despite its role as a largely "feminine" object in the contemporary Western world, is not innate to womanhood. In fact, Naomi Wolf's *The Beauty Myth* discusses how "[a]mong the Nigerian Wodaabes, men spend hours together in elaborate makeup sessions, and compete—provocatively painted and dressed, with swaying hips and seductive expressions—in beauty contests judged by women."[5] While makeup has complex origins in larger schemes of beauty around the world, its reality for many cisgender women hinges on feelings of inadequacy. Wolf joins other scholars who perceive makeup as a tool of patriarchal oppression: "The beauty myth is not about women at all. It is about men's institutions and institutional power," and "the qualities that a given period calls beautiful in women are merely symbols of the female behavior that the period considers desirable."[6] Even among the Wodaabe men, makeup is a tool to establish social ties, desirability, and connections to those in power (in this case, women) rather than offering the wearer a more abstract sense of confidence, comfort, or acknowledged identity. While the Wodaabe men's makeup practices point to the fact that gender norms are culturally and socially constructed, these artificial constructions still have very real impacts on people's lives. Therefore, I do not want to invalidate the concrete realities of misogynistic female beauty ideals and makeup by implying that these same beauty standards are, in and of themselves, fluid and subjective. Nonetheless, too many of these scholars have failed to directly connect the ways in which these social stigmas of beauty and makeup harm both cisgender and transgender people.

As previously discussed, past feminist approaches to makeup tend to highlight the social pressures women face to achieve a standard of beauty and how the industry harms cisgender women's self-esteem by advertising unrealistic appearances. This interpretation is not incorrect; in fact, the UK women's empowerment group Girlguiding released a study in 2013 chronicling girls' anxieties around beauty. James Meikle of *The Guardian* reported details of the Girlguiding study, writing that "some girls, influenced by the media and advertising, are spending substantial sums on beauty products. Among 11-to-16-year-olds, more than six in ten wear makeup to school . . .

[of 7-to-11-year-olds] half wear makeup."[7] With these harrowing details of how women face increasing pressures to conform, one can empathize with the growing celebration of "all natural" women who shirk makeup altogether. Nonetheless, we must change the makeup narrative from its recent binary perspective to include trans representation in the contemporary age. Women and trans people both receive similar criticisms about makeup. The same school, job, and DMV policies that dictate dress codes and cosmetics for cisgender women also block trans women from makeup, long hair, pronoun changes, and other avenues of gender expression. These norms, meant to limit transfeminine people to their assigned-at-birth masculinity, also impact cisgender women and build an ideological gender segregation by policing women's appearance. For whoever wears makeup, no matter the person's gender, that individual participates in some form of self- and cultural expression. That person is choosing how they[8] want to look, but members of the public also perceive makeup styles as symbolizing elements of that person's identity or femininity. Makeup is a marked look; heavy makeup, correctly or incorrectly, conveys a different social stereotype than light or no makeup. For people who do not "pass" as cisgender women, though, makeup takes on a different marking and is perceived as an attempt to perform femininity or escape masculinity, and the adornment may evoke confusion and, at times, mockery in society.

Performing gender involves myriad aspects; likewise, many people perform nontraditional gender expression (especially those expressions leaning toward the feminine) by applying makeup. Judith Butler[9] addresses some of these complexities of performance in the figurative and, as with makeup, literal masquerade of "being" and "appearing" masculine/feminine in her classic *Gender Trouble*:

> If the "being," the ontological specification of the Phallus, is masquerade, then it would appear to reduce all being to a form of appearing, the appearance of being, with the consequence that all gender ontology is reducible to the play of appearances. On the other hand, masquerade suggests that there is a "being" . . . prior to the masquerade, a feminine desire. . . . On the one hand, masquerade may be understood as the performative production of a sexual ontology; on the other hand, masquerade may be read as a denial of a feminine desire that presupposes some prior ontological femininity regularly unrepresented by the phallic economy.

As Butler establishes, "being" and "appearing" female are two very different sides of the same coin;[10] a "tomboy" is not male because she "looks boyish." Likewise, a cisgender drag performer may capture the appearance of femininity onstage, but his mask does not alter his internal masculinity.

When considering the "all natural" makeup movement, we must question how the idea of "natural" interacts with the two elements of gender: being and appearing. Which women can pass as "all natural," and what are the punishments for the women who cannot? Before approaching these questions, let us first define the "all natural" makeup movement. Aptly named, the "all natural" trend encourages women to flout the oppressive beauty norms perpetuated by the beauty industry by wearing minimal or no makeup. While the idea of women capturing their "natural" beauty seems to empower since it relieves some of the burden of women worrying about the male gaze, the very notion of "natural" feminine beauty is rife with biological essentialism. Superficially, "all natural" advocates assume that women wear makeup to attract partners or to appear more appealing to the external world, and they hypothesize that these women will find more self-confidence and body positivity when they do not wear makeup. For some, perhaps this positive prediction is true. While this speculation ignores the evidence[11] that cisgender women are labeled as unprofessional or slovenly when they do not wear makeup, it also fails to acknowledge the gender performance role of makeup. While makeup is, of course, not intrinsically feminine and some trans people also do not wear it, many transgender women do utilize cosmetics to both appear and perform their internal gender in a society that largely presents makeup as a feminine item. Without these beauty tools (and, sometimes, even with them), many of these women may not be publicly recognized as female because of secondary sex characteristics otherwise associated with masculinity: a broad face, thinner lips, boxy jawline. Since gender consists of both public and personal elements, makeup is a valid tool for many transgender women to bring to the surface of their skin what they perceive to be hidden inside; quite the opposite of "all natural" practitioners, these transgender women use makeup to evoke what is "natural" to them, the image of femininity that they visualize but may not see reflected in the mirror. To say that wearing makeup is a mask that hides someone's "natural femininity" is to imply that all women are born with bodies that match their identity, and such an argument disregards the dysphoria of transgender women who use these beauty products to actively convey and encourage the world to also see their gendered self-image.

As a preface to the remainder of this chapter, I distinguish the motivations—and, therefore, the enforced levels of oppression—behind the "all natural" makeup movement. Some women do choose to wear less or no makeup for personal empowerment; my critique of this particular movement concerns the assumption that all women should or even can live an "all natural" beauty lifestyle, therefore ignoring the utilitarian need of many trans women who depend on makeup and the lasting patriarchal fears of women having the power to change their own appearance in a male-driven society. The privilege in the "all natural" makeup movement is that most cisgender women, especially those who already have idealized feminine facial features, who choose not to wear makeup may face social stigma, certainly, but they will most likely still be recognized as women. These women's gender will not be in question without the makeup that helps them adhere to beauty norms. Transgender women, on the other hand, encounter a "catch 22" when they do or do not wear makeup. For many transgender women, as with cisgender women, makeup is not intended to attract partners or fit an abstract standard of "sex appeal." Uniquely for transgender women, makeup offers the opportunity to present the desired gender characteristics in public that these people feel internally. These women may find more confidence when they can navigate the world appearing more stereotypically feminine, their beauty products enabling them to pass as their gender. Nonetheless, when transgender women cannot pass publicly as female, they are often mocked or demeaned for the perceived gender transgression of a masculine-appearing person wearing makeup. In short, how can a transgender woman, who normally relies on makeup, maintain her public femininity bare-faced, "all natural," when many people around her believe her womanhood is, in and of itself, "unnatural?"

All women encounter prejudices under the same umbrella of patriarchal beauty norms that both unfairly sexualize cisgender women while barring transgender women from being recognized completely as female; however, the "all natural" movement is often, unfortunately, co-opted into a larger social system that pits women against one another, compelling them to police one another's adherence to their supposed gender norms. Steve Craig analyzes women's sociological responses to makeup and concludes, "For radical feminists, the social pressures on women to be 'beautiful' were an example of a patriarchal society's treatment of women as chattel."[12] This Second Wave view of beauty as a tool of gendered oppression, the same perspective that engendered an interest in "all natural" makeup, fosters tension toward transgender women who seemingly uphold and perpetuate these commodified attitudes about women's beauty.

As women in the 1970s stopped supporting the beauty industry, companies began to specifically cater to the "New Women," feminists critical of traditional beauty products and ideals, by designing makeup meant to only "highlight" or "promote" women's "natural features."[13] Of course, these "natural" aspects of beauty are culturally arbitrary, bringing out the facial elements already valued in Western women: high cheekbones, rosy lips and cheeks, matte skin, trimmed eyebrows. While these "all natural" makeup products advertise a return to a supposedly innate allure, they work to reinforce existing expectations about the way a woman should or should not look; however, this imposed appearance becomes more complex because this beauty ideal is now established as an *organic* trait, and, therefore, people who do not possess these traits (smooth skin, delicate facial features, etc.)—like many transgender people who use makeup to achieve this look—cannot participate in this "natural" womanhood. A young trans woman, whom I will call Erica throughout the course of this chapter, describes her experience with cosmetics: "I started experimenting with makeup and gender expression overall in college, and most of the negative reactions I have received have been from cisgender women."[14] Erica elaborates the following:

> During my senior year, for the first time in public, I wore mascara, eyeshadow, lipstick, and foundation. I did not think that I was wearing a lot of makeup, but I suppose it stood out. All I knew is that I felt nice. I felt like myself, like a girl. That was the first time that had ever happened to me. In one of my sociology courses, a female classmate who sat across from me stared at me throughout the period. She whispered to a male friend who sat beside her, and she gestured to her lips and eyes with one hand while she pointed at me with her other hand. They both laughed, and they continued pointing at me throughout the class. I never wore makeup again at my college. I would apply it in my dorm room and take selfies to remind myself of what I looked like, and how I liked what I looked like, when I wore makeup. I was too scared to do much else. The classmates never threatened me physically, but I worried that other students might.

These disparaging actions from a female classmate may hinge upon the beauty mythology that the "all natural" movement seeks to escape but unwittingly reinforces. Some women may feel forced to wear makeup because these items are perceived as integral to idealized feminine expression, value, or even corporate success. When a cisgender woman who has embraced the traditional Western woman's beauty mythology sees a non-cisgender person wearing makeup, a traditionally "female" statement, perhaps that woman feels attacked or uncomfortable. She may realize that her entrenched ideas of femininity, such as the caricature of long eyelashes or bright lips, is fragile and applies to many people outside of essentialist womanhood. Some cisgender women may police trans women's makeup use out of a misconception that these trans women are appropriating female beauty, washing off the makeup like a mask to return to their more masculine appearance and "male privilege" whenever they so choose, otherwise avoiding the misogyny of living as a woman.

This belief poses a problem for several reasons, but it does present a potential train of logic for the opponents of transgender people expressing themselves through makeup. On an economic level, certain cisgender women may be opposed to transgender women wearing and, therefore, promoting beauty products that seemingly perpetuate women's sexualization and oppression. The "all natural" movement does work to alleviate some of these beauty norms for women, but it still operates with a privileged perspective of body acceptance. Erica also pondered the following:

> While Third Wave feminism tells cisgender women that they should embrace their "natural" beauty and need not wear makeup, there is still significant

> pressure for many of us in the trans community to look as feminine as possible to pass as female and to alleviate our own gender dysphoria. Makeup helps many of us accomplish these goals. These movements seem to run parallel to each other: that women should accept their bodies and be "natural," but it seems that trans folks like me are actively ignored. My physical "natural" is five o'clock shadow, and it is not my spiritual "natural."[15]

To include narratives like Erica's into the ethos of the "all natural" makeup discussion, we should reflect on how adornment has historically served a role of utility and survival for people whom we may, in hindsight, consider to be transgender or gender nonconforming. By briefly tracing this history, we can weigh this complex ancestry of beauty with the patriarchal sexualization of these products, therefore recognizing how the "all natural" movement has never been a possibility for people who do not otherwise conform to cisgender norms or labels.

While it would be ahistorical to claim that people who dressed or lived as another gender were necessarily transgender, since transness is a relatively modern construction, drag and gender socialization do present an interesting window into how past people chose to present themselves, whether by identity or otherwise, as being women in as "natural" a way as they could. Much like how contemporary makeup often complements the socialized feminine traits, emotions, and behaviors that a transgender person exhibits, people throughout various points in history have used clothing and makeup to explore gender presentation. On stage during the English Renaissance, male actors dressed in drag as female characters. Most of these actors were probably cisgender, only stepping into femininity for their performance; nonetheless, throughout the duration of the play, an actor would "become" female. Makeup was crucial to this performance, and a young male actor lightened his face, painted his lips, and de-emphasized his heavy jawline. The audience would recognize him as a woman, at least in terms of his character, and he would act as a woman while in the new "reality" of the plot.

Historical gender performance and identity often exceeded these temporary instances of drag. In the Japanese Edo period, like in Renaissance England, men were the only actors in Kabuki. For many of these actors, performing womanhood became a permanent endeavor; the actors would dress and live as female on and offstage. In this situation, makeup and adornment do not *make* one a woman, but they do help one be *acknowledged and socialized* as female. Makeup accompanied literal and figurative performance as assigned-male actors transitioned, for all intents and purposes, into a life of femininity. Gender performance was not limited to theater, though. Even among the Greco-Roman populations, people assigned male at birth would remove their genitalia and take on female identities to worship the wilderness and mountain goddess Cybele. For these worshipers, clothing and makeup were not meant to trick audiences for a play but to reinforce their own status as women. From the hijra communities in India to the Two Spirit Native Americans, people have long sought to distance themselves from male labels to live as women, often using makeup and other trappings to bring out these female features that correlate with their lived gender roles and behaviors.[16]

Like with Erica, past people who did not conform to their expected or social gender binaries as assigned at birth frequently wore makeup or participated in other beautification processes. Unlike the contemporary, heteronormative misconception that women wear makeup to attract men, this ornamentation performed more practical purposes, often directly supporting people living as women. In these historical situations, wearing makeup was an act of social belonging and identity exploration, whether for an hour onstage or for a lifetime. Transgender women continue to wear makeup as an outlet of expression and safety; trans women can protect themselves from potential harassment when they can better pass as cisgender. Trans women face assault at work, in bathrooms, and in other public spaces if others suspect that they are trans. Therefore, makeup can assist many transgender women in two ways: relieving gender dysphoria and promoting their safety and satisfaction in public life as other people more easily recognize them as their preferred gender. This passing often requires transfeminine people to change their clothing and their features to conform to the expectations of how a woman "should naturally" look.

As previously discussed, the word "natural" is, in and of itself, a misnomer based on patriarchal and cultural norms because there is no one archetypal, concrete image for a cisgender woman. Not every woman who is "natural," bare-faced or otherwise, looks traditionally feminine. For example, many women produce more or less body hair than is considered typically beautiful. Preaching that women should embrace "natural beauty" privileges those women who already appear and navigate life in a traditionally feminine way. Women living "all natural" oftentimes purchase products that continue this subtle beautification. These items, such as tinted moisturizer, lip plumpers, mascara, bronzer, and toners all continue to occupy women's time and money, some of the original Second Wave complaints against makeup, while promising a flawless appearance. The illusion of flawlessness is, in and of itself, paradoxical to "all natural." The Western idea that beauty is innate rather than something to be cultivated juxtaposes with the repeated images of typically "beautiful" women in media. This paradox in cultural attitudes toward beauty fuels two different tensions: the resentment of women who openly wear heavy makeup and the social pressure to continue conforming to these beauty standards in even more inconspicuous ways (wearing an "all natural" makeup look or by striving after other markers of idealized femininity, such as glowing skin or shinier hair). Ultimately, this perspective harms all women and reminds us of centuries-old patriarchal stigmas surrounding makeup and women's appearances.

The "all natural" makeup emphasis is not new, although its feminist approach may be. The distrust of women who wore makeup stretches back to the Renaissance. Men such as Richard Brathwait condemned women who wore makeup as being "unnatural." Brathwait wrote, "Lascivious Idoll, that with painted cheeke, / Sinne-drawing eye, thy sacred vow doest break / With thy Creator."[17] Ironically, these protests against women painting their faces disagree with the social admiration of art as an accurate representation of reality. In the Renaissance, scholars perceived painting as a platform to capture the appearance and emotional state of a subject, the *truth* of the subject. We can argue that today's makeup holds this same power in revealing truth for transgender women. Nonetheless, many women and men at the time believed that wearing makeup was a sin against God, an attempt to trick and seduce men with a facade. Farah Karim-Cooper elaborates on the Renaissance fear of women who wore makeup to claim autonomy over their appearance: "it was believed that witches could transform themselves into anything they wanted to deceive men. To bewitch was to charm, seduce, and entrap, to render a man powerless."[18] Much like today, women who wore makeup were believed to have been hiding something about themselves since such women supposedly wore cosmetics to conceal their predatory sexual nature toward men. By making themselves appear more beautiful than they were in reality, such women threatened the social order. Makeup was an abomination in a society in which, in all other ways, men held physical and figurative control over women's bodies. Karim-Cooper explains the depth of this focus on a woman's "natural" appearance: "a law was passed by the English Parliament in the late eighteenth century which attempted to impose on women the same penalty for adornment [including makeup] as for witchcraft, freeing up their husbands who had married them under such false pretences."[19] Such laws appear unreasonable to a contemporary reader; however, in 2015, *Yahoo!* subscribers found a similar mentality after the website was duped into publishing a false story about a man who sued his new bride for fraud after he saw her for the first time without makeup. This persisting fear of women "tricking" men by wearing makeup emerges from a male perspective of women as, in a sense, merchandise. The "all natural" movement, just as it seeks to free women from the male gaze, likewise evokes dehumanizing language that women who wear makeup are guilty of "false advertising." When coupled with transphobia, the push toward no or minimal makeup cuts through intersections of anti-woman logic.

The backlash against makeup demonstrates that when both cisgender and transgender women wear makeup, they risk being labeled as promiscuous or untrustworthy. *Mamiverse*, a beauty and fashion website, published "The Chic of Natural Beauty: 10 Reasons Why Men Hate Makeup" to encourage their readership to join the "all natural" movement; however, as demonstrated by the title, these motivations to go bare-faced are centered around men's opinions of women rather than the Second Wave focus on bodily acceptance. The first reason is as follows: "They [men] wonder what you are hiding."[20] The article continues to list "Makeup is messy" and "Will he recognize you in the morning?" as male concerns around makeup. The *Mamiverse* writers conclude, "Authenticity is lovely . . . you'll attract higher quality candidates [dates] if you're presenting yourself as genuine, honest and confident. A ton of makeup doesn't really say those things, does it?"[21] In reality, women wear makeup for many reasons other than the sexual due to numerous social and personal motivations. While these factors for using cosmetics may be different for each person, spanning a spectrum from professional confidence to establishing social belongingness and avoiding violence, strands of the "all natural" movement evoke centuries-old fears of men losing sexual control of women. For women who have internalized this misogyny, there is a subtextual expectation that women's appearances exist only for and by men. In this situation, the *Mamiverse* writers perpetuated ideas of men's sexual entitlement to women's images by portraying makeup as "messy" and camouflage—something that bars one from honestly representing herself rather than a mechanism for expression.

Transgender awareness and advocacy have increased in the late twentieth and early twenty-first centuries, compounding the existing patriarchal fears of men being "tricked" by women who wear makeup. Concerning these unaccepting ideas of the LGBTQ+ community, makeup is perceived as doubly "unnatural." In this male-focused emphasis on "all natural" beauty, makeup is a device for women to deceive. With makeup, a cisgender woman can manipulate her appearance to seduce an unwitting man. Likewise, transgender people who are often not recognized as "real" women can shape themselves into the image of femininity, subverting the ideas of heteronormativity and binary that are the undercurrents of hegemony. In short, makeup worn for gendered self-expression is a revolution against the patriarchal order and tradition with which many cis men and women have grown comfortable, and revolution is often met with violent suppression.

Violence exists on a spectrum from microaggressions to brute force. Trans makeup artists routinely face gendered critique, a form of soft violence, when they post their tutorials on sites like YouTube. In 2013, the popular makeup artist Joseph Harwood posted the video "Boy to Girl Makeup Secrets" to guide transgender women through cosmetically narrowing their faces and hiding excess hair. Some YouTubers responded with essentialist language, implying that Harwood was not a "real" woman, so to speak, and Harwood's[22] makeup was not a convincing enough gender presentation. This argument, then, points to the notion that gender is determined by external forces, by the audience who evaluates the performance of the person who is enacting gender. One commenter with the username "No past, no future" refused to refer to Harwood with any personal pronouns and said, "It doesn't look like a woman at all." This dehumanizing language, "it," is familiar to many transgender women who socially reside in a liminal space between the binary: not male but also not biologically, to use essentialist terms, female. Another user named "Alexie Muszczynska" complained, "You still look like a man with make up and wig. You don't have this womens cuteness in you face shape, and soft movements which women do. When i look at you i see a man in costume which moves heavy, nothing more." Some of these comments may be attributed to online trolls, people who intentionally post negative or hurtful comments to evoke conflict. Nonetheless, the mentality underlying these comments is nothing new: that a transgender woman is hiding her true self, her male body, with makeup, and the general population will not be "fooled" into believing the gender charade.

Another YouTuber named Stef Sanjati posted the 2016 makeup tutorial "Feminizing Make-up for Trans Women." Like Harwood, Sanjati spent nearly half an hour showing viewers how she used makeup to express her womanhood and be accepted as female. Users "Mich Michelle" and "Oscar Pinto" both commented, in order, "Your highlight looks like a clown nose" and "Funny, let me know when you transform your chromosomes." YouTube user "Kris J" responded with a comment that mirrors the previously discussed fears of cisgender men being "duped" into perceiving transgender women as potential sexual partners: "I saw your Adams apple and it surprised me." In a larger system of supremacy and violence, these comments may seem minuscule, but they build on the mythology of what an "all natural" woman should look like, as dictated by men, and work to punish those who do not fit this mold.

More seriously, the preoccupation with and demand for women to be "all natural" for men engenders mortal consequences. The trans panic defense, a legal argument thus far banned only by California and Illinois, is used by men who have beaten or even killed their sexual partners after discovering that these lovers are transgender. This cumulation of violence, the semantics of "panic," reminds us of the subconscious chaos that emerges when women have the autonomy to shape their own appearance and control their image.

Ironically, this same system that can kill transgender women for "tricking" men by wearing makeup, encroaching on traditional ideas of women's and men's appearances and roles in society, also eroticizes them. Trans women are popular adult video performers. While most of these actresses wear makeup and appear traditionally beautiful, some of the top porn website searches include terms such as "tr*nny," "Sh*male," "Man or Woman?," and, perhaps most striking in comparison to the trans panic defense, "Sheboy surprise." The result is a cultural emphasis on women's reproductive organs and bodies as the defining factor of femininity and a punishment/spectacle for those women who use makeup to "invade" or otherwise usurp this biological, patriarchy-driven definition of womanhood. Women, transgender women included, exist for the consumption of society and to please men, but only on these men's terms.

The threats against transgender and cisgender women who wear heavy makeup reveal the inadvertent transphobia of people who think that "no makeup" is a more genuine representation of the human form. This perspective of the "all natural" makeup movement shows a male entitlement to know and participate in the bodies and identities of women, to see past their faces and into their pants to judge them valuable or not. The backlash against transgender people wearing makeup shows a fear of this possibility in a heteronormative society. While the professional and personal consequences surrounding the forced[23] "all natural" makeup movement are different, institutionally, for most cisgender and transgender women, they are rooted in similar systems of patriarchal and cisnormative inequality that negatively harm both parties. In 2011, Ellie Krupnick of *The Huffington Post* published the satirical article "Sofia Vergara or Blake Lively: Who's Got the Tranny Look? (PHOTOS, POLL)." Before the article was pulled,[24] it asked readers to decide which celebrity was more likely to be transgender based on the two women's bright makeup and clothing choices. Associating heavy makeup with deception and, in recent decades, with transgender identity reinforces hierarchy because it places others in a position to deem what is "natural" about another person's appearance and, related in part, about their lifestyle. As in the above article, "tr*nny" and transgender identity become the butt of a joke about women who "try too hard," about people who cannot or do not conform to Western beauty and behavior norms; for transgender women like Erica, whom I interviewed earlier, this reasoning is particularly damaging. When trans women do not wear makeup, they are frequently perceived as "effeminate men" rather than women; however, when trans women do wear makeup, they risk mockery, stereotypes, and outright violence for being "unnatural" or inauthentic. Therefore, the "all natural" movement bars transgender women from alleviating their gender dysphoria and representing themselves as women in public. The irony behind this "all natural" exclusion inadvertently snags cisgender women, as cis women who wear heavy makeup are often called "tr*nnies" online.

Transgender women, wearing makeup or not, face scrutiny in a patriarchal society. According to *Reuters*' Daniel Trotta, a survey from the National Center for Transgender Equality found that 24 percent of transgender people in the United States had been questioned or harassed in public restrooms. However, the barriers of how society defines or does not define "real" womanhood, an entirely subjective term, are unreasonable for many cisgender women, too. Since the rise of the "all natural" makeup movement in conjunction with transgender awareness, more cisgender women have faced harassment for, in fact, going bare faced in women's public spaces. For example, Matt DeRienzo of *The Danbury News Times* reported on Aimee Toms, a cisgender woman sporting a bare face and short hair. Toms was harassed in a public restroom, called "disgusting" and told that she "doesn't belong here [the women's bathroom]" after another shopper mistook her for a transgender woman.[25] Toms is not the only cis woman who, while looking "natural" without any makeup, has been confronted or asked for proof of gender identity. With these instances of cisgender and transgender women being questioned, assumed as not "real women," the fantasy of "all natural" female beauty unravels.

The "all natural" makeup trend as we know it began in the 1970s as Second Wave feminists sought a respite from oppressive male beauty norms and insecurity. Despite this empowering motivation, a more malicious undercurrent of "natural" beauty lingers back to the Renaissance when men condemned makeup as an abomination, second to witchcraft, that concealed a woman's true intentions and countenance. This later interpretation of makeup builds on binary and unstable cultural definitions of gender to further stigmatize transgender women who choose to wear makeup to present what is "natural" to them, an internal femininity not otherwise apparent in their bodies. These patriarchal perspectives of makeup as "hiding" a woman's true beauty may pit some cisgender women against one another and against transgender women, encouraging them to police one another to ensure their gender compliance. Ironically, though, this message of a woman embracing her "natural beauty" by abandoning makeup boomerangs back to impact comely cisgender women who, themselves, are not privileged by the "all natural" makeup movement. Many young women face mounting social pressure to wear makeup and meet unrealistic beauty expectations as mirrored by photoshopped models; nonetheless, many transgender women wear makeup as a utilitarian tool, as throughout history, to explore gender expression and identity. When women feel forced, by dress codes or through social messages that makeup is a temptress's trick, to not wear makeup, they miss the opportunity to portray their bodies with an authenticity deeper than skin level.

Whether we choose to wear makeup or not, we can acknowledge its function for those who use it to express their identities. Ultimately, one must critically analyze the motivations behind the drive to go without makeup and criticize others who do choose to wear it. In this discourse, we can recognize that transgender and cisgender women are both well served by a definition of "all natural" beauty that transcends minimal makeup and essentialism: the autonomy of women to control their bodies and public image, with or without the blue eye shadow.

NOTES

1. Content warning to readers: This essay references negative online comments, slurs, and other abusive language used against transgender people. To find support, please contact local LGBTQ+ organizations near you or visit GLAAD's online transgender resources at https://www.glaad.org/transgender/resources.

2. Throughout this paper, "all natural" refers to the trend to wear no or very little makeup, not to the organic processing or sustainability of those makeup products.

3. Mary Wollstonecraft, *A Vindication of the Rights of Woman,* digitized Amy E. Zelmer, Col Chat, and Sue Asscher (Oxford Mississippi: Project Gutenberg, 2002), http://www.gutenberg.org/cache/epub/3420/pg3420.html.

4. Sandra Bartky, "Foucault, Femininity, and the Modernization of Political Power," in *Feminisms and Foucault: Reflections of Resistance*, ed. Irene Diamond and Lee Quinby (Boston: Northeastern University Press, 1988), 64–68.

5. Naomi Wolf, *The Beauty Myth* (New York, Harper Collins, 2009), 13.

6. Wolf, *The Beauty Myth*, 13–14.

7. James Meikle, "Growing Number of Girls Suffer Low Self-Esteem, Says Report," *The Guardian*, November 28, 2013, https://www.theguardian.com/society/2013/nov/29/girls-low-self-esteem-rising-girlguiding-report.

8. I use "they" here as a more inclusive pronoun.

9. Judith Butler, *Gender Trouble* (New York: Routledge, 1990), 47.

10. Readers may also reference Candace West and Jon H. Zimmerman, "Doing Gender," *Gender and Society* 1, no. 2 (June 1987), https://www.gla.ac.uk/0t4/crcees/files/summerschool/readings/WestZimmerman_1987_DoingGender.pdf.

11. Readers may also reference the conference notes from the symposium *Makeup, Identity Performance, and Discrimination*, 2006, at Duke University School of Law, https://scholarship.law.duke.edu/djglp_symposium/2006/events/.

12. Steve Craig, "Feminism, Femininity, and the 'Beauty' Dilemma: How Advertising Co-opted the Women's Movement," Presentation at the Southwest/Texas Popular Culture/American Culture Association Conference at Lubbock, Texas, in January, 1998.

13. Steve Craig, conference paper, 1998.

14. Erica, personal conversation with the author, 2018.

15. Erica, personal conversation with the author, 2018.

16. While not directly referenced here, readers may also find the following pieces for further reading about the history of transgender representation, drag, and gender-nonconforming beauty: G. G. Bolich, *Transgender History and Geography: Crossdressing in Context* (North Carolina: Psyche's Press, 2007); Martin Cannon, "The Regulation of First Nations Sexuality," in *Queerly Canadian: An Introductory Reader in Sexuality Studies*, ed. Maureen Fitzgerald and Scott Rayter (Toronto: Canadian Scholars Press, Inc., 2012), 51–63; Whitney Davis, *Queer Beauty: Sexuality and Aesthetics from Winckelmann to Freud and Beyond* (New York: Columbia University Press, 2010); George Haggerty, *Encyclopedia of Gay Histories and Culture*, Vol. 3 (New York: Routledge, 2012); Jeffrey Masten and Wendy Wall, *Renaissance Drama, New Series 32* (Chicago: Northwestern University Press, 2003); Beatrice Medicine, "Directions in Gender Research in American Indian Societies: Two Spirit and Other Categories," *Online Readings in Psychology and Culture, Unit 3*, vol. 3 (2002); Serena Nanda, *Neither Man Nor Woman: The Hijras of India*, Second Edition (California: Wadsworth Publishing Company, 1999); Andrea Pelleschi, *Transgender Rights and Issues* (Minnesota: Adbo Publishing, 2016); Susan Stryker, *Transgender History: The Roots of Today's Revolution*, Second Edition (Boston: Da Capo Press, 2017); Barbara Summerhawk, Cheiron McMahill, Darren McDonald, *Queer Japan: Personal Stories of Japanese Lesbians, Gays, Bisexuals and Transsexuals* (Norwich: New Victoria Publishers, Inc., 1998).

17. Richard Brathwait, *Time's Curtain Drawne* (London, 1621), A5V.

18. Farah Karim-Cooper, *Cosmetics in Shakespearean and Renaissance Drama* (Edinburgh: Edinburgh University Press, 2006), digitized Google Books, https://books.google.com/books?id=-bBvAAAAQBAJ&printsec=frontcover&dq=Cosmetics+in+Shakespearean+and+Renaissance+Drama,&hl=en&newbks=1&newbks_redir=0&ppis=_e&sa=X&ved=2ahUKEwj

Eo_m0grHnAhUro1kKHRwtB6cQ6AEwAHoECAMQAg#v=onepage&q&f=false.

19. Farah Karim-Cooper, *Cosmetics in Shakespearean and Renaissance Drama,* n.pg.

20. "10 Reasons Why Men Hate Makeup," *Mamiverse*, June 28, 2017, https://mamiverse.com/benefits-of-natural-beauty-73364/.

21. "10 Reasons Why Men Hate Makeup," *Mamiverse*.

22. I use Joseph Harwood's name rather than pronouns to avoid misgendering Harwood.

23. I use "forced" here to reiterate that my argument concerns the strands of the "all natural" movement that seek to persuade or pressure women to not wear makeup because it seems unnatural or unappealing or demonstrates a woman's dishonesty. I do not apply this argument to those who *personally* choose not to wear makeup while acknowledging that makeup can serve an important role in others' identity.

24. See record of this article at Adam Clark Estes, "HuffPosts' 'Tr*nny' Joke Didn't Go Over Too Well," *The Atlantic*, November 9, 2011, https://www.theatlantic.com/business/archive/2011/11/huffposts-tranny-joke-didnt-go-over-well/335703/.

25. Matt DeRienzo, "Woman Mistaken for Transgender Harassed in Walmart Bathroom," *The Danbury News Times*, May 16, 2016, https://www.newstimes.com/local/article/Woman-mistaken-for-transgender-harassed-in-7471666.php .

BIBLIOGRAPHY

Bartky, Sandra. "Foucault, Femininity, and the Modernization of Political Power." In *Feminisms and Foucault: Reflections of Resistance*, ed. Irene Diamond and Lee Quinby, 33. Boston: Northeastern University Press, 1988.

Brathwaite, Richard. *Time's Curtain Drawn.* London, 1621.

Butler, Judith. *Gender Trouble.* New York: Routledge, 1990, 47.

Craig, Steve. "Feminism, Femininity, and the 'Beauty' Dilemma: How Advertising Co-opted the Women's Movement." *The Feminist eZine*, January 1998. http://www.feministezine.com/feminist/fashion/The-Beauty-Dilemma.html.

DeRienzo, Matt. "Woman Mistaken for Transgender Harassed in Walmart Bathroom." *The Danbury News Times*, May 16, 2016. https://www.newstimes.com/local/article/Woman-mistaken-for-transgender-harassed-in-747.

Harwood, Joseph. "Boy to Girl Makeup Secrets." YouTube, December 10, 2013. https://www.youtube.com/watch?v=T2KVBpLm30c&list=PLhKjB16yszdsEfmXTOa6pr6dCXOAIxPzD&index=11.

Karim-Cooper, Farah. *Cosmetics in Shakespearean and Renaissance Drama.* Edinburgh: Edinburgh University Press, 2006, 103.

Mamiverse.com. "10 Reasons Why Men Hate Makeup." June 26, 2017. http://mamiverse.com/benefits-of-natural-beauty-73364/7/.

Meikle, James. "Growing Number of Girls Suffer Low Self-Esteem, Says Report." *The Guardian,* November 29, 2013. https://www.theguardian.com/society/2013/nov/29/girls-low-self-esteem-rising-girlguiding-Report.

Sanjati, Steph. "Feminizing Make-up for Trans Women." Youtube, December 3, 2016. https://www.youtube.com/watch?v=fi7_6SqretM.

Trotta, Daniel. "U.S. Transgender People Harassed in Public Restrooms: Landmark Survey." *Reuters*, December 8, 2016. https://www.reuters.com/article/us-usa-lgbt-survey/u-s-transgender-people-harassed-in-public-restrooms-landmark-survey-idUSKBN13X0BK.

Wolf, Naomi. *The Beauty Myth.* New York: Harper Collins, 2009, 13–14.

Wollstonecraft, Mary. *A Vindication of the Rights of Woman*, Chapter 3. London: Courier Corporation, 1792. Bartleby ebooks. http://www.bartleby.com/144/3.html.

Chapter Seven

"What's the Point in Covering Them Up?"

Visible Disability and the Invitation to Stare in YouTube Makeup Tutorials

Katherine Anderson Howell

Visible disability can disrupt the common tropes of YouTube makeup tutorials, including application, voiceover, and visible display. The nature of the tutorial, and of YouTube itself, invites looking, and staring, which, as Garland-Thomson notes, "makes things happen between people."[1] Staring is not passive for the starer or the staree. The three young women whose makeup-focused YouTube channels I explore in this chapter have visible disabilities and disrupt our expectations about what people who live in disabled bodies should do and be. They engage in a form of activism that uses popular culture and invited stare to connect with other makeup fans, create fans of their own, and generate changed thought and action in both groups. MakeupJunkieG, whose real name is Georgia, has a form of dwarfism that causes her to live with chronic pain and use a wheelchair. MakeupArtistGorda66, also known as Marimar, has cystic hygroma, and her tumor is on her face, preventing her from eating and speaking orally or fully closing her mouth. She uses a throat tube. Isabelle Weall is a quadruple amputee whose amputations resulted from early childhood meningitis. Each shows her disability clearly on her channel, and each engages with it in multiple videos. Georgia directly addresses how makeup has changed her interactions with people and her experience with chronic pain; she has also done "routine" videos showing how she lives her life. Marimar has done a video explaining her condition and has posted it as the home video on her channel; she also signs using American Sign Language in every video. Isabelle talks openly about her amputations, the reasons for them, disability etiquette, and the beauty of scars.

YouTubers with visible disabilities present a form of visual and fan activism that offers opportunities for subversive expression and inclusion in digital spaces. Postfeminist critiques of YouTube makeup tutorials shut down these possibilities. However, I will show through both Brough and Shresthova's conceptualization of fan activism[2] and Garland-Thomson's understanding of staring and disability that, while YouTubers with visible disability may reinscribe certain elements of typical beauty culture, they offer subversive alternatives to it as well.

Postfeminist critiques of beauty culture focus on "white femininity"[3] and "performative consumption" as a way of selling makeup.[4] The notion of white, feminine performative consumption fits neatly into a postfeminist view of the created self as a branded commodity for others to view and become fans of or consume. Opel offers the audience, or potential fans, an essential element of self-branding: "A critical component of self-branding, then, is the feedback that social networking spaces offer (as in the comments section)."[5] This feedback occurs in Instagram and Facebook likes and comments, Twitter threads, and YouTube views and comments. Search terms, hashtags, and the platforms' own suggestions define the community providing these likes and comments. If one commonly watches makeup tutorials on YouTube, one can expect the platform to suggest similar channels for further watching. Thus, YouTube partially creates a fandom community. Opel argues that "the can-do girl in this fan community participates in self-branding in participatory culture through the construction and circulation of . . . essential postfeminist cultural performance—a can-do girl who chooses through her tastes and lifestyle preferences a unique subject, but also chooses to broadcast this choice in a technologically savvy manner."[6] This self-branding applies to makeup tutorials in the sense that each person's YouTube channel has a distinct aesthetic reflecting their tastes and that their channel reflects their lifestyle in the way that they desire. The notion that, however, the self becomes a brand and commodity in a postfeminist manner reflects, as Opel suggests, white femininity, and, I would argue, abled, mainstream feminism.

Affuso argues that YouTube videos offer inclusive opportunities for women "of all ages, races, and body types" to create "resistant fan activity with tutorials providing adaptive measures."[7] Affuso also sees these adaptive measures as "indoctrinating larger numbers of women to opt-in to consumer citizenship,"[8] part of the postfeminist view of beauty culture. Brough and Shretshova, however, argue that "fan participation in and through commercial entertainment spaces is not predetermined to be resistant or complicit—in fact, it is often both—but its political significance lies in part in the changes in relations of power that may occur through such participation."[9] In fact, simple reductions of commercial/noncommercial are "too simplistic to be analytically useful."[10] Brough and Shresthova argue that the power relations between fan and producer (or YouTuber and makeup brand) or fan activist and consumer (or YouTuber and viewer) matter significantly in commercial or commodity activism. More than self-branding, they argue that "we need to pay attention to how particular actors construct, use, and circulate their voices through the production or reproduction of cultural content, as well as whether and by whom content is consumed and engaged."[11] In this case, we might consider how disabled people construct their bodies and lives through the experience of cosmetics and how others look at that construction.

Garland-Thomson points out that looking as an act of consumption is not new: "In late capitalism, the predominant form of looking, the mass exercise of ocularcentricity, is what we might call consumer vision."[12] This kind of experience of the world through the view of consumption "requires looking at commodities, not people."[13] This way of looking is the "casual visual cruising of window-shopping or Web surfing."[14] Moving through the world, in particular the world of makeup on YouTube, which combines both window-shopping and Web surfing, means that visual stimuli inundates us. And thus, the disabled, differently bodied YouTuber—or to use Garland-Thomson's phrase, "novel person"—grabs our attention and disrupts our postfeminist narrative of self-branding, commodity culture in two ways.

First, postfeminist critique may not apply to actions done by people that white, abled feminism has left behind. Second, as Garland-Thomson has pointed out, "extraordinary-looking bodies demand attention. The sight of an unexpected body—that is to say, a body that does not conform to our expectations for an ordinary body—is compelling because it disorders expectations."[15] Georgia, Marimar, and Isabelle have unexpected bodies, and, in a space like YouTube that focuses on visual attention, they allow their bodies to be visible and control the attention that their bodies demand.

Garland-Thomson argues that "beauty is a perceptual process and a transitive action: it catches interest, prompts judgment, encourages scrutiny, creates knowledge."[16] The videos discussed below engage in this process of beauty. Those who find novelty in the bodies of these YouTubers and engage with their tutorials may find themselves engaged in the process of visual activism: "look, think, act. First [the differently bodied] use the human urge to look at new things to make people look at them. Second, they use . . . the way we look at them . . . to ask the public to think differently about people like them. The last step depends on their starers' receptiveness. If their visual politics of deliberately structured self-disclosure succeeds, it can create a sense of obligation that primes people to act in new ways."[17] The "invitation to stare"[18] is a political act, one which crafts disability as a part of the everyday beauty process.

MakeupJunkieG, or Georgia, is white, uses a wheelchair, and is, according to YouTube, about thirty inches tall. Garland-Thomson reminds us that "anything that looks too big or small assaults our sense of what is proper"[19] and that our world has "embroidered certain minority forms of embodiment" into tales through which society can self-examine, yet "often lost in this exchange is a sense of the particular lives and looks of the people whose shapes have across history given rise to these stories."[20] Thus, "the most spectacular form of visual novelty that can prompt stares are breaches of human scale and shape,"[21] and Georgia uses her small stature, and the stares it brings, to her own advantage.

In her video titled "Real Life Elf on the Shelf for 24 Hours *Caught on Camera,*" she demonstrates a willingness to use her body and her disability in subversive ways. The video was posted on December 16, 2018. As of January 2, 2019, it had 148,083 views, approximately 4,700 likes, and 205 dislikes. Georgia has tagged the video elfontheshelfisreal, elfontheshelf, and 24hourchallenge.

The first shot of the video shows Georgia duct taped to a wall in an elf outfit. The tape crosses over her body in a large X, and one long strip covers her mouth. She screams, but she could be screaming with laughter or tears; we cannot tell.[22] Her muffled words also appear on the screen: "I just fell"[23] and "I'm scared."[24] Then the video cuts to a color test screen[25] and the true opening, where Georgia sits, poised and calm, on a white desk, in the same elf outfit. She wears her hair half up, but mostly down, with a jingly elf hat in her hair. She has full red lips, dark, full "instagram" styled brows, and false lashes. She wears a green dress with gold buttons, a red collar, and red-and-white striped sleeves. She also has red-and-white socks on. She clearly plays on the tales that Garland-Thomson mentioned, as well as the commercial Elf on the Shelf dolls. Before the action begins, a card appears on the screen that reads, "Roll the clips of me looking about two years old dressed as an elf just for your entertainment . . . Enjoy."[26]

Georgia then tells the viewer that the first Elf on the Shelf scene will involve the following props: a toy Storm Trooper, a toy Darth Vader, and some colorful, numbered sacks. The Storm Trooper and Darth Vader are nearly Georgia's size. Next, a card on the screen appears, with the words "Star Wars Sack Race" and an image beside them of Georgia and the Star Wars toys in sacks, mimicking a race on the floor. The image, as are all the Elf on the Shelf scenes, appears to be "taped" at the corners with festive tape, as if in a scrapbook.[27] The next scene, "Drunk with Darth Vader," follows the same pattern: Georgia describes the props and then shows the scene on a card with writing and the image; this one shows Georgia curled up beside Darth on the couch, holding an empty wine bottle and an empty glass.[28] Georgia's elf fishes for "goldfish," in the form of cheese puffs, in the toilet,[29] and plays Connect 4 with a toy T-rex, of which Georgia says she "share[s] something in common: [we] both have very short arms."[30] She follows this with a huge giggle,[31] regardless of whether it is "proper" to do so. The next scene shows Georgia "grating a snowman's ass,"[32] using marshmallows as the grated-up snow. Then Georgia pretends that her dog has wrapped her in tinsel.[33]

The next scene describes Georgia "held hostage by storm trooper"[34] and shows her sitting on a stool,[35] with the Storm Trooper toy from earlier in the video in front of her and crisscrossed in duct tape. We have a replay of the opening of the video, and we realize she is laughing to the point of crying, and words appear on the screen stating, "crying over realization of what I'm doing for YouTube."[36]

The final scene shows Georgia drawing a moustache and the words "Elves Rule" on her father's face while he sleeps, or pretends to, on the couch, using eyeliner, staying true to the makeup theme of the channel.[37] At the end, Georgia returns to the desk and says to the viewer that the video is "only for a bit of fun just before Christmas"[38] and that she "thought why not dress up as an elf, because we love an extra queen."[39]

Under the video, Georgia has pinned a comment by YouTube user Light-Dreamer that reads, "You don't look 2yo girl. Cute is for all ages. You look festive and A-MA-ZING." A few comments down, Shannon W comments, "Girl . . . the little people community is going to come for you for this," and Georgia replies to this comment with the cry-laughing emoji. She seems to suggest that the little people community does not necessarily represent her or her choices; hers is the life behind her stories, and the makeup community is the one she has chosen to engage with in this video.

Initially, this video presents a challenge to watch, in part because the first view we have of Georgia's position and cry/laugh/scream is disconcerting and sets an ominous tone, but also because it feels incorrect and uncomfortable to watch a little person perform as an elf. We see how we have been embroidered with the images of different embodiment, and we want to resist our temptation to stare.

Georgia seems to know this, as she reassures us at the end of the video that it is "only for a bit of fun." After all, "characters with unusual forms and sizes abound in our folktales, literature, art, and material culture,"[40] and Georgia knows that. However, she intentionally sets up a potentially subversive tone at the opening by inviting people to look at her laughter or crying or discomfort out of its context. Georgia makes the editing choice to disrupt our perception of her vulnerability and of the performative politics of the video by intentionally ripping the duct tape scene out of context and removing it from the reassurance that she sits securely on a stool.

Her sarcasm in the video that she looks like a two year old, when she wears bold makeup, including dark long nails, offers a clear preemptive rebuke against those who might feel that a little person dressing as an elf is infantilizing: her small stature allows people to play out the cultural myth that "the miniature invites stewardship and appropriation."[41] Her pinning the comment by LightDreamer reinforces this rebuke; all ages can experience cuteness and festivity, and, by implication of the video, all bodies can as well. Georgia, on her channel, is unabashedly adult—not in a pornographic or erotic way—but in a way that presents a persona unafraid to put the disabled and different body on display. The video, while perhaps in part reinscribing stereotypes, gives a subversive, tongue-in-cheek, middle finger to those who might limit her self-expression.

In contrast, her video, posted September 30, 2018, titled "The *Real* Me. . . . The Power of MakeUp" offers a more sincere view of how Georgia views her role and the role of makeup and performance in her life. The video is twelve minutes and nineteen seconds long, and only Georgia appears in the video. She has tagged the video with thepowerofmakeup, transformation, and storytime. As of January 2, 2019, the video has 126,624 views, 4,500 likes, and only seventy-eight dislikes. The comments vary in tone yet are mostly positively intended, but, aside from liking many of them, Georgia doesn't respond much or pin any. The word "cute" fills the comments, as do variants of the idea that Georgia does not need or should not wear makeup to be beautiful, entirely missing one of her larger points about disability and pain.

To this point, Thoreau reminds us that "stereotypical beliefs about disabled people are encoded in our culture through language as well as images."[42] The Disneyfication of "exaggerated eyes and lashes"[43] encode cuteness as well. Thus, when Georgia insists on the power of makeup, and her commenters miss the point by discussing her cuteness, they, perhaps unwittingly, undermine her power. However, she uses the tools of YouTube, via the lack of pinned comments, to reclaim it. Unlike the Elf on the Shelf video, where she pinned someone else's comment to make her point and replied with implied laughter at someone else to further it, in this video, she allows the point to reverberate on its own. If the commenters miss it, they miss it, and miss her engagement as well.

The video[44] opens with Georgia center screen with no makeup on. It does appear that she has done her brows because she has had them microbladed, a process she also documented on YouTube. She introduces the concept of the video, that she will discuss the power of makeup, but she does not warn the viewer that she will only do half her face, leaving a clear demarcation between "empowered" Georgia and regular Georgia. The rest of the video follows the usual genre conventions of a GRWM (get ready with me) video, as she narrates what she does with the makeup and describes the products she uses while also talking about her life and her makeup philosophy. She tells the viewer that "instead of doing a really extreme glam look, I wanted to do my everyday makeup"[45] because this seems more real.

Georgia's thoughts in the first half of the video could be the thoughts of any socially liberal twenty-year-old in 2018: people wear makeup for themselves, not for others; makeup has no rules; makeup enhances; makeup empowers; makeup has no gender. She uses typical influencer slang like "sip tea," "sis," "queen," and "ya girl." She mentions her insecurities, which are, again, typical: she dislikes her eyes, her freckles, and the redness of her skin. These attitudes reflect what many influencers might say; memes circle often about how girls do not wear makeup for boys, and makeup has become increasingly a genderless hobby as influencers like Jake Jamie (in the United Kingdom) and James Charles (in the United States) make names for themselves. Georgia strives for this ordinariness, it turns out. She talks about how putting on lashes is her favorite part of makeup[46] and how putting a darker color in the outer corner of her eye "makes [her] eyes look super sultry and sexy and I love that,"[47] again refusing cuteness. In these ways, we see that Georgia is, in many ways, an ordinary twenty-year-old.

Later in the video, Georgia states directly, "makeup breaks the barrier for me."[48] People who once might have ignored her or looked away from her in her chair now engage her and talk to her about her makeup. In fact, she says that the precise way they look has changed: "It [makeup] makes people be a lot more positive toward me so instead of staring at me because I'm in a wheelchair, they stare at me because of my makeup. . . . They approach me because of my bright red lipstick or my lashes."[49] For Georgia, as well as for others "who inhabit such bodies," the world "misfits" them "in the literal sense of the word."[50] Garland-Thomson explains the ignoring that Georgia has faced: "the cultural imagination thus ever threatens to thrust those who are too large, too small, or too irregular outside of the circle of common humanity."[51]

Makeup has become a social act for Georgia, but, instead of a simple performance of femininity or of conforming to sexual or gender norms, makeup allows her to insist that people acknowledge her as a full person, not simply a disabled body, or a chair in the way, or someone difficult to look at or engage. When people see her wearing lashes, the differences seem easier to bridge.

Georgia also takes pleasure in makeup. She says, "I absolutely love transforming my face. I love playing with makeup."[52] This transformative play is a kind of fandom. While applying highlighter to her skin, she elaborates on this idea: "When I'm in pain and I have the worst grey dull skin, my glow is the most important to me."[53] Georgia lives with chronic pain, which she describes as "honestly never ending."[54] She says as she shows the finished look that "honestly when I thought I was falling apart and I literally felt like I had no purpose in life but pain, makeup for me was a huge distraction in life. It gave me something to focus on."[55] For Georgia, part of the power of makeup is control over the appearance of pain, and over the experience of it.

She can refuse to show the pain that she experiences and can create the experience she wants to show on her face. She states, "I don't want pain to rule my life,"[56] and she shows us how the process of everyday beauty helps her regain control.

Multiple things happen in this video. Georgia participates in a community effort to explain the power of makeup, and her ideas reflect the ordinary ideas of that community until they become personal. That ordinariness demonstrates the extraordinary power of Georgia's invitation to stare. She chooses to invite the stare by presenting herself in public the way she wants, with bold, microbladed brows, false and full lashes, a contoured and shimmery face, and a glossy, or even sometimes red, lip. As she repeats herself and stumbles over words, she also lays claim to her agency and her sex appeal.

We may think that in the world of makeup tutorials having a typical, perfect face matters most. The face is a central metaphor to human language, and "faces are consequential texts that we read attentively" as they "reveal our roots and histories."[57] A person with an unorthodox face finds power in "manipulating the eyes of the starer to end, extend, or relocate the encounters . . . thus [enlisting] the potency bestowed by someone's fear and [converting] it into a form of personal authority inflected by either generousity or command can enlarge the self in ways that are psychologically beneficial and socially effective."[58] MakeupArtistGorda66, or Marimar, has used her unorthodox face as a means to reclaim authority in her own life. She is a Latina YouTuber with facial tumors that have required multiple surgeries and that necessitate the use of a throat tube.

Marimar's "IDK Eye Look Tutorial"[59] has no sound except for occasional background noise and the sounds of the palettes. The video, published on January 3, 2019, has 5,232 views, 336 likes, and eleven dislikes as of January 14, 2019. The background is dark. In a room with wood paneling, Marimar sits among stacked boxes with pictures on the wall. The only light comes from the light she uses to light her face. She puts the names of the shadows she uses and the palette they come from at the top left of the screen. She chooses the shadows she will use by swatching them on her hand, but, unlike other YouTubers, she does not show her audience the swatches. However, she does show the outside of each of the three separate palettes she uses to her audience. Most of the video focuses on her eyes, and, when she needs to see them up close, she uses a small handheld mirror.

When Marimar finishes her eyes, she signs, "Finish up my face then come back,"[60] and the video fades out then back in to her with a full face, including lashes. She uses a tissue to wipe her mouth, including some inside her lips, then applies a liquid lipstick and provides the signs and captions for the name and brand. During lipstick application, her soft palette is fully visible. The video follows similar genre conventions to other GRWM style videos, except that Marimar doesn't tell a story or pretend to chat with her viewers. The pleasure of makeup and the beauty process are the points.

The silence of the video makes the ads alarming. Hearing viewers may be accustomed to the noise and sound of YouTube ads, which can even interrupt speakers midsentence. However, in the silence of Marimar's videos, the ads come through as blaring disruptions, not simply interruptions, thus providing another level of resistance to postfeminist critique. Combined with her visible differences and her invitation to stare, Marimar's video resists easy categorization as part of can-do girl culture.

Marimar's comments often say that she should not have moved out of her family home. Videos like those titled "Need Y'all Help" and "Homeless at McDonald's" often result in encouragement to return to her mother's home and to leave her boyfriend, Jamal. Documenting her financial struggles results in ableist calls to return home, classist calls to stay on Supplemental Security Income (SSI), and racism toward her boyfriend. Jamal, who is Black, often faces stereotypical call-outs in the comments, such as that he needs to get a job, that he is taking advantage of her, or other racially charged implications. We see that while Marimar creates her own identity, her comments section "also allows the people [she interacts] with to do the same."[61] So, in some ways, "the reality of the Internet may not be as emancipatory for disabled people as has been claimed."[62]

In the video "Why Did I move out!? [chin in hand emoji]"[63] posted December 29, 2018, Marimar answers back to all of these comments. The video, as of January 4, 2019, had 43,429 views, 1,200 likes, and one hundred dislikes. The pinned comment from Marimar reads, "A lot of my family are getting mad at me for post this video by it not no disrespect and the bad part I didn't even say nothing bad so if you haven't talk to me over a year don't talk to me stay bless [three praying hands emojis]." The video is filmed in the car. Marimar signs, and the video is captioned. Marimar does not do her makeup in the video, so our attention focuses on her hands and the words on the screen. Garland-Thomson argues that "hands attract intense looking when they act as instruments of linguistic intercourse. The art of oratory extends the word from mouth to hand and bonds hand to eye."[64] This intense looking extends even further for sign languages "because they do all the work of communication rather than augmenting speech. One listens to speakers; one stares at signers."[65] Marimar's mechanism of communication invites our stare, and she uses that to her advantage in the beginning of the video.

She opens with saying that she is trying not to cry, and she defends Jamal, stating that he "is the one I truly trust when it come to health, emotion, and mind."[66] She discusses wanting to move, and YouTube provided her with income, and she regarded it as a career. Her mother discouraged her YouTube career because of concerns over her SSI, which might have been stopped or decreased if she had an income.[67] Marimar describes her mother as "low key controlling [her] life."[68] She mentions her family making her go to a restaurant when she would rather not.[69] Not only can Marimar not orally consume food, we find out later when Jamal enters the video that Marimar hates going to restaurants: "A lot of places she won't go in, especially, like, if you eating."[70]

Marimar explains that her family treats her like "a baby"[71] while she sees people her age (she is twenty-four in the video) living independently.[72] She wants to know how to live on her own before her mother dies, but she states that her mother expects her to live with family, such as her sister, if her mother does pass away.[73] At the end of her explanation, she blows a kiss and signs I love you.[74]

When Jamal enters the video, he says that Marimar asked him to recap for people who don't like reading,[75] a sign of inclusivity and an understanding of her audience. Jamal does so, and touches on other moments of ableism in Marimar's life. He doesn't use the term ableism, likening the experiences to racism.[76] He says to the audience, "People don't understand what you [Marimar] have to go through when we go out in public. . . . There is people who just stare to the point it makes me mad."[77] He describes an experience where Marimar and his mother went to get their nails done, and the technician ran and hid from Marimar.[78] Marimar was told to get out.[79] Jamal's mother was angry and wanted to react, but Marimar wanted to go home.[80] Marimar did return to the place, with Jamal, who sat and made them do her nails and eyebrows for half off. He then mentions that they go to places like the salon at Walmart where Marimar is accepted and even recognized from Facebook.

The experiences of Marimar and Jamal point to the ways that race, class, and disability truly intersect, both in real life and in the internet comment sections. Marimar is trilingual (English, Spanish, and ASL) and hard working; YouTube is challenging. Still, however, both her family and her commenters infantilize her. She feels safe with Jamal, but her commenters despise him largely for racialized reasons. She does not want to rely on SSI but is expected to do so. The social expectation that a twenty-four-year-old with disabilities should return to her family profoundly differs from the social expectations of most other twenty-four-year-olds. Her videos allow her to use her fannish interest in makeup and her skills to both resist the racist, classist, and ableist push toward home and isolation and to use the stare for her own authority.

If Marimar's signing hands attract intense stares, then Isabelle's amputated hands invite the stares of people accustomed to seeing people with amputations both as people who are lacking and people who have gained intense trauma: they lack the amputated limbs, but they have the trauma and the associated story. Society finds itself riveted by amputations "when they are at work. Ordinary activities, such as eating, drinking, grooming, or manipulating objects become spectacles of interest when unusual hands accomplish them . . . surprise might initiate a stare, but in the case of unusual hands encountering a usual task, curiosity about human ingenuity often sustains this visual inquiry."[81] Isabelle Weall is a teenaged white YouTuber whose amputations are a result of meningitis at age seven. Her videos show her doing ordinary tasks and advocating for disability rights.

Isabelle's video "AM I A MAKEUP ARTIST?? Candy Cane Makeup Look!,"[82] posted December 12, 2018, offers a straightforward makeup tutorial. As of January 6, 2019, the video has 3,991 views, 389 likes, and five dislikes. Isabelle opens the video by stating that she will do a look she saw on Instagram, and she doesn't know if she is "talented enough to recreate it because I'm not a makeup artist."[83] Isabelle's limbs are visible in the video, as she uses her elbows to push back her hair and her joints to hold brushes and tools. She mentions that she has filmed six videos in a day to keep up with her Christmas series, a difficult feat with school also going on. She opens palettes and packages with her mouth nonchalantly. She holds the brushes between her two arms to blend and has her own technique involving moving both the brush and her head. She encounters usual tasks, solving them unusually. She chats during the video about the colors just as a typical fifteen-year-old might: "In the picture they've used green glitter, but I don't have green glitter. Who has green glitter, apart from this makeup artist?"[84]

She applies a Christmasy green eye shadow look and a white winged eyeliner with a red stripe: a candy cane makeup look. Toward the end of the video, her younger brother comes in, and she asks him to "come say hi."[85] The situation demonstrates an ordinary sibling relationship, comfortable and kind. This quotidian interaction suggests that this beauty process is usual for their family. She ends the video by stating cheerily, "I think this look is super cool. Anyone can do it. Even I can do it, and I don't have any hands, so of course you can do it. That's so bad for me to say."[86] Her dark humor undercuts her participation in the history of "many armless people . . . displaying to the typically handed the ways they accomplished quotidian tasks."[87] Isabelle's videos do not mention the disability history of her makeup career, but she seems aware of the position she holds and the awe that people have in her confidence and abilities. She shows this awareness in the frequency with which she makes videos about what not to say to amputees, things she does differently, and how she loves her different body.

"How to Love Yourself with Scars!? My Scar Story,"[88] demonstrates Isabelle's activism. The video was posted December 10, 2018, and has 11,142 views as of January 6, 2019. The video has 779 likes and six dislikes. The pinned comment by Isabelle states, "Never be ashamed of a scar. It simply means you were stronger than whatever tried to hurt you [pink stacked heart emoji]." In the opening of the video, Isabelle states that "for some reason, scars are such a like taboo subject."[89] She lists many of the ways to get a scar, including having a child or getting meningitis. She begins to show her scars, saying, "literally I've got hundreds."[90] She explains how she got her scars, again demonstrating her dark humor with a smirking face: "it's kind of a bit gross . . . I am aware. I know."[91] Her scars come from the symptoms of meningitis, medical tubes, amputations, and a different shoulder surgery. She speaks of them with humor, stating that she has a "selection."[92] She speaks with irritation about scars' perception as flaws: "obviously it's not a flaw in the person, it's a flaw in how society views them."[93]

Isabelle tells a story about visiting the plastic surgeon after leaving the hospital. The surgeon wanted to reduce her scarring with more surgery, and Isabelle could not understand why he wanted to do that or why surgery would be necessary for just a scar.[94] She doesn't understand why she should hide her scars or keep them secret. In her case, she could have scars or could have died: "In that way, they're sick" (in the slang sense of awesome).[95] Here, Isabelle enters into a cultural phenomenon of others who have childhood stories of medical interventions. McLaughlin and Coleman-Fountain tell the story of another such young woman, stating that the "scars on her legs were material testimony to this reshaping, letting past surgeries speak through the body,"[96] and, as her surgeries saved her life, Isabelle questions, "What's the point of covering them up?"[97] She then invites people to share their scar stories in the comments section, joining again with disability history by mimicking others who have "[used] the visual pull of their stareable bodies as public announcements that people with significant disabilities have good lives and make valuable contributions."[98] Isabelle's engagement with this history shows how her visual novelty puts her outside of postfeminist beauty culture and into the realm of visual activism, and Isabelle's commenters follow up on her invitation, sharing stories and offering support.

All of these YouTubers present a form of visual activism in which people in extraordinary bodies live ordinary lives. Of course, as Garland-Thomson reminds us, "the risk of all activism is that it will not make this last leap from intent to effect,"[99] and we see in the persistent comments toward Georgia regarding cuteness and toward Marimar that she needs to return home that some viewers miss the point. However, the participation of people with disabilities in visual narrative and online storytelling puts control of the language and of "individual and collective identity" in the hands of the person with disabilities,[100] as Isabelle's comments and community demonstrate, and, as McLaughlin and Coleman-Fountain[101] argue, all bodies, disabled or not, novel or not, come with narratives. The bodies that Georgia, Marimar, and Isabelle present online are bodies that both participate in the "'ordinary' bodywork of everyday life"—in this case makeup—but also are bodies in which "medicine has a heightened presence"[102]—Georgia's wheelchair, Marimar's throat tube, and Isabelle's scars.

Those who live in novel bodies do not seek the ordinary as simply an imaginary or discursive practice: "They also should be understood as having effects on the things people do to their bodies to enable them to be recognised within such imaginaries. From turning everyday activities into opportunities for working on body strength and agility, to undergoing painful surgery and physiotherapy, discursive validation of normality is embedded literally on to the body itself."[103] In other words, the ways that young people with disabilities, and these YouTubers, in particular, want to participate in the world and imagine their futures literally shape the way they present their bodies to the world in the present.[104] They don't do this without critical thought or consideration, however; they explicitly present "some challenge to others to see a 'normal' life as possible while differently embodied."[105] They are not "can-do" girls; they display their physical pain, their family grief, and their harassment at the hands of others. They do not have it all.

While tempting to view these disabled YouTubers as trying to fit into a postfeminist mold, we see that, instead, they resist this perception. If we view them as visual activists, in Garland-Thomson's sense, we see how they invite the stare with their novelty. However, if we view them as participating in commodity activism, which Brough and Shresthova see as "[complicating] our understanding of resistance,"[106] we begin to see still even a more complex picture emerging. They invite the stare with their novel bodies, and they continue the stare with their embrace of a beloved popular-culture object, makeup and the makeup tutorial. This "strategic deployment of popular culture content" is activism[107] and uses "play, performance, spectacle, and affect."[108] These things "motivate civil action,"[109] even though they are disregarded as discursive tools. Brough and Shresthova also point out that "transmedia storytelling [is] a catalyst for collective identity formation and mobilization."[110] Thus, deploying the novel body, engaging the stare, participating in the fandom community and the beauty culture, and telling their stories moves these disabled YouTubers out of the realm of postfeminist self-commodification and into that of visual and fan activism.

NOTES

1. Rosemarie Garland-Thomson, *Staring: How We Look* (Oxford University Press: Oxford, 2009), 33.

2. Melissa Brough and Sangita Shresthova, "Fandom Meets Activism: Rethinking Civic and Political Participation," *Transformative Works and Cultures*, eds. Henry Jenkins and Sangita Shresthova, special issue vol. 10 (2012): https://doi.org/10.3983/twc.2012.0303.

3. Dawn S. Opel, "Self-Representation in Literary Fandom: Women's Leisure Reader Selfies as Postfeminist Performance" in "Performance and Performativity in Fandom," eds. Lucy Bennett and Paul J. Booth, *Transformative Works and Cultures*, no. 18 (2015): 4.7, http://dx.doi.org/10.3983/twc.2015.0607.

4. Elizabeth Affuso, "Everyday Costume: Feminized Fandom, Retail, and Beauty Culture" in *The Routledge Companion to Media Fandom*, eds. Melissa Click and Suzanne Scott. (Routledge: New York. 2018), Ebook.

5. Opel, "Self-Representation," 4.7.

6. Ibid.

7. Affuso, "Everyday Costume."
8. Ibid.
9. Brough and Shresthova "Fandom Meets Activism," 4.9.
10. Ibid., 4.4.
11. Ibid., 4.9.
12. Garland-Thomson, *Staring*, 39.
13. Ibid., 29.
14. Ibid.
15. Ibid., 37.
16. Ibid., 187.
17. Ibid., 193.
18. Ibid., 191.
19. Ibid., 162.
20. Ibid., 167.
21. Ibid., 161.
22. MakeupJunkieG, "Real Life Elf on the Shelf for 24hours *Caught on Camera*" YouTube Video, December 16, 2018, https://youtu.be/WmajlBZ43Fg, 0:03.
23. Ibid., 0:06.
24. Ibid., 0:08.
25. Ibid., 0:10.
26. Ibid., 1:24.
27. Ibid., 2:15.
28. Ibid., 2:40.
29. Ibid., 3:01.
30. Ibid., 3:17.
31. Ibid., 3:22.
32. Ibid., 4:07.
33. Ibid., 4:30.
34. Ibid., 4:56.
35. Ibid., 5:02.
36. Ibid., 5:03–5:13.
37. Ibid., 5:21.
38. Ibid., 5:33.
39. Ibid., 5:38.
40. Garland-Thomson, *Staring*, 161.
41. Ibid.,162.
42. Estelle Thoreau, "*Ouch!* An Examination of the Self Representation of Disabled People on the Internet," *Journal of Computer-Mediated Communication*, Vol. 11 (2006): 445, doi:10.1111/j.1083-6101.2006.00021.x.
43. Garland-Thomson, *Staring: How We Look*. 163.
44. MakeupJunkieG, "The *Real* Me . . . The Power of Makeup," YouTube Video, September 30, 2018, https://youtu.be/Vn1LLVKrL6Q.
45. Ibid., 2:23–2:29.
46. Ibid., 5:44.
47. Ibid., 4:00–4:08.
48. Ibid., 9:49.
49. Ibid., 9:11–9:26.
50. Garland-Thomson, *Staring*, 167.
51. Ibid.
52. MakeupJunkieG, "The *Real* Me," 8:08–8:12.
53. Ibid., 10:03–10:11.
54. Ibid., 10:37.
55. Ibid., 10:48–11:00.
56. Ibid., 11:18.
57. Garland-Thomson, *Staring*, 98.
58. Ibid., 107.

59. MakeupArtistGorda66, "Idk Look Tutorial [chin in hand emoji]" YouTube Video, January 3, 2019, https://youtu.be/6jniY_bOQT0.
60. Ibid., 16:42.
61. Thoreau, "*Ouch!*," 443.
62. Ibid.
63. MakeupArtistGorda66, "Why Did I Move Out!? [chin in hand emoji]" YouTube Video. December 29, 2018, https://youtu.be/saHLB9YaZ1w.
64. Garland-Thomson, *Staring*, 120.
65. Garland-Thomson, *Staring*, 121.
66. MakeupArtistGorda66, "Why Did I Move Out!?" 1:27.
67. Ibid., 2:58–3:51.
68. Ibid., 5:16.
69. Ibid., 4:51–5:14.
70. Ibid., 29:01–29:06.
71. Ibid., 3:58.
72. Ibid., 4:18.
73. Ibid., 5:40–5:55.
74. Ibid., 10:55.
75. Ibid., 11:32.
76. Ibid., 24:45, 24:52.
77. Ibid., 24:20–24:42.
78. Ibid., 25:47.
79. Ibid., 26:01.
80. Ibid., 26:27–26:29.
81. Garland-Thomson, *Staring*, 132.
82. Isabelle Weall, "Am I a Makeup Artist?? Candy Cane Makeup Look!" YouTube Video, December 12, 2018, https://youtu.be/NP1LhlT30uE.
83. Ibid.
84. Ibid., 2:28–2:37.
85. Ibid., 5:58.
86. Ibid., 20–6:28.
87. Garland-Thomson, *Staring*, 133.
88. Isabelle Weall, "How to Love Yourself with Scars?! My Scar Story," YouTube Video, December 10, 2018, https://youtu.be/nce_Fw1ixI8.
89. Ibid., 0:16.
90. Ibid., 1:30
91. Ibid., 2:00–2:07.
92. Ibid., 2:50.
93. Ibid., 4:07–4:13.
94. Ibid., 4:17–5:29.
95. Ibid., 6:51.
96. Janice McLaughlin and Edmund Coleman-Fountain, "The Unfinished Body: The Medical and Social Reshaping of Disabled Young Bodies," *Social Science and Medicine*, vol. 120 (2014): 79, http://dx.doi.org/10.1016/j.socscimed.2014.09.012.
97. Weall, "How to Love Yourself with Scars?!," 8:27.
98. Garland-Thomson, *Staring*, 135.
99. Ibid., 193.
100. Thoreau, "*Ouch!*," 445.
101. McLaughlin and Coleman-Fountain, "The Unfinished Body."
102. Ibid., 80.
103. Ibid., 83.
104. Ibid., 84.
105. Ibid.
106. Brough and Shresthova "Fandom Meets Activism," 4.7.
107. Ibid., 2.3.
108. Ibid., 5.2.

109. Brough and Shresthova "Fandom Meets Activism," 5.2.
110. Brough and Shresthova "Fandom Meets Activism," 5.5.

BIBLIOGRAPHY

Affuso, Elizabeth. 2018. "Everyday Costume: Feminized Fandom, Retail, and Beauty Culture." *The Routledge Companion to Media Fandom*. Edited by Melissa Click and Suzanne Scott. Routledge: New York. Ebook.

Brough, Melissa and Sangita Shresthova. 2012. "Fandom Meets Activism: Rethinking Civic and Political Participation" *Transformative Works and Cultures* edited by Henry Jenkins and Sangita Shresthova, special issue. Vol. 10. https://doi.org/10.3983/twc.2012.0303.

Garland-Thomson, Rosemarie. 2009. *Staring: How We Look*. Oxford University Press: Oxford.

MakeupArtistGorda66. 2018. "Why Did I Move Out!? [chin in hand emoji]." YouTube Video. Posted December 29. https://youtu.be/saHLB9YaZ1w.

MakeupArtistGorda66. 2019. "Idk Look Tutorial [chin in hand emoji]." YouTube Video. Posted January 3. https://youtu.be/6jniY_bOQT0.

MakeupJunkieG. 2018a. "Real Life Elf on the Shelf for 24hours *Caught on Camera,*" YouTube Video. Posted December 16. https://youtu.be/WmajlBZ43Fg.

MakeupJunkieG. 2018b. "The *Real* Me . . . The Power of Makeup." YouTube video. Posted September 30. https://youtu.be/Vn1LLVKrL6Q.

McLaughlin, Janice and Edmund Coleman-Fountain. 2014. "The Unfinished Body: The Medical and Social Reshaping of Disabled Young Bodies." *Social Science and Medicine* Vol. 120 pp. 76–84. http://dx.doi.org/10.1016/j.socscimed.2014.09.012.

Opel, Dawn S. 2015. "Self-Representation in Literary Fandom: Women's Leisure Reader Selfies as Postfeminist Performance." In "Performance and Performativity in Fandom." Edited by Lucy Bennett and Paul J. Booth. *Transformative Works and Cultures,* no. 18. http://dx.doi.org/10.3983/twc.2015.0607.

Thoreau, Estelle. 2006. "*Ouch!* An Examination of the Self Representation of Disabled People on the Internet," *Journal of Computer-Mediated Communication.* Vol. 11 pp. 442–468. doi:10.1111/j.1083-6101.2006.00021.x.

Weall, Isabelle. 2018a. "Am I a Makeup Artist?? Candy Cane Makeup Look!" YouTube Video. Posted December 12. https://youtu.be/NP1LhlT30uE.

Weall, Isabelle. 2018b. "How to Love Yourself with Scars?! My Scar Story" YouTube Video. Posted December 10. https://youtu.be/nce_Fw1ixI8.

Part III

Makeup and the Individual: Navigating Culture with Makeup

Chapter Eight

Not Just for the Boys

Some Aspects of the Grotesque in Men Selling and Wearing Makeup

Michael V. Perez

It is highly unlikely that Southern Gothic author Flannery O'Connor, in her short, difficult life, ever saw a drag queen or even knew what drag was. Somehow for me, the literary grotesque element she espoused, masked in distortion and featured in her legendary essay "Some Aspects of the Grotesque in Southern Fiction," codifies some of the symbols and actions her frequently misunderstood cast of misfits and supposedly-upright citizens caught in comically violent encounters represent. The word *grotesque* itself has become a go-to code for many of my analyses, no more so than when applied—literally—to the intersection of aspects of makeup tutorials and drag queens, now fifty-five years after O'Connor's premature passing.

How this discussion shifts from her literary canvas—a territory where countrified serial killers can murder a baby as part of a doomed family whose car is appropriated and whose inhabitants become merely human refuse, to a traveling salesman stealing a girl's wooden leg in the guise of seduction—is my goal herein. What constitutes the surface of O'Connor's grotesque plot points, the tacit binary tensions inherent in the grotesque—such as *I'm attracted / I'm repulsed by a man painted like a lady, and vice versa*—has become a larger intrinsic canvas for me that allows current makeup tutorials founded by drag queens, in both makeup and verbal applications, to form a basic foundation herein for analysis of faces well beyond the concern of O'Connor's literary treatises. These are all the more germane and useful because of their markedly different yet similar resonances, contours, and applications—a grotesque face that blends grace and distortion equally, often delivered online by men that present and identify as gay, non-binary, or queer.

What the literary grotesque masks, however, is often misapplied when O'Connor's dramatis personae are grappled with. I will shamelessly remove the layers of religious doctrine at work in O'Connor's writings about writing and expose the superficial appearances of the facial grotesque as the actual core and base of what we see, learn, and buy when men—and women—teach us makeup in 2019, be it via selfie, tutorial, or community. The grotesque, Southern or otherwise, is alive and well and helping to sell product while blowing up social media to sustain a digital facial pedagogy founded in drag essentials and foundations; O'Connor's writings become mission statements in how and why makeup tutorials are fundamentally grotesque today and show no signs of being softly blended away, much like the slash of a garish cheek contour on Kim Kardashian's Instagram-ed mug.

This chapter also uses a personal narratology approach to analyze the covert inherent grotesqueness where beauty and revulsion—or at least an ugly edge—coexist. Men and makeup have coexisted for centuries; it has been one method in which homosexuality has been signaled to the appropriate audience and is reflected herein by the concept of the Southern Grotesque to men made-up around us (and not only for tutorial purposes). The act of men in makeup, due to its compositional and inherent gender fluidity, has, as its base (pun intended), a fundamentally grotesque edge, one wherein contours are not always blended and lines not always blurred. This grotesque effect then finds its way into makeup tutorials, elements of which are predicated on terms, tricks, and language ticks derived from the drag communities of the past fifty years and most recently (from 2009 onwards) in the parlance and shade(s) espoused on the Emmy-winning cultural phenomenon *RuPaul's Drag Race*, as of this writing showing no signs of deceleration.[1]

No one would conflate O'Connor's aesthetic with drag queens and the distortion prevalent in current makeup tutorials—unless, like myself, you grew up in the South and came of age in drag bars of various repute and names such as The Sweet Gum Head, The Answer, and The Locker Room Disco Showplace Bathhouse. The grotesque and comic ways seen in these bars (and back behind them in their respective alleyways) created a way of seeing and recognizing that reading O'Connor's fiction and nonfiction years later unexpectedly fulfilled and sharpened. O'Connor, in her essay "Writing Short Stories," espouses a writer's viewpoint that I see as easily morphing into a current makeup aesthetic, in tutorials, on the street, or via the resplendently painted, shaded, slash-contoured and "boy-browed" young man behind the counter saying "hello" to you as you enter your local ULTA, pushing the limits of "credulity" and made-up expectations: "I would even go so far as to say that the person writing a fantasy has to be even more strictly attentive to the concrete detail than someone writing in a naturalistic vein—

because the greater the story's strain on the credulity, the more convincing the properties in it have to be."[2] I exchange "making a facial fantasy" for "writing a fantasy," with emphasis on the kind of concrete detail all tutorials apply to freshly-cleansed skin and, ultimately, men who instruct them thusly, not as drag queens, but as business men good at making faces pop. The naturalistic movement in makeup, since the advent of the internet and the increased visibility of drag aesthetics or from the inception of YouTube to RuPaul's media blitz (roughly 2005 to the present), has segued to a more convincing "strain" of maquillage whose base is in the sharper lines and chiaroscuro inherent in what is known today as "Selfie Makeup," sponsored by a drag queen near you. In this way, O'Connor and her brilliant comments regarding her writing could be applied to the facial texts espoused by psychological and biological women.

Totally out of context as this application may be, the concept of the grotesque at work in O'Connor's fiction nonetheless works as a rubric for not only men in makeup but men who make tutorials in varying levels of makeup, aka "face." To "beat face"—to use gay slang—when discussing the application of makeup in or out of a tutorial circa 2019—enables a larger legacy to remain intact and to morph in its application, namely, the heritage enacted in the Harlem drag ball circuit, upheld in the 1989 documentary *Paris Is Burning*, and reworked and reapplied for codification and membership signification during the eleven seasons of *RuPaul's Drag Race* (*RPDR*). The continuum continues to land in social media, what is now being dubbed as "selfie makeup" or "Instagram face," also working as a grotesque reference in drag queens making up (or "beating") their faces for YouTube exposure and, ultimately, arriving as an integral aspect of tutorials by Jeffree Star, Manny MUA, Shane Dawson, Wayne Goss, and James Charles—not to mention female makeup tutors, thereby conflating the concept of drag-derived grotesque makeup elements as rigidly gendered depending on who is doing the applying (literally and figuratively). O'Connor's concept creates a foundation for makeup mentoring and tutorials at this commercial point in time; I often wonder what she would have thought of Jeffree Star's skin canvas of tattoos, having created a very different and conflicted skin canvas for the titular character of her short story "Parker's Back." What Parker the character creates on his body charts an embodied space and commentary that moves, as he accumulates more tattoos, from the profane to the sacred, for which he is ironically shunned (for filling the only space left on his back with an "idolatrous" image of Christ in order to impress a radically Bible-Belt woman he wants to marry). Star's body, or what we see of it in his tutorials, is a crowded canvas that assumes a grotesque effect even before makeup is discussed and applied.

THE APPLIED GROTESQUE AND O'CONNOR

Two "mission statements" I fashion for applying the grotesque—or perhaps more accurately, distortion—derive from (of course) Flannery O'Connor. Her discussion of some of her strategies and technical foundations for her brilliant fiction come under the title of the Southern Grotesque—to which I am liberally applying my own shady foundation in reviewing the relationship between drag and makeup tutorials:

> I would not like to suggest that this kind of writer, because his interest is predominantly in mystery, is able in any sense to slight the concrete. Fiction begins where human knowledge begins—with the senses—and every fiction writer is bound by this fundamental aspect of his medium. I do believe, however, that the kind of writer I am describing will use the concrete in a more drastic way. His way will much more obviously be the way of distortion.[3]
>
> *(Here, replace the word "fiction" with "makeup"):*
>
> It's not necessary to point out that the look of this fiction [makeup] is going to be wild, that it is almost of necessity going to be violent and comic, because of the discrepancies that it seeks to combine.

My argument is that every current daily painted face seeks to combine these discrepancies, be they matte, shiny, or otherwise; that faces seek to combine their parts with the whole effect, be they "real" or highly scaffolded and evidently constructed (read: contoured). With decidedly different outcomes and causes, O'Connor's analysis could not care less about the art of make-up—yet the effect remains as useful when applied (liberally) to makeup itself—not a case (with all due respect) of souls at stake in O'Connor's creative oeuvre, but faces, sister, faces, in touch with degrees of distortion: the slash at the cheekbone, the frosted highlighter swipe, the contoured, reimagined nose or jaw-line, all paying attention to the man behind the curtain, that is, the camouflaged queen giving orders, drawing and distorting lines, and making fire rise a la *The Wizard of Oz.*

You can win *RPDR* and YouTube followers by not painting for the back row of a barroom or theater but painting, instead, for "the cash checking store down the street," as Trixie Mattel quipped in her first season of *RPDR*.[4] Mattel would eventually win an All-Stars season and a place in the Drag Hall of Fame, but it took audiences a cool minute to warm up to her brand of "Anime Barbie-on-amphetamine" drag grotesque effect. Anime and Barbie and a denim skirt with pink fringe: these are the discrepancies Mattel seeks to combine; now, we are all the more conditioned to react to the grotesque, and the discrepancies of painting a face to the extreme, by simply emulating and testing what we see on our clean primed faces in preparation for a daily upload and post—wherein the stage has become the proscenium of the iPhone pic.

Where does a common language come from when gay men beat face that can be "mopped" (stolen) and used to guide the construction of a (biological or psychological) female mug? One word: the aforementioned "SISTER(S)!" featured on James Charles's YouTube channel as his salutation catch-phrase, and also featured prominently on his merch (on the back of his caps, on his T-shirts, etc.), which all hearken back and forward at the same time as lexical and cultural components of a distinctive vocabulary.

"BASE"-IC SLANGOLOGY

Shade, mug, beat, read, snatched, shook, sister, werk: these are words that have entered the makeup community through queens' making faces inside our screens; this linguistic palette enables the origins of drag makeup, now also referred to as selfie makeup, to thrive via social media while also giving the young girl or boy following along on YouTube a sense of context and historicity, as well as membership in a community that expands its followers every time a Jeffree Star vlog is uploaded to YouTube.

Current makeup tutorials are gender fluid and grotesque by nature, assessing our tolerance and expectations for whom we accept when we look at men in makeup teaching us so-called "feminine" skills; this aspect draws its line from male makeup pioneers including Way Bandy and Kevyn Aucoin as well as the glamorously grotesque Mr. Star and his less-distorted but still resonantly genderqueer fellow artisans John Kuckian, Manny MUA, James Charles, and Wayne Goss. Painting the canvas of a tutorial face shows the scaffolding inherent in the process that may not be fully blended to create a "snatched" effect of rising cheekbones casting a shadow on the chin line on either side of a face—thus earning a new meaning for the word *foundation* as the facial equivalent of a lit house not afraid to reveal some facets of its construction. I call this a "grotesque lite" effect created by men who do not identify as drag queens and allow their faces to do the work, being themselves but male in fluctuating increments (with Mr. Star as one end of a continuum and Mr. Wayne Goss as the other end, with stops for James Charles and the scruffed and painted Manny MUA and John Kuckian along the way, all white males indeed, but who, for the purposes of this analysis, are being reviewed due to their prominence on the beauty community scene as of 2019 and for the gender they identify as). What we expect from male tutorials inherits the baggage of our forebearers, for sure; a current YouTuber may not even sense the grotesque at work while watching Manny MUA—and that's a good thing—but this chapter builds its foundation on the expectations such engendered baggage foments and how that historicity informs our choices for learning, buying, and wearing makeup.

It is noteworthy that one of O'Connor's most potent anti-heroines has a face with a naturally grotesque appearance, none other than Mary Grace from the late story and masterpiece "Revelation." Mary Grace, who instigates a pivotal moment of grotesque violence, is, indeed, hard to like even before she hurls a book called "Human Development" at the devout and jolly Mrs. Turpin, who is praying out loud as they sit in a doctor's waiting room. Mary Grace's face is riddled with blue-black acne and acne scars; the character is beyond made-up redemption. That O'Connor signifies the ugliness of an exterior as indicative of its interior in such a deceptively readable way shows her usage of the grotesque beyond mere symbolism—indeed as having one's soul worn on the face and not just through an eye's portal. How we can be seen while serving face that is clearly delineated as artifice changes from tutorial trend to product trend, from year to year, and upload to upload. Yesterday's bad makeup application can morph into today's hyper-real promo spot for Maybelline. In the spirit of grotesqueries, facial or otherwise, I hear and apply O'Connor's words to define my inquiry into all of my "made-up" themes:

> In these grotesque works, we find that the writer has made alive some experience which we are not accustomed to observe every day, or which the ordinary man may never experience in his ordinary life. We find that connections which we would expect in the customary kind of realism have been ignored, that there are strange skips and gaps which anyone trying to describe manners and customs would certainly not have left. Yet the characters have an inner coherence, if not always a coherence to their social framework. Their fictional qualities lean away from typical social patterns, towards mystery and the unexpected. It is this kind of realism that I want to consider.[5]

I want to consider the strange skips and gaps a tutored/tutorial face exhibits in a social framework that does not always cohere but currently celebrates mystery and the unexpected via the artistry of makeup to be taught by and for anyone with decent Wi-Fi—a social framework O'Connor might have thought of as grotesque by nature, grotesque in its inner coherence of outward discrepancies and distortions. Furthermore, there is a direct correlation between the visibility of the grotesque in drag platforms (and I mean more than heels here) and the actual winners and runners-up of respective *RPDR* seasons; here are some ground rules to build a foundation that clearly sets the lines and lineages for men in makeup, on or off the show, in or beyond the tutorial, and equally applicable to the rise of social networks from 2008–present:

FOUNDATIONS: BASE(-IC) RULES

1. A boy in makeup is grotesque (if here we mean *blurring binaries*).
2. A boy presenting as distorted cisfemale, blending genre expectations, is grotesque.
3. A boy applying makeup while still remaining primarily cismasculine is *bro*tesque.
4. A boy instructing in fully made-up face and no need for a wig is *way*brotesque (after Way Bandy, who did not instruct us in discernible full face).
5. A boy discussing product with affected diphthongs (high gay dialect, e.g., Sisters!) and final syllables and no sense of the difference between Angola and Ebola is James Charles.

And Jeffree Star (resplendently in his own showy, amorphous category; I dub this the *showtesque*, such as a vlog that includes the ragged cutting up of a Vuitton bag).

WHAT'S IN A PALETTE: READING AND MAKEUP (WHEN YOU ARE THE BOOK)

It's time to look at men who look at makeup from every possible angle, shade, and applicability and render grotesque effects through product, and not always consciously. Note that, as of March 2019, Shane Dawson—not really a grotesque example, but more of a delightfully camp one, unless you consider his sense of humor grotesque—is rumored to be bringing out a palette, a possibility that resulted in an explosion on the "Interwebs"; (Wayne Goss is the exception who has only brushes thus far on the market, and no palette product as of yet). Palette fever and its discontents feature prominently in the discussion of makeup grotesques, especially when a new palette allegedly causes an allergic reaction in a beauty vlogger and a grotesque yelling reaction is then posted.[6] The extended "dis" by beauty vlogger KodeeRants is reminiscent of drag legend Crystal LaBeija's[7] 1967 rant, showing us that *Palette Is Burning* might be the correct name for some of the pigments used in James Charles's eye shadows. The rant, the product, the read, the usage of drag lingo—these are all at work in 2019 on YouTube and uphold the tradition of grotesque makeup lessons, especially when the YouTube ranter shows the blisters that formed on her lids and underneath her brows for the global beauty community to gawk at, ostensibly because of a red pigment pressed as part of Charles's inaugural palette. Suffice it to say that KodeeRants sounds a lot like a mad drag queen, calling him "Sister" repeatedly in a mocking tone as well as using profanities not safe for this chapter. Should makeup come with a blatant disclaimer, and, if so, how much caution should be used in using a product supposedly to transform (but not stain) its user? When product distorts the line between real and artifice, gender and fluidity, not to mention performatively normal in accepted beauty parameters and their violations, the grotesque can obviously irritate more than skin, and cause its own grotesque reaction and retribution as exemplified by KodeeRants, an online beauty vlogger who may not be aware as to how her use of beauty queen-speak participates, and, indeed, perpetuates, fundamental elements of queer tutorial protocol even as she attacks Charles and his palette. There's a linguistic link at w(e)rk here, evident in the *Hello Sisters!* greeting young internet beauty maven James Charles uses as his makeup tutorial sign-on catch phrase. The word "sister," used regardless of gender, is a classic way to signify and show membership in queer communities, especially those where drag factors in as much as Max Factor. Charles also wears the slogan in other videos on his T-shirts and sweatshirts worn while he makes face, beats his mug, becomes snatched—all components of gay and drag dialect that are now common in the online beauty vlog community. What this language upholds is the lingo palette one must use to show membership and community, if not a sisterhood. Charting this beauty gayspeak must start with an obscure documentary reference, 1967's *The Queen*.

If a tutorial can be also about what not to wear, I posit Crystal LaBeija from *The Queen* as a forerunner of makeup assessment for the camera in the form of verbal tutorial reading, as follows: a late 1960s beauty, with heavy eyeliner wingtips, darkened lids, white lipstick a la Brigitte Bardot, and a cascading fall of hair, is in the middle of a ferocious, scorching rant, directed at a young, blond pageant contestant, indeed, the one who has just won the pageant to our raving beauty's third runner-up placement. The winner is very lithe, naturally feminine, with delicate features evident even with minimal and misapplied makeup: she is Harlow, perhaps most famous on YouTube now for being the recipient of a stream of hatred and "reading" (gay slang for "assessing" an opponent in the most shady yet accurate way: "exaggerating a flaw," according to Dorian Corey,[8] in your opponent and then running with it, usually with an audience present and observing). In this case, the reader is Crystal, mother of the House of LaBeija; the text being read is Harlow, and the core of the read as follows: "I didn't say she wasn't beautiful but she wasn't looking beautiful tonight. . . . Look at her makeup, it's TE-RRIBLE!" This moment could be called the first drag queen anti-tutorial caught for posterity as an upload, but resonating much louder and longer for the content of the words as much as the volume of them: "I AM BEAUTIFUL and I KNOW I AM BEAUTIFUL DAH-LING!" An indirect citation of LaBeija's sustained read can clearly be heard in vlogger KodeeRants's diatribe against the first palette brought out by James Charles where beauty, reality, and the grotesque blend into an Angry Queen citation for the painted ages, and a place to start, like a primed face or a primed vlogger enacting an under-acknowledged classic queenly revenge.

A FIRST TUTORIAL

My first encounter with a man teaching me how to use makeup was Alice Cooper, the legendary glam-rock-death-metal icon, in the pages of *16 Magazine*, an old school teen fanzine devoted to featuring the latest pop heart-throbs. Cooper had recently had a Top 10 hit with "School's Out," which would locate the teen mag feature on him as somewhere in the summer of 1972 as the iconic song ascended the pop charts to #7.[9] I was all of nine years old and thrilled to have the magazine in the first place; I knew I was crossing a line where I would be free to look at pics of early 1970s dreamy male television stars such as Bobby Sherman (my favorite), but this issue had something new and even more thrilling: an article with step-by-step pics of Cooper applying Maybelline eyebrow pencil onto his eyelids and underneath his eyes to achieve his signature look, finished with a vertical slash through each eye that ran above his brow bone to finish just to the left or right of his nostrils. The article was equal parts text and pics, with Cooper taking us from bare eye to "Alice lids" in easy steps, all with the same product, always rotated toward the camera lens so that the Maybelline logo was seen. At one point next to the first pic, the text had Cooper exhorting, "Do be careful, boys and girls!" presumably to caution his fans from over-zealous makeup-pencil application that could enter the eyes if not applied with care. I loved that Cooper was directly talking to us and did not even question his authenticity—who does at nine? Though I didn't understand the word *earnest* at the time, I felt it—not unlike the earnestness displayed, forty-seven years later, by today's male makeup digital rock stars.

BROWS, FRAMES, AND BOYS

Either using glue-stick to block and set and start a face through making-up, or the words of a story to pin down and prime a narrative, one might as well begin with eyebrows.[10] When 2018 Streamy Award-winner James Charles emerged on the makeup tutorial scene in 2016, having gone from high school senior photo notoriety to sometimes blundering and culturally insensitive YouTube sensation, he brought the enhanced visibility of a thicker, painted brow on a boy as a model in more ways than one—not plucked, but painted, matte, yet still somehow wet. What might have been easily attributed to glue stick and primer and then cream paint or even appropriated eyeliner a la Dusty Springfield became a sensation—easily spotted at the food court on a

Chick-Fil-A female employee, a student, a case worker, a pharmacist—the true litmus test for tutorial success: in the work-face and -place. Who was the boy who might have been responsible for this, with brows like a hybrid of Joan Crawford and Boy George, and how did he come to exert such influence? Better yet, what do we want and what exists in men who guide us, queer Obi-Wan-Kenobi style, to face our own gender-fluid palettes?

What we get from queen-painted faces is the fulfillment of engendered expectations, where desire and object merge in more ways than one. My premise is this: an eyebrow says it all, traced backward to a Weimar Republic/Silver Screen "face quote," as opposed to an air quote, or, as we shall see with Wayne Goss, eyebrows considered as frames for the daily painting of a face.

There's a direct leap from the directive of beauty vloggers to influencers and the L'Oreal face-out display at CVS (Goss's video blog on contouring and highlighting a la Kim Kardashian, for example). At the same time, the leap can also happen backwards from the makeup continuum, when Goss, for instance, effuses in a vlog as to the subtleties and legendary effects found in Way Bandy's seminal makeup textual tutorial from 1977, *Designing Your Face*.[11] Thus, the influence reflects back at the same time it moves forward—an example also being of the eyebrow *on fleek* that Joan Crawford could have worn, or the Hedwig-upturned pencil slash worn by Liza Minnelli in *Cabaret* that also cites the drawn-sideways exclamation points of both Jean Harlow in the 1930's and Aquaria, winner of season 10 of *RuPaul's Drag Race*. This forward-back approach is not an effect of facial stasis; indeed, it is indicative of a practical everyday art form that uses a multi-shaded foundation to move forward.

WHEN "SELFIE MAKEUP" IS DRAG MAKEUP

How[12] did drag queen aesthetics become a direct influence for internet makeup trends—or, if paying homage to women's constructed beauty is understood as an active reference as a queen paints for the evening, how did the roles switch from product user to product maven—from consumer to influencer on multiple media platforms? In late 2018, *ELLE*'s "BEAT. CONTOUR. SNATCHED: How Drag Queens Shaped the Biggest Makeup Trends" provided a chorus of voices as acknowledgment, ranging from *RPDR*, season 9 winner Sasha Velour to legendary NYC 1990s drag legends Vivacious; and Pyramid Club party hostess Linda Simpson to Kryolan's senior makeup artist, Tim Pearson, all weighing in on how women came to emulate men emulating a highly stylized and crafted "woman." For some, this is an inherently grotesque act. This is similar to some of the students I teach in an upper-level humanities university course who, while watching

Trixie Mattel narrate a brief drag history, cannot get beyond her distorted Anime Power-Puff Barbie Girl face with its extreme contours and enlarged blocked-and-distorted eyes and brows, no matter how clear and contextual the content she delivers happens to be. One student talked to me after class and said he felt uncomfortable asking himself, "Is that a GUY??" I hesitate to point to the following quote again, that O'Connor's Southern Grotesque palette is unknowingly at work here; I remind myself that she stated that "it's not necessary to point out that the look of this fiction [i.e., makeup] is going to be wild, that it is almost of necessity going to be violent and comic [e.g., Trixie Mattel's mug], because of the discrepancies that it seeks to combine."[13] A made-up face is a combination of shadows, light, contour, matte, shine, shades, highlights, base and porous acquiescence, artifice and realness in the face of beauty and cultural expectations. As in O'Connor's world as it is in Kylie Jenner's, the distortion of discrepancies will always have been sought in ever-changing, boundary-blending expectations.

According to *ELLE*'s clip, the rules changed when RuPaul emerged in his third season; suddenly, contouring and shading were less blended, with browns and tans used to show, in varying degrees, the architectonics or scaffolding that goes into making a face for a drag stage. Highlighting became ubiquitous—all to forge what makeup artist Renny Vasquez called "baby drag." Kim Kardashian, not surprisingly, becomes the go-to girl with her "beat" mug "snatched for the gods" (which is a good thing in gayslang).

The amount of makeup used increases, including the use of false eyelashes; contouring the nose and cheekbones and jawline, in varying degrees of blending, features prominently and can light beautifully from above for the "selfie" look. The link to RuPaul may seem an obvious one as the initial iteration of *Drag Race* on the Logo cable channel became more of a phenomenon, eventually moving to VH-1, while some contestants posted selfies on social media in advance of and after the airing of any episode. What's more revealing is the "complicity"—and lasting craft—of one early queen's impressive "mugology" from the show: the queen known simply as Raven,[14] season 2's *Drag Race* runner-up.

ELLE's clip shows legendary queen Vivacious giving a succinct backstory to how Raven became the cited face that queens started painting for tutorials on social media (starting, say, in 2010, after two seasons of *Drag Race*). Vivacious calls Raven's drag face a "mold" first of RuPaul's maquillage strategies (created by the iconic artist Mathu Anderson, a fixture on the NYC Club Kids scene since the advent of grotesque promoter Michael Alig), and then the mold for tons of queens, in drag or not—with minimal yet artful blending, blocked and painted eyebrows on fleek, highlighting and swipes of shading on the forehead and chinline, with darker shadows and white brow bone "realness"—a face very much in tune with the concept of chiaroscuro and the legendary Mr. Way Bandy:

> It could perhaps be argued that what René Descartes did for modern philosophy, Way Bandy did for contouring. A pioneer of the method in contemporary beauty application, Way insisted that we "reveal to our mirror only our best angles and most flattering illusions of reality, as seen through blurred vision and whatever other tricks we have at our disposal." He urged us to forget what we think we know (that is, the assets we wish we possessed) and familiarize ourselves with the true form of our facial structure; from the fat pads of our cheeks to the transparency levels and "drape" of our skin over bone. Bandy's techniques ultimately seek to create what he refers to as a "Personal Sculpture Portrait" through contouring with "light and dark." Did somebody say chiaroscuro?[15]

Thus, Raven, via Way Bandy, actually broke the internet of selfies and her fellow *RPDR* contestants by creating a beat mug fully in sync with tenets of drag makeup that became tenets of selfie makeup—who needs a crown when the shaded, contoured face you've created becomes a brand that launches a million imitators in search of the perfect product at CVS to render that face as theirs and ready to be posted? Here it is useful to recall my elucidation of male digital participation in makeup, tutorials or otherwise, when I stated earlier that a boy instructing in fully made-up face and no need for a wig is *way*brotesque (after Way Bandy, who did not instruct us in discernible full face).

By extension, a tutorial that starts with a day-painted bearded Englishman exclaiming "Winged eyeliner . . . ughhhh!" that then proceeds to modify the title of his video must be the clever clickbait strategy of Wayne Goss. Goss, whose tutorials arrived onto YouTube in 2009, may not know or care that his full beard hearkens back to a queer era in San Francisco around 1970 where "genderfuck" drag ruled as a performative aspect of street theater and protest, or maquillage as protest—with bearded cross-dressing queers as members of the Sisters of Perpetual Indulgence or The Cockettes. I argue that Goss's much more understated yet equally gender-fluid beard, moustache, and goatee create a facial citation back to these more flamboyant and less product-focused forebearers, thus forming a sort of grotesque-lite effect and resonance. His clips, which showcase the direct talking head of his matte, subtle mug, are a study in cool disdain that matches the tan tones and minimal highlighting comprising the effect of his makeup strategy—he always exhorts or paints himself to display the antidote to the "forbidden" areas that his subsequent clips address, but always with a nudge-in clickbait title to get you into his video in the first place, ostensibly to hear a rant or at least a strong dislike and decree.

Goss practices what he paints; he does not become a despot, but (as in the case with winged eyeliner) says, "You do you!" even while he starts the clip with a sound akin to a cat coughing up a hairball. Goss thus plays it both ways, not unusual for a makeup tutorial; he will make his point and modify the clickbait title to say that, indeed, winged eyeliner "WITH EYESHADOW" is actually what he dislikes. Mission accomplished: we're in his video clip under the auspices of seeing him lay down the law; what we get is a much more congenial approach to the subject. Furthermore, comments are occasionally disabled for certain topics and pages, creating a passive-aggressive forum in which the possibility for rebuttal is removed. This aspect is not utilized in every Goss clip, however; the effect is one wherein he is definitely not having it, sister, and will let you know where and when he is. Goss always emphasizes that the dislikes he's discussing are his and his only—not meant to be dismissive of his viewers' preferences if they oppose his (often accompanied by monosyllable sound effects of disgust) exhortations. This grotesque effect—encompassing uneven elements of attraction, repulsion, artifice, and realness, all rendered into an often gloriously non-binary effect beyond binaries, gender or otherwise, that masterfully brushes up against the line of gendered expectations—is unique to any man successful in makeup tutorials. My use of the word grotesque, here and elsewhere, is always intentional, and, as we have seen, integral to understanding anyone performing as male performing and instructing good face.

Wayne Goss encompasses all of the above made-up "bro-grotesqueries." Usually his clips announce (and herein lies the clickbait) their content in all caps, such as "THE BIGGEST EYESHADOW MISTAKE WE [note the inclusive and perhaps reductive 'clickbait-ian' emphasis on 'We' here] ALL MAKE" or "MAKEUP TRENDS THAT NEED TO DIE IN 2017." In the thumbnails of his tutorials, Wayne Goss appears to want it both ways: to tell you what not to do and then, once you're in his clips, give a disclaimer saying, basically, if you like what I'm telling you not to do, by all means do it—it's just makeup. This applies to clips as rigidly titled as "MAKEUP TRENDS THAT NEED TO DIE IN 2017," wherein the dark, heavy, James Charles boy-brow is given the "heave-ho," with Goss making a legendary simile comparing brows to frames on a canvas. For Goss, the boy brow is the "ugliest buggeriest frame."[16] For Goss, "EYEBROWS = PAINTING FRAMES, and who wants ugly frames?" His clip reveals the dark eyebrow trend as already prevalent in 2017; Goss is not having it, however. He is not having it in 2018 as well when he declares the "MAKEUP TRENDS THAT NEED TO DIE IN 2018." Ultimately, this can be seen as saying *You do you, as long as you click on my video first.*[17]

Goss, partially-bearded (more so than Manny MUA's clips wherein Manny is scruffed and painted), tests the line of grotesque "comfort" that exists when a male tutorial is delivered from the flawless mask of a beautiful face that could "pass" for female from the chin line upwards. While I do not presume that Goss is more effective a salesperson than Star, Manny, or James Charles, the way I have just introduced these men forms its own continuum, from revulsion to genderqueer lite—Charles having a traditional glamour mug beaten back, (as we used to say at North Carolina School of the Arts in 1982), while still recognizably in boy drag, sans wig, *sans accoutrement*, that reads as female. I obviously posit Star as a purveyor of the glamorous grotesque and, thus, at the far left of the continuum, owing to the way he can look like a Rodeo Drive celebutante influencer in one YouTube clip and a gorgeous alien descending upon WalMart in a fashion challenge aided by Shane Dawson in another clip. Ever-present is the painted, inked canvas of his well-primed skin covered with his celebrated aforementioned pastiche of tattoos, one of which appears to be crawling up the side of his neck like some industrial foliage or vine outside of Marilyn Manson's house.

"EASY BREEZY" SOCIAL PROGRESS

If men selling makeup is inherently grotesque (read: comic and violent, cismale yet cisfemale, butch yet femme all at once), even to a shimmering degree, it's been a great run for male visibility in the makeup industry since at least 2014. Here is where Star (the much-earlier veneer pioneer, of course, embodying gender blurring as a continual rethinking of contour, blending, and integrated color), Manny MUA, and Charles have become three wise men who, through their tutorials, endorsements, and ground-breaking spokesperson gigs, have brought the idea of made-up men from an oddity to a reality, albeit with some of the problems that plague the makeup industry (and body-face shaming perpetuation) intact. Star continues to expand his brand into his own cosmetic line, a long way from the days of posting pics on MySpace; his former bestie, San Diego's own Manny MUA, became the first Maybelline boy spokesperson for mascara, a natural choice seeing as how he has naturally long lush lashes; and James Charles became the first boy of CoverGirl, thanks to a Snapchat that went viral of him sitting for his high school senior photo and re-posting a better lit re-do photo once he saw the results of his first sitting; both pics were also posted to Instagram with the better lit (and much more highlighted, it must be said) pic receiving so many hits that Ellen DeGeneres had Charles on her show to recount the process he had gone through from senior pic re-do (and re-touching) to CoverGirl and, thus, her show.

Note the social media trajectory here: from Jeffree Star's MySpace exposure and dominance to Manny's YouTube tutorials to Charles's command of Instagram leading to a spot on the original funny girl CoverGirl's show—almost a twenty-first-century primer (emphasis on the word *primer*) in how to rule social media, beat some face, and get paid for product endorsement—preferably your own. *Marie Claire*'s website brings together the Made-Up Boys and enables their backstories and current activity on Instagram as a lovely fugue for product and men who perform beauty without the need for the title (if not the strategy and techniques, a la Raven or RuPaul, or Nina Flowers or Nina Bo'nina Brown, all alumni, of course, of the Ru-Vealing *Drag Race* sisterhood) of drag queen. A major beauty mag devoting such time and space to male makeup selfies via their continual Instagram presence speaks nicely to the expanding conflation of men in the online beauty world of 2019 as more than just a grotesque fluke in need of a wig for comprehension by the consumer—indeed a great way to help a company sell the hell out of some product.

MORE STORIES, OR APPLIED LAYERS

I'm about thirteen, living in suburban Atlanta, and not fitting in—at home or school—but especially at home, where I tend to take solace from the day's difficult navigation by locking my parents' bedroom door and putting on my mother's makeup. What an array there was—blushes, foundation, powders, mascaras, eye shadows, a shimmery gold highlighting crème that refused to wash off and which caused me to mimic Judy Garland's open-mouthed, heavy-lidded later-day "Man That Got Away" image relentlessly in the makeup mirror, and the forbidden fruit itself, lipstick—especially forbidden because the color I loved the most, Crimson Lies, bled so badly when I tried to remove it that I sat at the dinner table looking like I'd been in a fight, which (turning crimson and lying, just as the label said) I said I had.

This lightly grotesque anecdote needs participation from my older brother, a real prince but, at the time in question, still working through what it was like to have a sissy for a younger brother (again, suburban Atlanta circa 1976). His was the voice at my parents' locked bedroom door clocking me by saying, "You're putting on MAKE-UP!!" How he knew is beyond me—unless he knew the true colors of what went on behind that door as a mélange of painted attempts never quite cold-creamed off in time. That voice for me problematized fluidity in gender, both in appropriating cosmetics and when he watched me apply hand cream to my elbows on the way to the bus stop and asked me why, to which I responded, "It makes the rough parts soft," and he retorted, "They're supposed to be that way!" Suddenly, a product meant boy, or girl—or even both at once.

I hear his voice—a consistently benevolent one that would pummel more than one bully after school who had asked him why he had a fairy for a brother—as an indicator of a line that I hear and see drawn when boys and men wear makeup or over-rely on product, *not* grooming, *not* Dove Men + Care (whatever that means). I hear his voice as a reminder of how the grotesque is an integral part of men in makeup—his reaction, his drawing of the gender line between boys and girls, and how the grotesque is functioning in several ways currently as we are inhabiting an unprecedented era, one where boys can play with makeup and still be boys, ostensibly—yet the echo of that voice delineating a grotesque nature engenders and informs this current era in several exciting and problematic ways.

The "annuls makeup-mirabilis" that blessed high-school beauty logger James Charles in 2016 with both fabulous and controversial "Interweb" exposure revealed a different kind of exposed highlight in March of 2017, when Charles was revealed to have faked his own senior photo re-shoot, featuring a plethora of creamy shimmery highlights at the top of his already-monumental cheekbones.[18] The website *We the Unicorns*, a subsidiary of *PopBuzz*[19] (not affiliated with *Buzz Feed*, which had previously posted a rave chain of videos and pics on Charles, initially celebrating his *chutzpah* in demanding a pic re-do at his high school), let Charles have it, also conflating his faked shimmery pic with his lack of understanding, in subsequent tweets, the difference between Angola, Ebola, and Africa as he prepared for a senior trip to what he wasn't sure was a continent or a country, as well as tweeting an online AIDS joke, apparently not beneath a sixteen-year-old high school student about to embark on a high school senior trip out of the country—all predicated on the swish of a brush with an incandescent sparkle good for any place on any face, regardless of the country of origin.

I look at my high school photos expecting very little—I went to a performing arts high school, and I sat for my photo after a dance class that ran long, still in sweats and tights and leg warmers and a droopy perm. Walking the hallway to the session was a statement made in sweaty haste. When I looked at the initial photo proofs, I was amazed—my skin looked smooth and matte, not shiny and. . . . Wasn't there something missing? I forgot about it until the yearbook came out late in the school year. What wasn't missing, now, was any trace of my acne scars, which the yearbook photo faithfully kept: my face looked like it was highlighted with blush, which was actually just the roseate traces of both former and current acne. I learned a basic lesson in Makeup for Boys 101: Be Prepared, Demand A Re-Take, or Stage Your Own Pic Event and Call It "Realest."

Note that fellow makeup purveyor and Englishman John Kuckian became, in March 2017, a whistleblower who rebutted many of Charles's claims; it seems than Kuckian, a beauty indeed, has yet to achieve instant(-gram) legendary status; one could make the viable claim that his role as minor (bitchy) gadfly is in reacting, not acting, to male makeup celebs,[20] as opposed to the overall gadfly activity regarding the beauty industry of Wayne Goss, from the usage of lighting in tutorials to the behavior of certain "pancake" influencers and what he sees as their potentially negative impact.

The best summation of the state of the union in the beauty genre, besides Wayne Goss's early 2018 declaration that (perhaps) "There is no genre more ugly than the beauty genre," *Marie Claire*'s "The Beauty Boys of Instagram"[21] keeps you up to speed with the guys and their backstories and products, including that other "star," Patrick Starrr.

My later attempts at integrating makeup, especially blusher, after a stint at a performing arts college where older queens taught me how to put on "day face" that would withstand the heat of a ballet or modern dance class, proved to be, unfortunately, clockable by the man I was dating when I came over to his place one night in 1984. He grabbed my face, turned it from side to side, and said, basically, "Take that stuff off NOW!" When I asked why, he said, "You don't need it." I disagreed, and proceeded to go out nights "with my face beat to the gods," to paraphrase Vivacious again, until, one night on a dance floor, an older queen did a double take at my slashed blush, penciled brows, and copper-toned strokes of highlights to say, loudly, "GIRL! Get a wig!" Needless to say, I needed the *Marie Claire* (not to mention the internet) in my life to allow me to embrace makeup without a wig and without anyone in the unruly queer tribe of which I was a confused member finding me weird or (you guessed it) grotesque. I should mention that Flannery O'Connor herself would have had decidedly more negative words at the sight of any man discussed herein (if she, stricken with lupus and conserving her precious energy to create her devastating range of Southern Grotesque characters and situations, could even be bothered to pay attention to such nonsense—nonetheless, I conjure and apply her words and observations as preciously as my vintage jar of Clinique loose-pressed powder, concealer, and silver collapsible brush).

Working at a department store in Atlanta in 1984, I met Terry (not his real name), a very pretty man who worked the Clinique counter at an adjacent store. He told me I had fabulous cheekbones and wanted to "do my face" whenever I had the time. I picked my next shift's dinner break—with no real idea what was about to transpire. Terry sprayed primer, and, with huge flourishes of his hands, applied foundation and loose powder, penciled in my eyebrows, and finished me off with a matte eye shadow—what I would learn later was called "smoky"—and two small but noticeable upturned wings at the edge of each eye. I thanked him, and—late from my dinner-less break—ran all the way back to my store, stopping on the way to wipe off as much of his evident artistry as possible in the "black mirror" reflection of any dark adjacent store window. That was when I really noticed the men in my store's makeup department wearing subtle but noticeable variants of what I had just wiped off.

The in-store tutorial is an unsung element of men at work alongside women at countless makeup and beauty counters ever since there was a Macy's selling Arpege perfume next to Erno Laszlo product. The work entailed by these unheralded professionals—creating faces on the spot with less than a few minutes to assess the flesh canvas sitting expectantly in front of their particular line's counter—is a testimonial to selling and using product at once, live, in person, and lit ferociously from above. What our beauty super-vloggers continue to do in the tradition of their forebearers is to codify beauty and perform its applicable panache one time for relentless repetition, almost a reminder that Walter Benjamin's suspicion of artistic reproduction is improved upon insofar as the original "canvas" is not minimized in being copied but, indeed, is being preserved in its original state with its final effect intact. Technology is the conduit here that preserves "nature," or (arti-)face, in a way that Benjamin of course could not foresee (and might not, at any rate, have approved of, even if he had a reference to it):

> The mastery of nature, so the imperialists teach, is the purpose of all technology [*Technik*]. But . . . technology is not the mastery of nature but of the relation between nature and humanity. . . . In technology a *physis* is being organized through which mankind's contact with the cosmos takes a new and different form from that which it had in nations [*Völkern*] and families.[22]

Nations, families, faces—and tutorials online: these aspects conflate in the post-modern-day tutorial, with technology as "not the mastery of nature [read: face] but of the relation between nature and humanity." This is rather pretentious for a ten-minute Wayne Goss clip entitled "THE BIGGEST EYESHADOW MISTAKE WE ALL MAKE," but what Benjamin might have recognized most is the commerce between nature and technology happening in an accessible way. If Wayne Goss is correct in saying that the beauty industry online has the most anger and hatred, then he should be considered the ultimate gadfly in the machine, wherein what is seen representing beauty is not the truth,[23] in his eyes—a true "Debbie Downer" for a man without a line of product other than brushes at the time the videos discussed here were posted, a slightly grotesque touch indeed.

Like an unblended contour that slashes a cheek and keeps it neatly in check, what we may want, then, from boys to men in both makeup and tutorials, is an admission of the covert inherent grotesque where beauty and revulsion—or at least an ugly edge—can coexist. It's a bit like internalized homophobia, wherein a man who identifies as gay (and male) eschews what he perceives as effeminacy in other men, when there is a case to be made for a queer identity and visibility as being founded on the stacked backs of effeminate men in the first place. Acceptance is forthcoming, then, and it may be fleeting, as permanent as washing off the day's face to meet the faces around us. The crime is that the art in the artifice of beating face may be lost if only thought of as ephemeral, a glitch in popular culture. Men and makeup have coexisted for centuries; it has been one method in which homosexuality has been signaled to the appropriate audience, from the lower to higher levels reflected by my application of the O'Connor grotesque.

So the story goes as follows: just another day at the product counter (with the word *counter* suggesting a counter-argument at work): Manny MUA held to a relentless standard (with his five o'clock shadow retouched); James Charles staging an event as "retouching" when the actual pic was merely retouched; and the phrase "flawless coverage" inherently denigrating natural identity and reinforcing applicable beauty, not to mention a billion-dollar industry. As Michael Jackson's later face attests, separate, surgically enhanced hemispheres of feminine work topping the masculine hemisphere of jaw and jawline promote not only discomfort but bring to the makeup table an obvious question: Is the grotesque a prerequisite for accepting men in makeup or enhanced? Some aspects of makeup, tutorials, drag competitions, reality television, or otherwise, will always evoke a fundamentally grotesque reaction: the essence of what makes us expect gender as a painted event exclusive to one sex is the problem—sex is not the problem. Our gender expectations, now expanding as fast as any little boy can wander into his mother's makeup collection to paint and play and then find boys (and girls) like him on YouTube, are the problem that will never wash off for good, though Wayne Goss exhorts in one of his tutorials that if you don't agree with his statements or choices that "it's just makeup . . . it washes off."[24]

IT'S JUST MAKEUP

The most grotesque "tutorial" on YouTube is the fifty episodes of *Drunken Makeover*, a series hosted by Sasha Belle, a former contestant on *RPDR* who left relatively soon in the competition but decided to host a "show" wherein other former contestants from the show, as well as Belle's "drag daughters" (queens who take on her surname and regard her as their drag mother) are featured in a parody of beauty shows meshed with cocktail banter and consumption. What usually happens is that Belle, at the left of the screen, introduces her special guest—Katya, Myling Belle, Gina Belle, Butterfolds, Jaidynn Dior Fierce, Ginger Minj, et al.—at the right of the screen. Mayhem ensues. Makeup is trotted out and applied with varying degrees of insane application; the effect, and banter, are initially a hoot and then plain scary by the end of the "show." It must be seen not to be believed. The series establishes the grotesque firmly as steeped in hooch and applied to a mug that started out as the life of the party and ended as the party in the gutter: lines are drawn across any given face, sequins applied, colors splayed across cheekbones, as if a kid wandered into his big sister's palette and mistook it for kindergarten face painting. The Katya episode is the best example of the series,[25] probably because Katya, who doesn't drink, is as raucously funny sober as any of her sauced *Drunk Makeover* sisters by far. The stories she relays are beyond Not Safe for Work as she gets painted, or should I say abused, in the name of the opposite of beauty to entertain an audience as to the limits tutorials can push without earning too many dislikes.

As mentioned previously, *RPDR* All-Stars season 3 winner Trixie Mattel, true to her name, looks like a Barbie—if that Barbie had paid a visit to *Drunk Makeover*. Her face and drag are thrift-store action figure meets WalMart princess; her talents are prodigious, especially as a vocalist and guitarist; her cheeks are sublimely unblended; her eyes are used as a pupil effect, as her eye shadow and contouring stretch across her forehead (still unblended) and create an anime live-action Dollywood animatronic come to life. When Mattel dressed up Jeffree Star[26] to look like Trixie (or as the video clip states, "Jeffree Mattel") she mused—in the midst of product placement—"Do you ever think you're making fun of beauty?"

One might as well finish with the painted counter-argument of realness—and ponder if that sought visage is, indeed, the most grotesque aspect of makeup tutorials and selfies. No matter how *on fleek* our outsides realize, perhaps Way Bandy summed up the truest beauty treatment we all aspire to: "Real beauty is inner," he said in another interview in 1977. "By the experiences and opportunities of our lifetimes, we enrich our souls and earn our natural beauty."[27] Tellingly, this quote was used by the *New York Times* for Bandy's obituary.

This chapter, then, used personal narrative to frame a continuum of boys to men in makeup in order to turn a Cinderfella from a pumpkin into "something," to borrow the words of YouTube celebutante Chris Crocker as he feverishly applies highlighter to his entire face, saying "Oh . . . my . . . GOD!" as a mantra while he swipes and swoops away, likening his adorned face (cheeks, forehead, nose, chin) to a Krispy Kreme donut in the sun.[28] While this might be an example of grotesque-lite, Instagram users, while gagging at the video, asked repeatedly what the brand of highlighter was and where they could buy it.

Guys in makeup teaching us makeup are as current as your favorite grotesque queen from *Drag Race*, your niece's favorite pop star, your nephew's private YouTube tutorial or MP3 collection of "guy-linered" indie goth glamour punks, as a sub-genre of both makeup and music, intertwined. They always read and reflect as transformative, transcendent, and transgressive—and inherently grotesque, as long as women are held to a certain relentless standard of cosmetic reality, realness, and feminism that neglects foundations in favor of focusing on just highlights. The range of made-up men might start with Louis XV and shows no sign of ending with Jeffree Star or James Charles; a continuum is in order for made-up men who know what giving good face means, to paraphrase Madonna, as both a commercial and customized performance. How men who identify as queer trailblaze the way faces can be made up, (with gorgeousness and grotesqueness as fluid, constant references), continues to inspire the artistry and impact makeup constructs and promotes blended and blurred gender lines.

It is only right, however, that O'Connor should have almost the last word: "For the kind of writer I have been describing, a literature which mirrors society would be no fit guide for it, and one which did manage, by sheer art, to do both those things would have to have recourse to more violent means than middlebrow subject matter and mere technical expertness."[29] To paraphrase shamelessly and continue in my application of O'Connor's grotesque as a critical lens, facing the grotesque in any region of the United States and, indeed, the world, calls for a kind of unfit guide using a sheer artistry of facial "violence" and grace. This virtual palette of binaries coexists in a tweeted visage where the highbrow meets technical expertise in the many digital faces constantly under construction that make up "the face" of your chosen device-platformed tutorial of today. Here is where grotesque parameters and elements best allow us to constantly learn how to create the multifarious, digital lives we can face with a fingertip's press and caresses, fostering built identities that can jar us as much as allure us.

NOTES

1. RuPaul and her management team World of Wonder have indeed created a formidable franchise, through Drag Con fan/queen conventions, *Drag Race* spin-offs in the UK and Thailand, a revue on the Vegas Strip, and a proposed Celebrity All-Stars edition as well, not to mention the upcoming twelfth season of the main program and another season of "regular" All-Stars as an in-house platform for previous queens.

2. Flannery O'Connor, "Writing Short Stories" in *Mystery and Manners* (New York: Farrar, Straus and Giroux, 1970), 87–106.

3. Flannery O'Connor, "Some Aspects of the Grotesque in Southern Fiction" in *Mystery and Manners* (New York: Farrar, Straus and Giroux, 1970), 36–50.

4. An incomplete list of Queens from *RPDR* who play(ed) with the grotesque both as makeup drag and costume drag choices (in order of appearance on the show, with season winners *italicized*):

    1. Nina Flowers, or season 1 grotesque-glam queen ground zero
    2. Raven
    3. *Sharon Needles*
    4. The Princess
    5. *Raja*
    6. *Bianca Del Rio*
    7. *Sasha Velour*
    8. Nina Bo'nina Brown
    9. *Trixie Mattel*

5. O'Connor, "Some Aspects of the Grotesque."

6. Queen, Yass. YouTube Video, November 20, 2018, Accessed April 1, 2019, https://www.youtube.com/watch?v=vtv1PBeZYwU. This clip has unfortunately been taken down, but the YouTube channel Spill posted the following video that encompasses the situation and rant of KodeeRants versus Charles: Spill, "James Charles Attacked by Fan for Lying, Claps Back

on Twitter," YouTube Video, 7:24, December 2, 2018, https://www.youtube.com/watch?v=_9v9zc9tJks.

7. LaBeija was the mother of the House of LaBeija, one of the legendary houses of the Harlem Ball Circuit community; her heir, Pepper LaBeija, featured prominently in the 1991 now-legendary and controversial documentary *Paris Is Burning* (thus Charles's first palette earns the provisionary title and unfortunate pun of *Pigment Is Burning* due to KodeeRants's YouTube documented problems and apparently allergic reaction to the reds in the palette).

8. Starkeymonster, "Dorien Corey on Throwing Shade," YouTube Video, June 10, 2011, Accessed April 1, 2019, https://www.youtube.com/watch?v=Z2lEtUqxg44.

9. Songfacts, "School's Out by Alice Cooper," Songfacts, Accessed April 1, 2019, https://www.songfacts.com/facts/alice-cooper/schools-out.

10. Merriam-Webster made an eyebrow linguistically *on fleek*—(bonafide, on point)—https://www.merriam-webster.com/words-at-play/fleek-meaning-and-history.

11. Way Bandy, *Designing Your Face: An Illustrated Guide to Using Cosmetics* (New York: Random House, 1977).

12. *ELLE*. "BEAT. CONTOUR. SNATCHED: How Drag Queens Shaped the Biggest Makeup Trends | ELLE," YouTube Video, December 11, 2018, Accessed April 1, 2019, https://www.youtube.com/watch?v=g83SowqTi6c.

13. O'Connor, "Some Aspects of the Grotesque in Southern Fiction," 36–50.

14. WOWPresents. "M.U.G. with Naomi Smalls and Raven—Raven's Mug," YouTube Video, February 26, 2018, Accessed April 1, 2019, https://www.youtube.com/watch?v=19aeSXvir00.

15. Hannah Tindle, "Way Bandy's Guide to Living and Looking Beautiful," *AnOther*, http://www.anothermag.com/fashion-beauty/9014/lessons-we-can-learn-from-way-bandy.

16. Wayne Goss, "MAKEUP TRENDS THAT NEED TO DIE IN 2017," YouTube Video, December 28, 2016, Accessed April 1, 2019, https://www.youtube.com/watch?v=tKwz2Ob8CEE.

17. Wayne Goss, "MAKEUP TRENDS THAT NEED TO DIE IN 2018," YouTube Video, November 17, 2017, Accessed April 1, 2019, https://www.youtube.com/watch?v=vhnuZwRV_CI.

18. Charleyy Hodson, "James Charles Was Just 'Exposed' for Faking His Viral Yearbook Photos," *We the Unicorns*, March 6, 2017, Accessed April 1, 2019, https://www.wetheunicorns.com/news/james-charles-yearbook-fake-proof/.

19. Victoria Sanusi, "This Teen Retook His Senior Year Photo to Make Sure His Highlight Would Pop and Zendaya Is Here for It," *BuzzFeed*, September 6, 2016. Accessed April 1, 2019. https://www.buzzfeed.com/victoriasanusi/this-teen-retook-his-senior-year-photo-to-make-sure-his-high?utm_term=.or7leGxal#.ncarMW0Xr.

20. Kucki Tea, YouTube Video, February 17, 2017, Accessed April 1, 2019, https://www.youtube.com/watch?v=BS_uylRfeZg&t=733s. John Kuckian's video is no longer available, but similar clips and relevant discussion of him can be found in other YouTube videos and on other vlogger channels.

21. Koa Beck, "Meet the Beauty Boys of Instagram," *Marie Claire*, November 2, 2018, Accessed April 1, 2019, http://www.marieclaire.com/beauty/a20197/the-beauty-boys-of-instagram/.

22. Peter Osborne and Matthew Charles, "Walter Benjamin," *Stanford Encyclopedia of Philosophy*, July 22, 2015, Accessed April 1, 2019, SW1, 487, translation amended. https://plato.stanford.edu/entries/benjamin/#ArtTec.

23. Wayne Goss, "THE BIGGEST EYESHADOW MISTAKE WE ALL MAKE," YouTube Video, November 20, 2018, Accessed April 1, 2019, https://www.youtube.com/watch?v=aot3t_DdPeo.

24. Wayne Goss, "A VERY IMPORTANT VIDEO—PLEASE WATCH—THANK YOU," YouTube Video, January 1, 2018, Accessed April 1, 2019, https://www.youtube.com/watch?v=5EraAtPx0J4.

25. Sasha Belle, "SASHA BELLE presents DRUNK MAKEOVER Episode 39 with KATYA ZAMOLODCHIKOVA," YouTube Video, June 17, 2015, Accessed April 1, 2019, https://www.youtube.com/watch?v=n6tmMyFkK_0.

26. Jeffreestar, "TRIXIE MATTEL TURNS ME INTO JEFFREE MATTEL," YouTube Video, September 21, 2018, Accessed April 1, 2019, https://www.youtube.com/watch?v=MzaEd7JtjO8&t=22s.

27. "WAY BANDY, MAKEUP ARTIST AND BEST-SELLING WRITER, DIES," *New York Times*, August 15, 1986, Accessed April 1, 2019, https://www.nytimes.com/1986/08/15/obituaries/way-bandy-makeup-artist-and-best-selling-writer-dies.html.

28. Crocker's original video is not longer available in YouTube, though other videos spoofing his highlighter review can be found online.

29. O'Connor, "Some Aspects of the Grotesque in Southern Fiction," 1970.

BIBLIOGRAPHY

Bandy, Way. *Designing Your Face: An Illustrated Guide to Using Cosmetics*. New York: Random House, 1977.

Beck, Koa. "Meet the Beauty Boys of Instagram." *Marie Claire*. November 2, 2018. Accessed April 01, 2019. http://www.marieclaire.com/beauty/a20197/the-beauty-boys-of-instagram/.

Belle, Sasha. "SASHA BELLE presents DRUNK MAKEOVER Episode 39 with KATYA ZAMOLODCHIKOVA," YouTube Video. June 17, 2015. Accessed April 1, 2019. https://www.youtube.com/watch?v=n6tmMyFkK_0.

ELLE. "BEAT. CONTOUR. SNATCHED: How Drag Queens Shaped the Biggest Makeup Trends." YouTube Video. December 11, 2018. Accessed April 1, 2019. https://www.youtube.com/watch?v=g83SowqTi6c.

Goss, Wayne. "THE BIGGEST EYESHADOW MISTAKE WE ALL MAKE." YouTube Video. November 20, 2018. Accessed April 1, 2019. https://www.youtube.com/watch?v=aot3t_DdPeo.

———. "MAKEUP TRENDS THAT NEED TO DIE IN 2017." YouTube Video. December 28, 2016. Accessed April 1, 2019. https://www.youtube.com/watch?v=tKwz2Ob8CEE.

———. "MAKEUP TRENDS THAT NEED TO DIE IN 2018." YouTube Video. November 17, 2017. Accessed April 1, 2019. https://www.youtube.com/watch?v=vhnuZwRV_CI.

———. "A VERY IMPORTANT VIDEO—PLEASE WATCH—THANK YOU." YouTube Video. January 1, 2018. Accessed April 1, 2019. https://www.youtube.com/watch?v=5EraAtPx0J4.

Hodson, Charleyy. "James Charles Was Just 'Exposed' for Faking His Viral Yearbook Photos." *We the Unicorns*. March 6, 2017. Accessed April 1, 2019. https://www.wetheunicorns.com/news/james-charles-yearbook-fake-proof/.

Jeffreestar. "TRIXIE MATTEL TURNS ME INTO JEFFREE MATTEL." YouTube Video. September 21, 2018. Accessed April 1, 2019. https://www.youtube.com/watch?v=MzaEd7JtjO8&t=22s.

O'Connor, Flannery. "Some Aspects of the Grotesque in Southern Fiction." *Mystery and Manners*. New York: Farrar, Straus and Giroux, 1970, 36–50.

———. "Writing Short Stories." *Mystery and Manners*. New York: Farrar, Straus and Giroux, 1970.

Osborne, Peter, and Matthew Charles. "Walter Benjamin." *Stanford Encyclopedia of Philosophy*. July 22, 2015. Accessed April 1, 2019. https://plato.stanford.edu/entries/benjamin/#ArtTec.

Queen, Yass. YouTube. November 20, 2018. Accessed April 1, 2019. https://www.youtube.com/watch?v=vtv1PBeZYwU.

Sanusi, Victoria. "This Teen Retook His Senior Year Photo to Make Sure His Highlight Would Pop and Zendaya Is Here for It." *BuzzFeed*. September 06, 2016. Accessed April 01, 2019. https://www.buzzfeed.com/victoriasanusi/this-teen-retook-his-senior-year-photo-to-make-sure-his-high?utm_term=.or7leGxal#.ncarMW0Xr .

Songfacts. "School's Out by Alice Cooper." Songfacts. Accessed April 1, 2019. https://www.songfacts.com/facts/alice-cooper/schools-out.

Spill. "James Charles Attacked by Fan for Lying, Claps Back on Twitter." YouTube Video, 7:24, December 2, 2018. https://www.youtube.com/watch?v=_9v9zc9tJks.

Starkeymonster. "Dorien Corey on Throwing Shade." YouTube. June 10, 2011. Accessed April 1, 2019. https://www.youtube.com/watch?v=Z2lEtUqxg44.

Tea, Kucki. YouTube. February 17, 2017. Accessed April 1, 2019. https://www.youtube.com/watch?v=BS_uylRfeZg&t=733s.

Tindle, Hannah. "Way Bandy's Guide to Living and Looking Beautiful." *AnOther*. http://www.anothermag.com/fashion-beauty/9014/lessons-we-can-learn-from-way-bandy.

"WAY BANDY, MAKEUP ARTIST AND BEST-SELLING WRITER, DIES." *New York Times*. August 15, 1986. Accessed April 1, 2019. https://www.nytimes.com/1986/08/15/obituaries/way-bandy-makeup-artist-and-best-selling-writer-dies.html.

WOWPresents. "M.U.G. with Naomi Smalls and Raven—Raven's Mug." YouTube Vieo. February 26, 2018. Accessed April 1, 2019. https://www.youtube.com/watch?v=19aeSXvir00.

Chapter Nine

Hijabi Makeup?

The Muslim Female Face and the Practice of Exposure

Fatma Sagir

The cosmetics industry produces a plethora of products every year for women all over the world, targeting, in particular, the face as a palette of feminine beauty, but also including products such as nail polish, bodycare, and skincare products. However, women of color have criticized the lack of diversity within the range of beauty, cosmetics, and makeup products. In the last few years, popstars such as Rihanna, with her label Fenty, and Iraqi-American blogger Huda Kattan, with her label Huda Beauty, have introduced to great success these products for a broader range of skin tones, adding to the diversity, on-screen visibility, and body-positivity movements, while well-established and market-dominating companies such as L'Oreal or Lancôme have been rather slow in addressing the needs of nonwhite women. Modest Fashion bloggers are at the forefront in popularizing and, as entrepreneurial bloggers, selling these products tied to the fashion industry.

When Italian design lable Dolce and Gabbana launched its 2016 collection of Abayas and Hijabs, targeting the Middle Eastern city of Dubai, United Arab Emirates, not only did fashion magazine editors get excited, but, in particular, so did Muslim women within the targeted market region. Muslim women wearing the hijab[1] shape an ever-growing social media audience for fashion and lifestyle content. The Modest Fashion economy is a continuously growing market aimed at a woman from any faith "who wants to dress modestly."[2] With the emergence of Modest Fashion Week[3] in London, Jakarta, Dubai, Amsterdam and other places over the past years, Modest Fashion has experienced a buzz that sells to a well-established, extensive market[4] in cosmetics, fashion, and luxury items and has also contributed to the mushrooming growth of Muslim female influencers[5] via Instagram. In this chapter, I focus on the practice of makeup among Muslim Modest Fashion bloggers[6] who wear the Islamic headscarf and refer to themselves oftentimes as "hijabi." The Arabic term *hijabi* means, broadly translated, "someone with a headscarf."[7] In an increasing number of Muslim female bloggers' profile descriptions, the term "modest" (often used interchangeably with "hijabi" or "Muslim") does not appear anymore or, more frequently, never did. "Lifestyle and Beauty," "Fashion and Beauty," or "Beauty Enthusiast" are more commonly used terminology at the present moment (2020). The reason could be the rise in Islamophobia and online abuse toward women, in general, or it could reflect an effort to be "visibly invisible," for example, blend in as the "ordinary" and not the "other"[8] while still appealing to Muslim audiences.

Works on Modest Fashion, fashion, and beauty blogging offer valuable insights while providing a critical approach to issues of feminism, neoliberalism, and capitalist economies. I would like to add a microperspective approach toward the *practice* of makeup among Muslim bloggers and its multilayered offerings in meanings and insight toward the contradiction between the idea of modesty, represented through the hijab, and the practice of female body exposure that results through posing and makeup use.

I will do so, first, by focusing on the head (e.g., hijab) and, afterward, the face (e.g., makeup). I seek to shed light on the issue of performing identity as much as to discuss the complexity and contradiction between modesty and exposure by starting with an introduction to the background and context through which this transformation takes place, and then engaging with selected elements of makeup from my elected case-study samples from Instagram accounts and YouTube channels. I wish to discuss a series of questions connected to the practice of makeup with regard to its scene location, performance, and representation, tying it to questions of exposure and visibility of the Muslim female body.

MODEST FASHION BLOGGERS, THE HIJAB, AND MAKEUP

Much has been written about women in Islam, and, in particular, the headscarf. It seems to be the most popular topic to talk and write about in reference to Islam and its compatibility with modernity per se. The religious covering suggests a modesty that appears to be contested by the focus on the made-up face, and, subsequently, its sharp exposure and clear visibility is perceived to thwart the very idea of covering. Makeup is, in Islamic jurisprudency, as much controversially discussed and regulated as it is among lay Muslims.

A bit of autoethnography should help to highlight the issue. I grew up in a Muslim migrant family in suburban Northern Germany during the 1980s. Heavy makeup, or any makeup at all, was frowned upon. A Muslim woman should be "pure." Her faith and her modesty would allow her faith to glow; therefore, she would not need rouge or accessories. Her modesty, through her covering of her body and hair, would be her asset. To some extent, this understanding is still to be found in the many comments to blog posts by Modest Fashion bloggers when followers and readers do not approve of their appearances. The initial cause for debate is usually a string of hair that shows under the headscarf. As I grew up, I was surrounded by many assumptions about Muslim women and a multitude of expectations of how an ideal Muslim woman should act, which was ideally not to be heard and not to be seen. Almost everything about women's bodies—the way they moved, laughed, and talked—had to follow rules. The Muslim female body transformed through its "tabooization" into over-sexualized bodies. In addition, I lived in a non-Muslim Western environment in which the Turkish Muslim image in society was one where the Muslim community oppressed their daughters and women. To Western society, those women needed to be saved, especially if they wore a headscarf.

Next to the religious-gendered expectation and prejudice, I also was aware of the general expectations toward women entrenched in German society. Using makeup at school was forbidden, and most women around me had no makeup on, or at least none I noticed. What I clearly was aware of was that makeup was not seen as appropriate for a covered Muslim woman. If a Muslim woman wore the headscarf, it was expected she refrained from wearing makeup or attracting any type of attention to her physique. Almost thirty years later, things have changed radically. Before I started my research, I already had observed a shift in clothing and, tied to it, habitus as well. In the early 2000s, I noticed the change in Muslim girls' and young women's dressing. If they wore a headscarf and followed an Islamic dressing code, they did not wear the headscarf like I was used to seeing during my young adulthood. Long and loose-fitting abayas and coats were the rule, with trousers an absolute no-go, whereas, from the early 2000s on, a slow but radical shift in bodily and sartorial practices emerged. A new style of wearing the headscarf itself was in conscious opposition to how the young women's mothers formerly wore the headscarf. While their mothers wore it out of tradition or habit, their daughters, who carried an alternative awareness of headscarf meaning, wore it as a critique of traditional misogynist readings of the Qur'an *and* against prejudice and stigmatization as "the oppressed."[9] This awareness in young Muslim women living in the West was informed by the experience of growing up with questions of belonging and identity as much as with experiences of racism.

SAMPLES AND METHODOLOGY

My interest in the represenation of fashion, women in fashion, and fashion photography in digital culture started with my following *New Yorker* photographer Scott Schuman's blog *The Sartorialist* on street style. This was before the arrival of Instagram. At one point, he uploaded a picture of a Muslim woman with a colorful headscarf, which earned him many negative comments. At that time, only a handful of Muslim women's blogs were present.

A few years later, everything had changed. With the arrival of YouTube in 2005 and Instagram in 2007, young Muslim women started emerging on digital platforms. Many so-called Millenials started fashion blogging with a traditional blog, after which they moved on to YouTube. This development evolved from 2010 on, and, with the arrival of Instagram, an erruption in the sheer number of so-called hijabi or Modest Fashion bloggers was clearly recognizable. Bloggers from North America and the UK were leading the movement in numbers. However, there was also a strong emphasisis on bloggers from other countries such as Turkey, Singapore, Indonesia,[10] the UAE, and Kuwait. Dubai, in particular, grew in importance as well, becoming a luxury hub and the latest host to a Modest Fashion Week. In fall of 2018, the Fine Arts Museums of San Francisco showed the exhibition "Contemporary Muslim Fashions" with the exhibition catalogue published in the same year.[11] The Museum of Modern Art in New York included an entry under "H—049 Hijab" in its publication from the exhibition "Items: Is Fashion Modern?," referring to British blogger Dina Torkia and American fencer Ibtihaj Muhammad, who wears a headscarf and has appeared in the now-notorious #Mipsters[12] video.[13]

Images of covered Muslim women appeared in digital culture with headscarves, but now they were all "dolled-up" and "made up" through the use of advanced camera and lighting technology as well as retouching and filter apps on smartphones, making the women's images highly visible. Their images attracted views, with the fascination for this prevalent appearance causing irritation among Muslim and non-Muslim audiences alike. "But this is not Islamic!" and the ever-returning "This is not hijab" comments still hold their popularity. The issue of makeup is tagged to the issues of the hijab, performance, and scene setting of the Muslim female self by Modest Fashion bloggers.

Special focus is paid to the highlighting of the eyes, the contouring of the face, and the coloring of the lips. Nails and nail polish as well as jewelry such as earrings and nose rings, and, in the case of one blogger from the UK, tattoos are featured extensively. Another blogger's specialty is Marvel and superhero-themed makeup and hijab tutorials, although these two are rather the exception than the rule.[14] The majority of Modest Fashion bloggers stick to the usual blogging contents of makeup, fashion, lifestyle, travel, food, and self-help. Some couples give practical life advice on religious issues. "Ask Sid'n Dina," by British-Muslim blogger Dina Torkia and her husband Sid Khan,[15] gathers a big audience as Torkia and Khan dive into every taboo topic the Islamic community faces, including sexuality and relationships.[16]

Most bloggers started early in their teens while still living with their parents. At a later point, some bloggers continued broadcasting from their bedrooms, while others moved either to a bathroom where all the makeup equipment would be stored, or, in some cases, an extra room, such as a study or a boudoir surrounded by clothes and other fashion items. Over time, some bloggers—as is the case with Dina Torkia (UK), Nabiilabee (UK), Ascia (Kuwait), and Melanie Elturk (US)—became mega brands with big businesses, while others became brand ambassadors and influencers, turning their hobbies over time into their day-to-day jobs. Some bloggers left their parents' houses after getting married and started involving their husbands into blogging.

For this, I selected samples of entrepreneurial bloggers. Most of these YouTube and Instagram accounts belong to Anglophone women, with a majority from the United States, Canada, and the UK. Many bloggers have mixed-race backgrounds or a migration background, and a few are converts to Islam.[17] I chose samples from YouTube and Instagram accounts, and, in the case of British-Muslim blogger Dina Torkia (aka Tokio) and American magazine and blog *MuslimGirl*, I included extracts from their websites. I also selected samples from UK-based blogger Sabina Hannan, as she focuses on makeup; American blogger Nura Afia, who became the first hijabi CoverGirl woman; and other bloggers. I looked into their general makeup, bodily, and sartorial practices as represented on their social media accounts. Furthermore, I analyzed online comments by readers, viewers, followers, and opponents, organizing the chapter around two main aspects that are at the heart of this topic: the hijab and makeup.

Erving Goffman's concept of *face-work* entails the idea of image-preservation. In a broader context, this is true for Modest Fashion bloggers, in general, but particularly strikingly apt regarding the display of makeup. As Goffman suggests, "face is an image of self delineated in terms of approved social attributes—albeit an image that others may share, as when a person makes a good showing for his profession or religion by making a good showing for himself."[18] Although Goffman clearly proposes *face-work* as an analytical tool to understand practices of self- and image-preservation in social interaction, I would like to take this further into the actual everyday practice of the beautification of the female face to a literal sense in which they are *doing face-work*. The practices in hijabi makeup tutorials are entangled with a number of ongoing discussions about women, gender, religion, and Muslim women's bodies and rights, as blogger Nura Afia highlights:

> Growing up, I couldn't think of any major Muslim or hijabi girls in mainstream media that I could have looked up to. I've seen a lot of people take their scarves off, being in this beauty community and feeling like they need to change, to grow, so I decided to keep wearing my scarf. When CoverGirl picked me to be their brand ambassador, it was huge because it's this first mainstream American brand that wanted to show hijabis on like a different scale. Being that I am the first Muslim CoverGirl, especially during this political climate, I just felt that role, and I felt the responsibility that I have to show other girls that, no matter what's going on in the world, you stick to what you believe in. I am Nura Afia. I am a hijabi.[19]

MODESTY VERSUS EXPOSURE: THE HIJAB AND MAKEUP

In the winter of 2018, Muslim social media was buzzing with a "scandal." British Muslim fashion blogger Dina Torkia, aka Dina Tokio,[20] announced she would be removing her headscarf.[21] Dina Torkia rose to fame as a cross-media representation of young Muslim women living in an urban context in the West, although her followers and her influence reach far beyond this through the accessibility of digital culture. She started blogging in the early days of YouTube and later entered, with the BBC, a Muslim beauty pageant in Indonesia. Her bubbly and light-hearted YouTube videos quickly gained her a large, predominantly female audience, with her rise to internet and media fame mirroring the rise of the Modest Fashion market.[22]

For years, she had been telling her followers on various occasions how she, at times, had struggled to keep wearing her headscarf. To say "all hell broke loose" when she removed her headscarf would be a colossal understatement.[23] Over the last years, comments on her social media had become increasingly hostile, attacking her mostly for her choice of clothing but also for coloring and showing her hair, dancing, showing her ankles, wearing trousers, and other behavior considered by a section of the audience as immodest for a Muslim woman.[24] This, in turn, had led to blogposts by Torkia in which she adressed the men[25] attacking her, who were predominantly Muslim.[26]

Dina Torkia seems to receive more criticism than any other Muslim fashion blogger, especially compared with those who display heavy makeup or retouching of images on Instagram. Pages of comments regarding these posts reflect predominantly on the beauty, outer appearance, and technicalities of mastering the art of makeup application. Rarely are there references to her "Muslimness" found within the critical comments. There also seems to be a tendency toward directing criticism, verbal abuse, and hate comments toward more open and outspoken women. In most cases, whether the Muslim woman blogger is wearing a headscarf and showing her hair or not seems to be the single key criterion in deciding whether all her other habitual, sartorial, bodily, and beauty practices and, in the context of lifestyle blogging, her entire everyday life are to be considered allowed, and, therefore, Islamic, or not allowed, and, consequently, un-Islamic (which Islamic jurisprudence and theology term *haram*).[27] This evaluation of the Muslim woman leads to the question of whether she *is* a Muslim and whether she belongs to the Muslim community. Some comments regarding Dina Torkia's removal of her headscarf suggest she has left Islam.

Still, Torkia is, at the present moment (2020), among the biggest entrepreneurial Muslim fashion bloggers, garnering up to two million followers and sponsored through collaborations with household brands along with a variety of fashion and cosmetic labels.

THE HIJAB

The headscarf is considered by both Muslims and non-Muslims as the most prominent visible marker of a Muslim woman, and it, therefore, is associated with certain behavioral codes, rules, and habitus such as modesty and purity within both sexual and social contexts. The practice of covering the female body and head has a long history and a variety of practices depending on factors such as geographic region, school of thought, temporality, and societal and historical class stratifications.

For the sake of brevity, I refrain from a discussion of the colonial and postcolonial discourse of the veiling/covering versus the removing of the veil/the uncovering of the Muslim female body. Others have done that on a multitude of occasions, such as Saba Mahmood discussing the notion of agency in scholarly discourse on Muslim women[28] and Sirma Bilge arguing that many times agency is assumed with Muslim women either removing the headscarf or needing "to be saved" from oppression through the headscarf or having agency as an "aggressor" against the West.[29] Emma Tarlo offers a different angle by suggesting agency in the headscarf itself.[30]

Over the last decades, the headscarf has become the subject of political debates charged with issues of racism and postcolonialism in Europe, including France, where Muslim women are facing increasing hostility wearing it in addition to its being banned from most of the public sector; and in Turkey, where it was, until 2013, banned from public spaces, schools, and universities; as well as in Muslim countries such as Saudi Arabia, where women are forced to wear it due to societal pressure; or in Iran through state law. In European as well as other Western contexts, in reference to Muslim minorities, the headscarf has experienced a sharp shift in framework, displaying a multitude of meanings. Most significantly, it has been viewed as a tool for expressing Muslim identity against an increasingly hostile environment of Islamophobia after major incidents such as the UK's Brexit vote to leave the

European Union (2016), the election of Donald Trump as president of the United States (2016), and the flight of over three million Syrians from civil war to Western countries such as Germany, Canada, the United States, and Australia.

Against this highly political, tension-charged setting, lifestyle bloggers continue to post and pose. Muslim female lifestyle and fashion bloggers diligently declare their break with stereotypes through fashion blogging. As a result, big labels such as Lancôme, L'Oreal, Nike, and high-end indie fashion labels quickly recognized this market potential, due as much to the green-washing and hijacking of social activism[31] and the idea of diversity and body-positivity in that the market was now open to the "halalification"[32] of luxury products as well as high street labels. Whether to understand this as the crucial capitalist rule of the market or to see it as an increasing effort to include and represent "minorities" in the mainstream is a discussion with valuable arguments on both sides, with the end result of understanding that both elements of this development might be inseperably entangled.

The reality that, from 1920 on, mainstream makeup ads appeared targeting women's bodily and other "insecurities" as a tactic to sell beauty products is something that hijabi bloggers have utilized in order to begin addressing the "insecurities" of young Muslim women who wear a headscarf rather than the actual cosmetics labels or companies themselves. Sharing the commonality of being almost invisible on screen and in popular culture with their audience, these bloggers offered their tutorials in order to make themselves feel better and to demonstrate that "fashion goes with faith," in that Muslim women in a hijab could be beautiful too, which, in turn, had the goal of raising awareness about Muslims being "ordinary people."[33] Furthermore, these women provided their audiences with knowledge about their makeup and dressing practices from their everyday life experiences. Beginning in 2015, the Modest Fashion market skyrocketed, and Modest Fashion companies, such as Turkish company Modanisa, developed business relationships with hijabi influencers, and eventually other companies, retailers, and labels began to develop Modest Fashion lines targeting the Muslim pound or dollar.

SPACE: BEDROOM—BATHROOM—BOUDOIR ... AND BEYOND

Videos about lifestyle, fashion, or makeup typically show the female blogger in her bedroom, occasionally in her living room, but, in general, particularly for "hijab" tutorials or makeup as well as so-called hauls where the blogger shares the items she had purchased or been sent with her audience, blogging happens from the inside of her home. Beauty and fashion bloggers are filmed in their bathing robes with a full hijab on, creating a warm atmosphere through the use of lights and carefully selected colors for the frame they wish to set. Inside the privacy of their homes, with their nearest family around, Muslim women would not need to wear the headscarf. If we keep in mind that the term "hijab" can also mean a separation or barrier, when one is worn in the private space of a bedroom or bathroom, this practice not only transforms the private space into a public space where the blogging happens and is shared with the audience of anonymous viewers, but it also turns the body within this setting to a private space. This practice of simultaneously exposing the private to the public through the use of the face during makeup tutorials as a space for exposure while covering the body and the head per Islamic protocol creates a highly ambivalent image.

THE AUTHENTICITY-INTIMACY CURRENCY

Authenticity is the fundamental currency of social media, and most particularly within blogging. Bloggers who want to "sell" content and seek to garner larger audiences are extremely cognizant of this tool. Blogger audiences, on the other hand, seek authenticity due to the associated intimacy that develops through their viewing of the blogger's profile. In makeup videos and tutorials, intimacy can be created through a variety of practices, such as "Get Ready With Me" videos, in which bloggers show a before-and-after makeup face and address their audience while applying makeup as if chatting to a girlfriend and having a good "sit-down" and "heart-to-heart," reinforcing the idea of female friendship and community. The continuity of broadcasting videos and images as much as the use of constant features and elements such as the same introduction or ending of a video lend serialities to the posts that subsequently create a bond with audiences. An additional bonding technique is the methodology of makeup videos, as they are different from videos that help master a particular technique. Makeup videos offer an approachability through narrations of everyday life by the content creator. Therefore, some followers and viewers come back for the instructional tips while others return for entertainment and curiosity purposes.

The moment audiences sense a decrease in authenticity, they show their displeasure by first complaining about it through their posts. If the content creators do not make amends, viewers oftentimes move on to another blogger, or, in some cases, audiences have been known to accept the shift and change in the role of their favorite blogger. This shift in trust towards the "truth" and "realness" of a blogger generally occurs when they start advertising products or become "brand-ambassadors," which, in social media language, are known as "influencers." Nevertheless, the "staged-ness" of it all is, by and large, accepted if the blogger makes advertisement activities transparent. However, there is one aspect that is difficult to forsee, which is whether followers will continue their loyalty toward a Modest Fashion blogger or any blogger when the blogger alters their lifestyle or character development, as happened with Dina Torkia.

Torkia's headscarf had become a main component of her brand as an outspoken young Muslim woman and as one of the biggest Modest Fashion bloggers. Her headscarf was a prominent factor of her personal brand in various media outlets such as *Vogue*, national and international media coverage, and even a book titled *Modestly*.[34] What happens when the key elements of a blogger's business economy—their attitude, practice, and convictions—evolve over time? Although her follower numbers are not showing any decrease (2020) and she still keeps selling products and creating content, the continuing stream of online abuse under every single post, tweet, and upload suggests it will remain difficult for her to overcome this "brand change." The results of her actions are yet to be seen in the following years; the verdict remains open at this point.

FOCUS FACE: FROM THE "HIJAB TUTORIAL" OVER TO THE "MAKEUP TUTORIAL"

"Makeup for girls that wear hijab is extra special, 'cause it gives us a chance to play off our face."[35] The interest in hijab this quote from Nura Afia reflects is not new. Long before fashion bloggers, there was already a certain fascination with the "orient," the "harem," and the veiled "oriental" woman. Images of women covered except for their eyes are familiar images that are still used to represent Muslim women or Islam in general. If we look at romanticized imagery used as thumbnails for music videos on YouTube for "oriental" music, the fascination for an Orientalist eroticism and exoticism toward covered Muslim women continues to prevail through focus on the heavily made-up and highlighted eyes in an otherwise entirely covered face. This practice clearly echoes past Western and colonial obsessions with the Harem image involving veiled women and is a prime example of fascination with "The Other" as detailed by Edward Said in his scholarship concerning the phenonenom.[36] Many bloggers started by producing hijab tutorials, in which they show how to arrange and fold a scarf onto the head, and later added makeup tutorials and how-to-dress videos, as well as so-called "look books" displaying fashion items, certain styles, and dress combinations.

When looking at Modest Fashion bloggers' photos, one's focus is automatically directed to the face; however, the entire ensemble and setting might be "perfect," visually appealing, or interesting. Since the head is covered with a headscarf, all the attention of the onlooker or viewer is directed onto the face itself. Obviously, sometimes there is no hair to style. However, oftentimes bloggers find ways to include their hair,[37] be it the constant change of coloring the hair in accordance to the chosen outfit or how far it shows under the headscarf, sometimes being moved so far onto the back of the head that it is invisible or, due to the similarity in its choice of color to the actual hair, almost undistinguishable from it, causing at times "unrest" and "turmoil" in the comments sections. One example of this phenomenon is bloggers, like Sabina Hannan, not wearing a headscarf at their wedding but opting instead for a traditional South-Asian Dupatta-style shawl or veil. Another case is the founder-of-MuslimGirl-blog-turned-online-magazine-creator Amina al-Khatahtbeh. While her head is covered, her chest oftentimes shows a considerable amount of cleavage, which raises the prominent argument (against a religious rule to cover) that the Qur'an only mentions to cover the chest upside down.

A prominent example of a gradual change in hijab and makeup practices is Dina Torkia's case. The British blogger kept changing her hair color from brown to red and pink to blue. In her first videos from 2012 and 2013 her hair is not visible, but the headscarf is dressed in a giant hairknot style, creating a big head in comparison to the rest of the body, which once again directs the viewers' gaze to the head in its entirety. While in the 2012 and 2013 videos Dina Torkia has a noticeably bold way of painting her face in order to give herself an almost doll-like appearance, from 2014 on her style changes. Due to the introduction of new technology at this point, Torkia is able to blend her makeup colors more smoothly through the use of contouring, which at times creates a mask-like image.

From 2014 on Torkia uses a variety of headscarf styles, from those resembling the traditional style, which covers the shoulders and the front of the upper body, to a turban that shows a triangle of hair on top reminiscent of the iconic 1950s style. Popular styles are those that include the headscarf in the overall style of the outfit by draping it in a fashion similar to hair in addition to those that include a beanie or a hat. Still, today, Dina Torkia fashions a headscarf, mostly in a turban-style, when modeling for Modest Fashion label Modanisa, for which she still works even after removing her headscarf. Another example is Instagram makeup short videos that only show a demonstration of applying makeup, be it just onto the lips or the eyes, or an entire full makeup procedure, with only a music piece, oftentimes hip hop music, as a sound element. Some videos focus intensely on the lips, almost overexposing and aggravating the lips and their sensuality while applying lipstick. The impression these videos leave borders on an oversexualized aesthetic that is common in many Instagram pictures and videos, regardless of their religious or ideological affiliations.[38]

In all respects, the focus is purposely directed to the face, which is the "place" where makeup "happens" and where femininity is displayed most directly because ideally the rest of the body is covered with the intention to hide all femininity and signs of female sexuality. This is required within

Orthodox Islam, where sexuality is allowed only within the confines of marriage, so that the main aim of the covering is understood as preventing Muslim men from being distracted and attracted by the femininity of a woman.

THE EYES—LINERS, GAZES AND LASHES: "YOUR EYEBROWS ARE ALWAYS ON FLEEK, GURL!"[39]

Applying makeup is a very intimate thing to do in everyday life. We do it in the privacy of our bathrooms or bedrooms. We do it in the private space that we only share with those we know and trust. It is done in front of a mirror. It asks for certain hand movements and certain movements of the head, the eyes, and the lips. On the other hand, some individuals apply makeup while riding public transportation, while others in the privacy of their automobiles. Some stand while others sit. In addition, the movements utilized during the application of makeup are unique for the hands and the face as well.

In a self-experiment, I let my husband take pictures of me during the process of applying makeup before a night out. The movements and the overall appearance of my face and my entire self is, in one word, alienated. In particular, applying mascara is a bizarre image of movements to observe. During this application, the mouth is open, eyes are pulled up, and the gaze is directed upwards while one hand guides the mascara brush to the lashes. Applying makeup onto the eyes is a tricky business, and using eyeliner results in more bizarre movements. While one hand holds the pen and applies the line onto the eyelid, the other hand pulls the closed eye to the side to make sure the line is steady and perfect. We do not look like ourselves while applying makeup, and some of us do not look like our natural selves after finishing the process of "painting" ourselves. In all cases, we believe a "new," "better" version of ourselves emerges in front of the mirror. Similarly, in makeup tutorial videos, women sometimes create an entirely new version of themselves, which results in a stunning "before and after" moment.[40]

Within the Modest Fashion blogger accounts I analyzed, none of these women wear the face veil (Arab *niqab*) that leaves only the eyes visible,[41] but heavily made-up eyes are still among some of these women's most prominent features. The use of fake lashes is commonly accepted and practiced. In addition to eye makeup such as eye shadow, eyebrow pencils, eyeliners, and mascara, some bloggers use contact lenses in various colors, with the primary ones being blue and green. This bodily practice of highlighting the female gaze, making the eyes bigger, brighter, more seductive, and using bold colors and big lashes, thwarts the generally accepted social and religious norms in Islamic tradition that women and men should lower their gazes. This method of visual aversion is utilized, but certainly not in the abovementioned sense. At the end of makeup videos, women lower their gazes, turn their heads in a delicate "feminine" way toward their chins and to one side of their shoulder, displaying not only the final result of their makeup application efforts but also a generally accepted "feminine" move of their body. In this manner, they position themselves in a posture of desirable but passive femininity, which, again, itself echoes imageries of women in Western art history.[42]

THE LIPS: RED—THE "FORBIDDEN" COLOR

The color red is considered to be popular in many cultures, although with sometimes differing meanings.[43] Red is anthropologically very appealing to the human eye. It is generally associated with youth, sexual attractiveness, fertility, danger, blood, revolution, and rebellion, with differentiations depending on the cultural and religious context. As the following interview quote shows, red, among many Muslims, is known to be the "forbidden color." This social perception of the dangerous and amoral ramifications of red persisted, although theological discourse has always had a variety of positions toward Muslim women wearing red in public. Makeup, and red lipstick, in particular, continues to be both controversial and experimented with, as reflected in this interview between Nura Afia (NA) and *Marie Claire* (*MC*):

> *MC* : Many traditionalists in the Middle East don't think it's appropriate to wear makeup, how do you deal with that?
>
> NA: Growing up my parents were very conservative, so I experienced it firsthand in a sense. Makeup in the Middle East just has a very negative stereotype—especially red lipstick. They think that's what prostitutes wear back home. So every time I wear it it's like, oh god. But you know what, makeup washes off at the end of the day. It's just a matter of educating them. It's a normal thing here for most American women. I think a lot of people want to take cultural practices and make it about religion, but it's not religious.[44]

Blogger Nura Afia's approach to wearing red lipstick is not only entirely different from mainstream Orthodox positions but also offers a relaxed and practical approach because "at the end of the day you can wash it away," and she believes the way to change the stereotype lies in "educating them," noting she understands that the source of the misconception among Muslims toward the color red comes from making cultural practices into religious rules.[45]

THE PRACTICE OF LAYERING: IMAGES, BEAUTY STANDARDS, IDENTITIES

Putting together "a look" requires considering how the various parts work together as a larger whole, something Nura Afia also discusses in her interview with *Marie Claire*:

> *MC* : When you're creating a makeup look, how does it play into the rest of the look?
>
> NA: I've got a huge scarf collection, so I really enjoy matching my scarves to my eye look. I like to be matchy-matchy with the colors. So like a burnt orange scarf with a matching eye, or a pink scarf with a matching lip. (Nura Afia, *Marie Claire* 2017)

The practice of *layering identities* is a concept I would like to introduce for describing the sartorial and bodily practices of Modest Fashion bloggers/ Muslim female bloggers. Overlapping and layering two different and, depending on your point of view, two contradictiory or opposing images and ideals of women, such as the Western woman versus the woman in Islam or women with makeup and fashionable clothing, figure-hugging trousers, and bold colors and women following a specific Islamic understanding of how a Muslim woman should dress and, therefore, behave according to Islamic religious rules, most prominently summarized under the umbrella of the headscarf. The practice of *layering identities* offers a bodily practice that overcomes and dissolves this dichotomy, presenting a different all-entailing frame very much similar to the fashion and style practice of mix-and-match or the musical mash-up. These practices lead to new images, and, in the case of Modest Fashion bloggers, to a new understanding and a variety of contributions to Muslim identity.

I suggest the practice of applying makeup in addition to the practice of wearing the headscarf are an approach to fulfill two different and, to some extent, contradictory beauty standards and ideal images of women. With the blending in and layering of the two images and standards of a Western woman with makeup and a Muslim woman with a hijab, Modest Fashion bloggers not only make but perform a new Muslim identity. However, the entrepreneurial Muslim fashion and beauty blogger now is the more ideal "economic subject,"[46] as she now speaks to two beauty standards through the work on her body, literally from head to toe.

The practice of *layering identities* through beauty and bodily practices as much as sartorial practices mirrors the struggle and challenges of young Muslims in general, but in particular what young covered Muslim women face in times of Islamophobia, terrorism, and conservatism within Muslim communities. Although the creating of these new images might be considered a reproduction of conventional beauty, it actually works within the discoursive frame of diversity, representation, and body positivity.

Young women started layering their clothes beginning with a dress over trousers, eventually leading to continual headscarf style changes, and, over time, I observed in the streets of German cities, first, lightly made-up faces and then, later on, heavily made-up faces, but all still with wearing the headscarf. Over time, I saw Muslim women with headscarves in all sorts of spaces they had earlier not been spotted, such as cafes and public places, pubs, clubs, the sports field, and our local women's-only lido, doing all sorts of activities, including smoking, chatting, pushing prams, dancing, singing, walking through university school halls, and working from behind the desk of a pharmacy. The obvious change here was in *presenting* themselves and *perfoming* themselves in public spaces. This moment of cultural and societal transformation moved into digital culture when young Muslim women created their own spaces via the internet in which to present and represent themselves. Post 9/11, Muslim women living in the West felt the pressure and rejection within society through the rise of Islamophobia, which included images circulated in media reports about Islam, Muslims, terrorism, war, and crisis in the aftermath of the attacks. Young Muslim women growing up in London, Birmingham, Toronto, and New York have most frequently expressed the toll this atmosphere had on them while growing up. In addition, many Muslim female teens and young adults wearing the hijab dealt with misconceptions and traditional and Orthodox expectations within their own Muslim families or communities.

A third element of this frame of intersectionality is the life and the sorrows of teenagers and young adults adding to the challenge of what it is to be Muslim.[47] Entry by famous American blog #MuslimGirl contributor Rayyan Sokkarie demonstrates the struggle—and surprisingly, the role—that makeup plays in dealing with this complexity. After struggling at school with bullying and being an outsider wearing the headscarf, Sokkarie comes across makeup:

> Middle school was by far the hardest; I began wearing the hijab. (. . .) I was all over the place trying to find my place in this sea of middle school kids that did not understand why I wore the headscarf. (. . .) toward the end of those hellish three years, I discovered this thing called eyeliner and I went ham (halal ham, of course). (. . .) Eyeliner everywhere, on my eyelid, on my waterline, darkening my eyebrows. My mom was like, "Yeah, whatever! Have fun with that. We'll see where this goes." Meanwhile, my sister would low-key judge me, but she mostly just let me be.[48]

From this quote, we understand that within the same Muslim family the three women display different positions toward the application of makeup while wearing the hijab and choose to tolerate the others', however opposite, position. Continuing on, she describes how she *felt* after finding makeup tutorials on YouTube:

> My confidence skyrocketed; I became my own person. I played around with different types of lipsticks, messed up on my eyeliner wings a couple of times, but sure as hell felt bomb. *Insert the heavily repetitive joke about why I shouldn't say "bomb" as a Muslim.* What I'm trying to say is that this ain't about you, you, or you. This is about me.[49]

Sokkarie attributes the boost of self-esteem, a positive change in body awareness, and body sensitivity to her practice of applying makeup.

"CONTENTLESS FEMINISM": AGENCY AND EMPOWERMENT

I received the following comment from a male colleague: "They are simply not political. All they are interested in is their makeup; they don't want to talk about actual social problems. They just talk about the new eyeliner they got, and they are 'excited' about the new mascara. I don't understand it." It represents just one of many encounters I experienced during my research period. Colleagues, and many times students of mine as well, continue to express their puzzlement over these young Muslim women, many of whom refuse to talk about radical Islam, terrorism, or religious beliefs altogether, insisting on only wanting to speak about the topics they choose.

This "disobedience" in fulfillment of their currently established and adopted roles as the *other*,[50] however, is a first indication that a deeper concept is beginning to emerge. In the introduction to her study *Postfeminist Digial Cultures* (2015), Amy Shields Dobson addresses male contempt of female self-representation and female media and culture production, with its particulars of targeting the "female selfie" and the speaking to a camera by "cultural commentators."[51] As can be derived from the abovementioned quote, Muslim female bloggers, in particular, are uniquely judged for refusing to play to the dichotomy of "the West" versus Islam and subsequently rejecting the standardized role that is expected of them, but let us deconstruct the quote further. What does it actually say about the speaker's understanding regarding what Muslims—in particular, Muslim women—should be engaging with?

During our conversation, I realized that my colleague's assumption here is that there are far more urgent topics and problems for Muslim women to talk about than cosmetics and beauty, as dealing with the latter is deemed apolitical. Rosalind Gill and others suggest this phenomenon to be "contentless feminism,"[52] which becomes an entirely different meaning in the context and frame in which Muslim women and girls act. While a young, white, middle-class woman discussing makeup and beauty might be considered "contentless feminism"—a categorization which, again, needs to be the center of a critical discussion in itself, as do almost all feminism categorizations Gill debates—a young Muslim blogger applying makeup is full of "content" and offers a multitude of meanings. Further critique targets the consumerism, the following and mimicking of celebrity culture, the unapologetic display of adoration for luxury items and luxurious brands of fashion, and, as a seemingly particularly heavy "sin," the absence of the "political" in their blogging activities. We find here an intersection of the critique young women face on social media ("selfie-mania") and the dynamics entrepreneurial bloggers in beauty and fashion blogging experience, regardless of their ethnic or religious heritage, as becoming part of a neoliberal and capitalist frame for aesthetic labor, which Sarah Banet-Weiser explores in her essay on the girl's empowerment movement and beauty blogging.[53]

Muslim fashion and beauty bloggers, through their engagement as entrepreneurial bloggers with cosmetic companies and women's magazines, are part of this dynamic. Banet-Weiser deduces that the blogger's involvement is not contradictory but rather complimentary, as on one hand they are criticizing society and the media for forcing women into certain standards of beauty and body while at the same time they are advertising how they have overcome these beauty standards through women's empowerment and by reaching these standards of feminine beauty through the optimization of the female body. The argumentative frame Banet-Weiser refers to in her analysis is neoliberalist and capitalist, as, according to Banet-Weiser, it focuses on the role women's aesthetic labor and body play into the reproduction of conventional femininity. She argues that beauty blogging is particularly apt for the performance of the self in digital media.[54]

Minh-Ha Pham, however, offers, in her analysis of media criticism toward the "selfie-mania" and online "vanity" of women, the idea of "networked vanity" to boost visibility and representation of minorities and people of color who lack visibility in media and popular culture other than being depicted in stereotypical or stigmatized ways.[55] Pham evaluates the idea of "vanity" critics have asserted on the selfie and "vanity-culture" in digital media, critiques that target mainly young women. She argues that "vanity," however, within the context of minorities' visibility and visual representation, offers cultural, societal, and political power for participation and representation. For groups such as Muslim women, who, in general, are either not positively seen in media and popular culture or are depicted as stereotyped—stigmatized as a threat (the terrorist) or as a "project" (the oppressed Muslim woman)—Pham demonstrates that being visible in digital culture offers a way to be visually present, but warns that even then "visibility doesn't always remedy inequality."[56]

CONCLUSION

Many young Muslim women who wear the hijab have found a space in digital culture to present and represent themselves and so have become more visible through fashion, beauty, and lifestyle blogging. The wish to be more visible in this manner rather than through stereotyping and stigmatizing images led these young Muslim women to create their own unique images and, thus, alternative narratives of the Muslim female self in media and society. Through their bodily and sartorial practices of following their religious standards regarding the covering of their bodies while simultaneously following "Western" beauty practices and standards, these women blend two opposing beauty standards and ideas of the ideal woman. However, both of these ideals, the covering versus the exposure, seek to achieve the goal of the "perfect woman" through body work.

Within the discourse of identity construction and identity performance, the practices introduced and discussed in this chapter can be summed up in the idea of *the practice of layering identities*. The sharing of these stylistic practices through the use of social media with a broadly based audience unfamiliar with their methods indicates a transformative understanding of the private and public to which objects, practices, and spaces belong. This is particularly evident in reference to the widely shared and, among large sections of Muslims, accepted specific Orthodox Islamic understanding of the private and the public. Young Muslim women's lifestyle blogging indicates a transfiguration in which the role of the hijab and associated habitus is challenged through the combination of what is considered non-Islamic, such as makeup and the exposure of the Muslim female body through online posing, and what is considered Islamic, represented in the symbol of the hijab.

NOTES

1. The Arabic term "hijab" has a multitude of meanings. In this text I use hijab and headscarf interchangably as both refer to the covering of the head/hair by Muslim women.
2. This may also refer to Jewish or Christian women.
3. Modest Fashion Week has been founded by two women fashion entrepreneurs and designers from two countries with a large Muslim population: Franka Soeria (Indonesia) and Özlem Sahin (Turkey). See https://www.modestfashionweeks.com/en/the-organizers/.
4. See also Shelina Janmohamed's work on the "'Muslim coin': Generation M. Young Muslims Changing the World" (2016).
5. Note the shift from the term "brand ambassador," commonly referring to celebrities, to the term "influencer," which only refers to content creators in digital culture. Both terms mirror the media channels in which they evolve.
6. I use the term "blogger" and "blogging" for all social media activities, be it uploading videos, posting pictures or writing blog entries. I do not differentiate between vlogging/vlogger and blogging/blogger, as I think it expresses the cross-media practice rather more aptly.

7. In this piece I use "hijab" or "headscarf" as interchangeable terms for practicality reasons. In Islamic theology *hijab* may also refer to a habitus with both female and male connotations.

8. Gayatri Chakravorty Spivak, "The Rani of Sirmur. An Essay in Reading the Archives," *History and Theory* 24, no. 3 (Oct. 1985): 247–272.

9. Nilüfer Göle, ed, *Islam and Public Controversy in Europe*, Surrey: Asghate, 2013; and Nilüfer Göle, *The Forbidden Modern: Civilization and Veiling*, Michigan University Press, 1997.

10. Indonesian entrepreneur Dian Pelangi is one of the most influential Muslim designers and bloggers with an Instagram following of five million and was included in the *Forbes* "30 under 30" list in 2018.

11. Jill D'Alessandro and Reina Lewis with Alex Aubry, Shiva Balaghi, Laura L. Camerlengo, Carla Jones, Su'ad Abdul Khabeer and Deena Aljuhan Abdulaziz, Remona Aly, Sariya Cheruvallil-Contractor, and Shelina Janmohamed (Eds.), *Contemporary Muslim Fashions*, published by the Fine Arts Museums of San Francisco, New York: Delmonico Books, Prestel, 2015.

12. "#Mipsters: Somewhere in America" is a short video clip from 2013 showing Muslim women of different ethnic backgrounds, mostly bloggers, in an urban setting in the United States, moving along to the sound of Rapper Jay-Z's "Somewhere in America," clad in bright colors and body-conscious shapes. The video caused considerable uproar and turmoil, with coverage from CNN to international media outlets, with critics contesting the women's Muslimness based on their outer appearences, sartorial choices, and bodily practices. The intersection of racism, sexism, and religious-motivated and legitimated misogyny is obvious in the entire debate. "Mipster" is an ironic combination of the terms Hipster and Muslim, now referring to the lifestyle movement.

13. Paola Antonelli and Michelle Millar Fisher, "Items: Is Fashion Modern?" Published in conjunction with the exhibition "Items: Is Fashion Modern?" by the Museum of Modern Art, New York (2017): 141–142.

14. Kuwaiti blogger Ascia Al Faraj (Ascia), with an Instagram following of up to three million, removed her headscarf in 2018/2019, revealing tattooed arms, whereas before this incident only tattoos on her hands were visible.

15. My case study "Having an Affair with the Imam" puts their YouTube channel and its videos containing advice into the center of my research on religious authority and everyday life. Blogger Ascia Al Faraj and her husband show on their YouTube account "The Hybrids" everyday life of a Muslim family. These, and other like-minded examples, are "side-products" to the evergrowing Modest Fashion and Mipster movements.

16. After Winter 2018, when Dina Torkia decided to remove her headscarf, the "Ask Sid and Dina" channel no longer answered questions relating to such topics; instead, they focused on lifestyle and everyday-life blogs, such as the renovation of their new home. This was mainly due to the negative comments and threats against the families after Dina Torkia's decision. However, on various occasions, they expressed their plans for eventually reinstalling these Q and A's.

17. The setting in which photos are taken and videos are produced as much as the locations visited, and other signifiers, give away information about social and economic backgrounds and reveal that the majority of Modest Fashion bloggers come from a middle-class/upper-middle-class milieu.

18. Erving Goffman, "On Face-Work: An Analysis of Ritual Elements in Social Interaction," *Reflections* 4, no. 3 (1967): 7.

19. "Nura Afia | About Face | ELLE," YouTube Video, 1:34, posted by *ELLE*, March 10, 2017, https://www.youtube.com/watch?v=jsQnlL6vQuk.

20. Dina Torkia has a mixed-heritage background of an Egyptian father and a British mother. She lives with her husband and two young children in her hometown, Cardiff.

21. Dina Torkia (DT) simply appeared on an Instagram post without a headscarf. She later adressed the issue in an hour-long video/podcast on YouTube, which has been viewed over 600,000 times. The constant stream of hate comment has not stopped, but DT has never again

adressed the topic (2020). "Dinatokio Drama," YouTube Video, 58:30, posted by Sid and Dina, November 3, 2018, https://www.youtube.com/watch?v=xHKzkvcKAZM.

22. The reason for this could be in the rise of Islamophobia and the opening to a bigger market. I use the self-referential terms "Modest Fashion" blogger as well as "hijabi," although the latter deserves a more in-depth discussion which I cannot provide here.

23. It is not possible to address the entire discourse in this chapter, but it is worth exploring in future research.

24. As a side-effect, the comment sections continue to display the debate on the issue of the hijab and, tied to, it questions of religious authority, Qur'anic exegesis, interpretation, lifestyle, tradition, and gender roles, among many other related topics, thus offering a platform, even if not mediated, for lively debate among Muslims, who, one might assume, would or could not get together in this particular way to discuss such a controversial topic (in real life).

25. The blog post titled "Muslim Men" addresses Dina Torkia's readers and Muslim men she feels criticized by regarding her dressing, makeup, and overall online presence. ("Muslim Men," *COVERD* [blog], posted by COVERD, October 17, 2017, http://www.dinatokio.com /life/muslim-men/.) In another post, Dina Torkia addresses her own makeup practices, particularly in the month of Ramadan, in which she refrains from using makeup, but not, as she insists, because she is overtly "religious"; it is because she feels exhausted. ("So Religious," *COVERD* [blog], posted by COVERD, June 11, 2017, http://www.dinatokio.com/style/so-religious/.)

26. Possibly most famously, conservative, self-described "Orthodox" British-Muslim bloggers "Ali Dawah" and "Muhammed Hijab." For example, see Ali Dawah's YouTube videos on the subject: "Reacting to Sids Immodesty—Sid and Dinas Podcast," YouTube Video, 23:24, posted by Ali Dawah, November 13, 2018, https://www.youtube.com/watch?v=lHg3oKsYKu0 and "Reacting to Dina Tokio Taking Hijab Off—The Y Files," YouTube Video, 26:16, posted by Ali Dawah, November 2, 2018, https://www.youtube.com/watch?v=ltLMszdn8bM.

27. However, *haram* has different layers of meaning in its vernacular use in everyday life of Muslims, using it in the sense of "forbidden" or as in many regional dialects such as Syrian Arabic in the sense of "how awful," "such a pity." In Islamic Theology and Philosophy (which does not separate in the same way as Western Theology and Philosophy) *haram* is used as a moral/normative category and as terminus technicus in the sense of "against the law" or "forbidden" or something that is "sacro-sanct," for example, to be protected. We still can see this latter meaning in the naming of the Great Mosque of Mecca, the Masjid al-Haram, and in the Turkicised Ottoman Harem. Today's lay Muslims, and especially those who are active on social media, either creating "Islamic" content or commenting, as in the case of Muslim fashion, beauty, and lifestyle bloggers, use the term almost entirely in the sense of "religiously forbidden."

28. Saba Mahmood, *The Politics of Piety. The Islamic Revival and the Feminist Subject*, Princeton: Princeton University Press, 2005.

29. Sirma Bilge, "Beyond Subordination vs. Resistance: An Intersectional Approach to the Agency of Veiled Muslim Women," *Journal of Intercultural Studies*, 31: no. 1 (2010): 9–28, DOI:10.1080/07256860903477662.

30. Emma Tarlo, "Hijab in London: Metamorphosis, Resonance and Effects," *Journal of Material Culture* 12, no. 2 (July 1, 2007): 131–156. https://doi.org/10.1177/13591835 07078121.

31. Nike's Colin Kaepernick advertisement on the occasion of Nike's thirty-year celebration of the "Just do it" campaign, which received mixed reactions that fell in two categories, exemplifies this. The first category celebrated the visibility and introduction of a political protest by a black athlete into popular culture. The second category criticized the hijacking of a seriously political cause and suspected Nike was out for "the dollar."

32. The term "halal" is the opposite of "haram"; it may refer to practices allowed religiously and to food prepared according to Islamic rules. It is also commonly used to describe a lifestyle, ideally an Islamic lifestyle. In reference to gender relations, a halal relationship refers to a relationship and encounter that is considered to stay within the rules of Islamic norms and traditions, such as no sexual relations before marriage or extra-marital affairs. See also note 2.

33. Dina Torkia produced a documentary series with YouTube's "Creator for Change" campaign in 2017 with the title "Your Average Muslim" to demonstrate this. "Your Average

Muslim | Full Documentary," YouTube video, 34:56, posted by Dina Tokio, November 7, 2017, https://www.youtube.com/watch?v=f14GtLR7O0Y.

34. Dina Torkia, *Modestly*, London: Ebury, 2018.

35. "Nura Afia | About Face | ELLE."

36. Edward Said, *Orientalism*, New York: Pantheon Books, 1978.

37. The youngest development (2020) or trend is a practice that I would like to coin as *hair-jab*: this term describes the sartorial practice of styling the headscarf/hijab like hair. Many Instagram accounts show images with this style almost indistinguishable from hair. As a second trend we can see more bloggers de-jab, a term that referes to those women who choose to remove their headscarves.

38. In how far pornography and its specific aesthetics are influencing the style, poses, and aesthetics in Instagram pictures and videos is worthy of future research and discussion, particularly in regard to the question of the male gaze in digital culture, lifestyle, and fashion blogging.

39. One of many comments next to makeup tutorials for the eyes or Instagram images of made-up eyes in general, also referring with the use of the slang term "on fleek" to perfection.

40. While on a 2017 field visit to London's Modest Fashion Week, I found myself in the awkward position of asking a member of the audience who happened to be a Modest Fashion blogger about the all-female blogger symposium members in front of us, as I could not match the images from Instagram/YouTube to those on a placard featuring the actual women that were discussing Modest Mashion blogging. Such was the difference in makeup styles online and offline. The women changed not only their appearences, apparently, but also their *faces* according to the setting they acted in. This practice, as such, is not surprising. However, it shows that within the space of digital culture a more playful and versatile approach to dress, face, makeup, and fashion is on display, while, one can only assume, the appearance in "real life" and the social interaction within this kind of public space demands a more careful approach and habitus.

41. Although one can find bloggers with niqabs.

42. John Berger, *Ways of Seeing*, London: Penguin/BBC, 1972.

43. Lisa Eldridge, *Face Paint: The Story of Makeup*, New York: Abrams Image, 2015.

44. Lauren Valenti, "CoverGirl Nura Afia on Makeup in the Middle East," *Marie Claire*, January 26, 2017, https://www.marieclaire.com/beauty/news/a25010/covergirl-nura-afia-interview/.

45. This line of thinking mirrors a common understanding among reformist Muslims: to separate between culture and religion.

46. Sarah Banet-Weiser, "'I'm Beautiful the Way I Am': Empowerment, Beauty, and Aesthetic Labour," in *Aesthetic Labour*, eds. Anna Sophia Elias, Rosalind Gill, and Christina Scharff (London: Palgrave MacMillan, 2017): 265–282, https://doi.org/10.1057/978-1-137-47765-1_15.

47. Kimberlé Crenshaw, "Mapping the Margins: Intersectionality, Identity Politics, and Violence against Women of Color," *Stanford Law Review*, 43: 6 (July 1991), 1241–1300.

48. Rayyan Sokkarie, "Sorry, Not Sorry: I'm Muslim, and I Wear Makeup," *#MuslimGirl*, 2016, http://muslimgirl.com/27340/hands-makeup-aint/.

49. Rayyan Sokkarie, "Sorry, Not Sorry."

50. Gayatri Chakravorty Spivak, "The Rani of Sirmur: An Essay in Reading the Archives," *History and Theory* 24, no. 3 (Oct. 1985): 247–272.

51. Amy Shields Dobson, *Postfeminist Digital Cultures: Feminity, Social Media and Self-Representation*, New York: Palgrave Macmillan, 2015.

52. Rosalind Gill, "Post-Postfeminism? New Feminist Visibilities in Postfeminist Times," *Feminist Media Studies* 16, no. 4 (2016): 610–630.

53. Banet-Weiser, "'I'm Beautiful the Way I Am.'"

54. Ibid., 266–267.

55. Minh-Ha Pham, "'I Click and Post and Breathe, Waiting for Others to See What I See': On #FeministSelfies, Outfit Photos, and Networked Vanity," *Fashion Theory* 19, no. 2 (2015): 221–242. DOI:10.2752/175174115X14168357992436.

56. Pham, "I Click and Post and Breathe."

BIBLIOGRAPHY

Antonelli, Paola and Michelle Millar Fisher. "Items: Is Fashion Modern?" Published in conjunction with the exhibition "Items: Is Fashion Modern?" by the Museum of Modern Art, New York, 2017.

Ashman, Rachel, Anthony Patterson, and Stephen Brown. "'Don't Forget to Like, Share and Subscribe': Digital Autopreneurs in a Neoliberal World." *Journal of Business Research* 92 (2018): 474–483. https://doi.org/10.1016/j.jbusres.2018.07.055.

Banet-Weiser, Sarah. "'I'm Beautiful the Way I Am': Empowerment, Beauty, and Aesthetic Labour." In *Aesthetic Labour*, edited by Anna Sophia Elias, Rosalind Gill, and Christina Scharff, 265–282. London: Palgrave MacMillan, 2017. https://doi.org/10.1057/978-1-137-47765-1_15.

Berger, John. *Ways of Seeing*. London: Penguin/BBC, 1972.

Bilge, Sirma. "Beyond Subordination vs. Resistance: An Intersectional Approach to the Agency of Veiled Muslim Women." *Journal of Intercultural Studies* 31: no. 1 (2010): 9–28. DOI:10.1080/07256860903477662.

Crenshaw, Kimberlé. "Mapping the Margins: Intersectionality, Identity Politics, and Violence against Women of Color." *Stanford Law Review*, 43: 6 (July 1991), 1241–1300.

D'Alessandro, Jill and Reina Lewis with Alex Aubry, Shiva Balaghi, Laura L. Camerlengo, Carla Jones, Su'ad Abdul Khabeer and Deena Aljuhan Abdulaziz, Remona Aly, Sariya Cheruvallil-Contractor, and Shelina Janmohamed (Eds.). *Contemporary Muslim Fashions*. Published by the Fine Arts Museums of San Francisco. New York: Delmonico Books, Prestel, 2015.

"Dinatokio Drama." YouTube Video, 58:30. Posted by Sid and Dina, November 3, 2018, https://www.youtube.com/watch?v=xHKzkvcKAZM.

Dobson, Amy Shields. *Postfeminist Digital Cultures: Feminity, Social Media and Self-Representation*. New York: Palgrave Macmillan, 2015.

Eldridge, Lisa. *Face Paint: The Story of Makeup*. New York: Abrams Image, 2015.

Gill, Rosalind. "Post-Postfeminism? New Feminist Visibilities in Postfeminist Times." *Feminist Media Studies* 16, no. 4 (2016): 610–630.

Goffman, Erving. "On Face-Work: An Analysis of Ritual Elements in Social Interaction." *Reflections* 4, no. 3 (1967): 7–13.

Göle, Nilüfer. *The Forbidden Modern: Civilization and Veiling*. Michigan University Press, 1997.

———, ed. *Islam and Public Controversy in Europe*. Surrey: Asghate, 2013.

Janmohamed, Shelina. *Generation M: Young Muslims Changing the World*. London: I.B. Tauris, 2016.

Lewis, Reina. *Muslim Fashion: Contemporary Style Cultures*. Durham: Duke University Press, 2015.

Mahmood, Saba. *The Politics of Piety: The Islamic Revival and the Feminist Subject*. Princeton: Princeton University Press, 2005.

Mora, Emanuela and Agnes Rocamora. 2015. "Letters from the Editors: Analyzing Fashion Blogs—Further Avenues for Research." *Fashion Theory,* Vol. 19. Iss. 2, 149–156, DOI:10.2752/175174115X14168357992274.

"Muslim Men." *COVERD* (blog). Posted by COVERD, October 17, 2017, http://www.dinatokio.com/life/muslim-men/.

"Nura Afia | About Face | ELLE." YouTube Video, 1:34. Posted by *ELLE*, March 10, 2017, https://www.youtube.com/watch?v=jsQnlL6vQuk.

Pham, Minh-Ha. "'I Click and Post and Breathe, Waiting for Others to See What I See': On #FeministSelfies, Outfit Photos, and Networked Vanity," *Fashion Theory* 19, no. 2 (2015): 221-242. DOI:10.2752/175174115X14168357992436.

"Reacting to Dina Tokio Taking Hijab Off—The Y Files." YouTube Video, 26:16. Posted by Ali Dawah, November 2, 2018, https://www.youtube.com/watch?v=ltLMszdn8bM.

"Reacting to Sids Immodesty—Sid and Dinas Podcast." YouTube Video, 23:24. Posted by Ali Dawah, November 13, 2018, https://www.youtube.com/watch?v=lHg3oKsYKu0.

Said, Edward. *Orientalism*. New York: Pantheon Books, 1978.

"So Religious." *COVERD* (blog). Posted by COVERD, June 11, 2017, http://www.dinatokio.com/life/so-religious/.

Sokkarie, Rayyan. "Sorry, Not Sorry: I'm Muslim, and I Wear Makeup." *#MuslimGirl*, 2016, http://muslimgirl.com/27340/hands-makeup-aint/.

Spivak, Gayatri Chakravorty. "The Rani of Sirmur. An Essay in Reading the Archives." *History and Theory* 24, no. 3 (Oct. 1985): 247–272.

Tarlo, Emma. "Hijab in London: Metamorphosis, Resonance and Effects." *Journal of Material Culture* 12, no. 2 (July 1, 2007): 131–156. https://doi.org/10.1177/1359183507078121.

———. *Visibly Muslim: Fashion, Politics, Faith.* Oxford: Berg. 2010.

Torkia, Dina. *Modestly.* London: Ebury, 2018.

Valenti, Lauren. "CoverGirl Nura Afia on Makeup in the Middle East." *Marie Claire*, January 26, 2017. https://www.marieclaire.com/beauty/news/a25010/covergirl-nura-afia-interview/.

"Your Average Muslim | Full Documentary." YouTube Video, 34:56. Posted by Dina Tokio, November 7, 2017, https://www.youtube.com/watch?v=f14GtLR7O0Y.

Conclusion

The chapters in this book provide a portrait of the beauty vloggers and online makeup tutorials as they have developed in recent years and situate the makeup tutorial as a point of intersection for artistry, self-expression, commerce, community, and social and cultural engagement. From considering how the vlogger acquires and maintains followers and uses that celebrity for economic gain and social commentary to analyzing how both the content creator and the content consumer use makeup and vlogs for individual expression and empowerment, the topics covered in this book reinforce the value of examining makeup tutorials and beauty vlogging more closely, now and in the future. While much has been touched on and explored here, there still are more subjects of great academic and social significance to be pursued, particularly as the landscape of the tutorial and digital media itself continue to change and evolve.

One such area deserving greater scrutiny now—and one that will only continue to expand in the future—is the range of social media platforms beauty influencers navigate and employ to gain, maintain, and interact with followers. To make the project more manageable and focused, this book employs a critical lens centering on YouTube specifically. This proves valuable as a way to follow the rise and popularity of beauty vlogging and makeup tutorials, which exploded on YouTube and launched many of the earliest beauty influencers, turning what, for many, may have started as a hobby into a full time career. With the pervasiveness of other social platforms like Instagram and Snapchat, the ways influencers employ these media to create content and connect with followers deserves further attention. Some beauty vloggers on YouTube even direct subscribers to follow them on these other platforms, making references to things viewers may already be aware of if they have been keeping up with their other social media accounts or even identifying these other sites as spaces for different sorts of content, more lifestyle-type and less exclusively beauty-related content, for example. These other platforms particularly appeal to younger audiences, but even the more mature YouTube channel host likely feels compelled to make use of a range of media to stay relevant and connect with newer audiences. The beauty influencer of today is just as likely to get a start and an audience through one of these other social outlets as through YouTube, so, clearly, much has yet to be mapped out and understood when it comes to makeup tutorials and vlogging in our modern digital world.

What's more, as audiences and regulations of YouTube continue to change, the platform may see audiences and even content creators begin to wane. Changes in recent years to YouTube's policies, regarding content regulations that could equate to censorship and certainly impact channel hosts' creative freedoms and opportunities for earning money, have led both vloggers and viewers to reevaluate their reliance on and use of the platform. The extent to which YouTube (and other platforms) control and evaluate content, from vlogger posts to viewer comments—the latter being something channel hosts themselves can block and so censor—deserves further study as well. How content is labeled and promoted or restricted not only impacts its potential for revenue but limits audience access and freedom of creation and expression. The ramifications of such policies further complicate the use and experience of digital media as a space where artistry, commerce, and community intersect.

While aspects of who vlogs and who views makeup tutorials certainly feature in the chapters included here, taking a closer look at statistics and trends based on makeup tutorial demographics, for both creators and viewers, would also enhance an understanding of the scope and impact of beauty vlogging more broadly. Analyzing the audiences consuming beauty content on YouTube (and via other social media platforms) as well as those posting such content in more depth could provide an interesting mirror of social identity, need, and interest and paint a clearer picture of what that resulting community "looks" like, so to speak.

How online makeup tutorials promote community building has been a recurring topic of this book, and almost every chapter includes comments from viewers expressing support or criticism of vloggers and even, at times, other viewers. These excerpted comments certainly represent significant trends and reactions to video content, allowing for a more comprehensive view of YouTube-channel interactions, but a more in-depth survey of viewer comments could further strengthen an understanding of this dynamic. Tracking and categorizing viewer posts and interactions, with both vloggers and other viewers, would provide a more detailed and complex picture of how these digital community spaces function and meet a social and creative need for those drawn to the sites. Even tracking specific viewers across channels could offer intriguing insight into the role of viewer interactions and how and why followers make use of these community/communication tools.

An equally productive outlet for more research would involve applying this sort of focus to individual beauty-vlogger channels. As touched on in some chapters here, beauty influencers often participate in a range of beauty-vlogging genres or categories of content, from "Get Ready with Me" (GRWM) and "Haul" videos, the latter of which might walk viewers through recent makeup product or even clothing purchases, to "Review" videos, weighing in on particular beauty products or brands, and "De-Cluttering" videos, in which vloggers invite viewers to see what products will be culled from their often expansive collections. Considering trends and the popularity of certain video types, which can involve cross-channel references and even collaborations, could enhance the study of this subject. Perhaps even more intriguing would be to follow specific beauty vloggers' trajectories and evolution on YouTube. An examination and analysis of the content trajectory of influencers could provide insight into the changing audiences and roles of beauty content and their creators. The seeming increase in lifestyle videos and general trend to diversify channel content, also referenced in this work, point to the evolving interests and tastes of both creators and consumers and so hint at other topics ripe for more in-depth analysis—analysis that might consider the motives (personal, creative, economic, etc.) and impact of such evolution and variation.

The important research and cultural studies included in this book embody the culmination of early and recent developments in the beauty-vlogging world of YouTube and represent how makeup itself fosters creativity, cultural engagement, and community building in the digital world of the twenty-first century. Each chapter enriches even as it complicates an understanding of the online makeup tutorial and all that it entails. Together they help to form a more comprehensive picture of the various ways individuals use beauty vlogs by considering how a vlogger gains and makes use of celebrity status, how and why consumers engage with content creators and other viewers, and how the individual can use makeup and the vlogging platform to create and embrace identity and self-expression while navigating cultural, religious, and gender expectations. The fact that there still are many questions and areas of academic and social significance left to explore only serves to further highlight the relevance of such topics now and far into the future.

The ways people find and create not only community but their own identities have expanded exponentially in this increasingly technological world, perhaps no more evident in the fascinating space of the online makeup tutorial. Pairing makeup—something at times controversial and often associated with artifice, restrictive notions of "beauty," masculine oppression, and even antifeminism—with the medium of the vlog has turned makeup itself into something that can be as progressive and boundary breaking as it is innovative and artistic, now on a much broader scale and with a much larger audience. Through the medium of the online makeup tutorial, individuals can find a voice and a space for instruction (social *and* practical) and connection. As this work demonstrates, though, this platform has its own complications as well, particularly given the inextricable links between content and commerce on most channels and certainly in the very makeup (no pun intended) of YouTube itself. While much has been explored in the pages of this book, makeup in the digital world, on YouTube and beyond, represents an exciting, culturally significant, and ever changing frontier—one that deserves, and should offer, great critical interest in the years to come.

Index

A. J. Crimson, 26
abayas, 185, 187
activism, 143, 144, 145, 153, 154, 155
activists, 48, 145, 155
Adam, 108
advertisements, 26, 49, 87, 105, 112, 151, 192, 193, 204n31
advertising, 17, 94, 105, 128, 135, 193, 201
advocacy, 48, 129, 136, 153
Afia, Nura, 189–190, 194, 197, 198
Africa, 46, 108, 176
Aguilera, Christina, 44
Aina, Jackie, 4, 25, 27, 28, 29, 34n40, 41, 50
albinism, 42, 43
Alig, Michael, 171
all natural movement, 10, 131, 132, 133, 135, 136, 138, 141n23
American Dream, 99n41
American Sign Language (ASL), 152
Americas, 108
amputations, 143, 144, 152, 153, 154
amputees, 143, 153
Anastasia Beverly Hills, 43, 51
Anderson, Mathu, 171
apologies, 20–25, 33n8, 34n29, 48, 49, 50
Aquaria, 170
Armani Jeans, 45
Armstrong, Nancy, 107, 123
Ashley, Alissa, 4, 26, 28, 41
Asia, 49, 108, 195
Aucoin, Kevyn, 165
Australia, 192
authenticity, 9, 17, 18–20, 20, 22–25, 26, 29, 31, 32, 66, 67, 68, 70, 71, 73, 75, 76, 78, 79, 80, 81, 85, 86, 88, 89, 91, 92, 96, 104, 105–106, 117, 119, 120, 136, 139, 169, 193

Bahrain, 41
Bandy, Way, 165, 167, 170, 171–172, 180
Banet-Weiser, Sarah, 123, 201
Barbados, 45
Barbie, 10, 98n40, 103, 105, 114–115, 116, 120, 122n47, 164, 170, 180
Bardot, Brigitte, 168
Bartky, Sandra, 128
Baudrillard, Jean, 114, 120
Beauty Bakerie, 26
BeautyGuruChatter, 67, 75, 80
BECCA, 5, 69
The Believe Foundation, 45
Belle, Gina, 179
Belle, Myling, 179
Belle, Sasha, 179
Berkowitz, Dana, 115
Bhatia, Aditi, 71
binary, 23, 42, 89, 90, 129, 136, 137, 139, 161, 162, 173
Bisognin, Marzia, 105
Blac Chyna, 26–27
Blandino, Jerrod, 50

Blaque, Kat, 48
BOMB (Black-Owned Makeup Brands), 26, 30, 41
Bordo, Susan, 114
Boy George, 169
brand, 1, 4, 5, 6, 9, 10, 12n10, 17–18, 18–20, 27–28, 28, 29, 30, 39, 40, 41, 43, 45, 45–46, 46–47, 48–49, 50, 51, 68, 71, 76, 77, 78, 79, 82n25, 85–88, 89–97, 97n4–97n5, 104, 106, 116, 144, 151, 164, 172, 174, 180, 189, 190, 193–194, 202n5
branding, 20, 84; self-branding, 10, 26, 32, 68, 85, 86, 87–92, 94–97, 97n8, 144, 144–145
Brathwait, Richard, 135
Brome, Alexander, 108
Brown, Nina Bo'nina, 174, 181n4
Butler, Judith, 97n8, 104, 120, 129
Butterfolds, 179
Bybel, Carli, 105

Cabaret, 170
Canada, 189, 192; Toronto, 140n16, 199
capitalism, 68, 89, 114, 115, 116, 120, 122n62, 145, 186, 192, 201
celebrity, 1, 7, 18, 25, 29, 37, 50, 66, 78, 80, 83n33, 85–86, 87, 88, 90, 91, 92, 94, 94–96, 97n2, 97n3, 97n5, 97n13, 98n21, 103, 105, 117, 118, 119, 138, 181n1, 201, 209, 210, 211. *See also* microcelebrity; star
channel hosts, 4, 7–8, 10, 18, 19, 26, 27, 29, 30, 32n1, 210. *See also* influencers
Charles, James, 105, 119, 149, 163, 165, 167, 167–168, 169, 173, 174, 176, 179, 180, 181n6
Charles, Prince of Wales, 45
Christianity, 107, 108, 202n2
cisgender, 127, 128, 133; men, 127; women, 127, 128–129, 129–131, 132, 134, 135–136, 137, 138–139
cisnormativity, 91, 138
Clara Lionel Foundation (CLF), 45
class, 9, 42, 65, 66–67, 68–69, 70, 71, 72, 73, 74, 74–75, 76–78, 79, 80, 81, 83n29, 109, 115, 117, 127, 132, 152, 170, 176, 177, 191, 201, 203n17
Cleopatra, 104, 117, 118–119, 120
Clinique, 177
Clinton, Bill, 23
The Cockettes, 172
Coloured Raine, 26
ColourPop, 5, 50
commercialization, 26, 65, 66–67, 67, 69, 74, 75, 78, 81, 91, 94, 96
community, 1, 3, 4–5, 7, 8, 9, 11, 13, 17, 19, 20, 22, 24–25, 26, 30–32, 37, 38, 40, 41, 46–47, 48, 49, 50, 51, 65–67, 67–68, 69, 70, 71, 73, 76, 77, 81, 82n5, 83n31, 88–90, 93–94, 106, 132, 136, 144, 147, 150, 154, 155, 162, 165, 167, 168, 182n7, 187, 189, 190, 191, 193, 209, 210, 211
conservatism, 197, 198, 204n26
consumers, 7, 8, 10, 11, 20, 25, 27, 29, 30, 31, 38, 39, 41, 42, 49, 51, 65, 67, 68, 86, 87–89, 91–96, 105, 115, 120, 144–145, 170, 175, 201, 209, 211
consumption, 88, 92, 96, 104, 107, 115, 138, 144, 145, 179
Cooper, Alice, 169
Corey, Dorian, 168
cosmetics, 41, 49, 65, 69, 71, 78, 82n25, 85, 87, 97n5, 104, 108–109, 110, 111, 112, 116, 119, 120, 128, 130, 132, 135, 136, 145, 175, 185, 192, 200; anti-cosmetic rhetoric, 106, 109, 113, 120; cruelty-free, 38, 85; selfie, 163, 165, 170, 171, 172, 200; vegan, 38, 85
Cover FX, 50
CoverGirl, 50, 105, 174, 189, 190, 205n44, 207
Crawford, Joan, 169, 170
Crenshaw, Kimberlé, 42, 53n58
Crocker, Chris, 180
cultural appropriation, 30, 49, 147
Curry, Ayesha, 50
cystic hygroma, 143

Dawson, Shane, 20, 34n29, 47, 79, 80, 83n31, 97n5, 98n36, 163, 167, 174
Deery, June, 68
DeGeneres, Ellen, 3, 174
de Jager, Nikkie, 2, 29, 31, 105
Del Rio, Bianca, 181n4
demotic turn, 1, 12n1, 13, 24, 68, 87, 88, 89, 90, 92, 94, 96

Designing Your Face, 170
Dior, 45, 50, 179
disability, 10, 42, 143–144, 145, 146, 147–148, 149, 151, 152, 153, 154–155, 173
disembodiment, 108, 113, 118, 120
Dobson, Amy Shields, 200
Dolce and Gabbana, 185
Donics, Byron, 105
drag, 2, 10, 129, 133, 140n16, 161, 162–173, 164, 165, 166, 167, 168, 170–171, 172, 173, 174, 179, 179–180, 180, 181n1, 181n4
drag queens, 90, 161, 162–163, 165, 167–168, 170, 174
dressing room, 10, 103, 110, 112, 115, 118
dressing room satires, 110, 112, 118
dwarfism, 143

Eburu, Chichi, 41
Egypt, 119, 127
Elturk, Melanie, 189
Emporio Armani Underwear, 45
Esteé Lauder, 50
Eve, 10, 103, 107, 108, 113, 120
Extreme Makeover, 115

Facebook, 105, 144, 152
face-work, 189
fame, 1, 24, 26, 43, 45, 48, 65, 66, 70, 77, 86, 89, 94–96, 117, 164, 190
fandom, 93, 144, 149, 155
fans, 5, 6, 8, 18, 20, 21, 23, 24, 25, 26, 28, 29, 49, 66–67, 67–68, 69, 70, 71, 72, 73, 74, 74–75, 75, 76–77, 78, 79, 80, 81, 83n29, 96, 97n5, 143, 144, 169
fashion, 11, 44–45, 80, 86, 87, 93, 105, 107, 135, 174, 185–186, 186, 187, 188, 189, 190, 191, 192, 194, 195, 197, 198, 201, 202, 202n3, 203n11, 203n13, 203n15, 203n17, 204n22, 204n27, 205n38–205n40
Feinstein, Joseph, 98n40
femininity, 104, 107, 114, 115, 127, 129, 131, 132, 133, 134, 136, 137, 139, 144, 149, 195, 196, 197
feminism, 42, 114, 132, 145, 180, 186, 200, 201, 211
feminists, 3, 42, 112, 114, 127, 128, 131, 135, 139, 144, 145, 151, 154, 155, 200
Fenty Beauty, 9, 28, 35, 37, 37–38, 38, 39, 40, 41–42, 43, 46, 48–49, 50, 51
Fenty 40, 37, 50, 51
Fierce, Jaidynn Dior, 179
Fine Arts Museums of San Francisco, 188
Flowers, Nina, 174, 181n4
food, 152, 169, 188, 204n32
food stamps, 76
Ford, Tom, 44
Forever, Alyssa, 26, 41
Foucault, Michel, 107, 123

Garland, Judy, 175
gender, 2, 3, 4, 8, 9, 10, 23, 32, 42, 78, 83n29–83n30, 90, 97n8, 105, 107, 109, 113, 115, 120, 127, 128, 129, 131, 132, 132–134, 136, 137, 138, 139, 140n10, 140n16, 141n22, 149, 163, 165, 168, 173, 174, 175, 179, 180, 187, 189, 204n24, 204n32, 211; dysphoria, 138; fluidity, 4, 162, 165, 168, 170, 172; identity, 98n36, 104, 127, 139; transgender, 3, 10, 31, 42, 127, 128, 129–131, 132, 133, 134, 135–139, 140n1, 140n16
Germany, 116, 186, 187, 192, 199
Gill, Rosalind, 200, 201
Girlguiding, 128
Givenchy, 48
Goffman, Erving, 189
Goss, Wayne, 25, 163, 165, 167, 170, 172–173, 176, 178, 179
Grammys, 44
Greece, 133
grotesque, 10, 107, 110, 161–164, 164, 165–166, 167, 167–168, 170, 171, 172, 173, 174, 175, 177, 178–179, 179, 180–181, 181n3–181n4
gurus, 1, 2, 9, 10, 17, 18, 20, 23–26, 26, 30, 32n1, 66, 69, 75, 80, 81, 83, 84, 85, 86, 87, 88, 90, 93, 94, 106, 121n17. *See also* influencers
Gutierrez, Manny. *See* MUA, Manny
Gutowski, Eva, 105

Hannan, Sabina, 189, 195
Harlow, 168, 170

Harvard University, 45
Harvey Nichols, 41
Harwood, Joseph, 136–137, 141n22
Haywood, Eliza, 112, 113, 115
headscarves, 186, 187, 188, 190–191, 191, 192, 193, 194, 194–195, 198, 199–197, 202n1, 203n7, 203n14, 203n16, 203n21, 205n37. *See also* hijabs
health, 41, 44, 86, 105, 151
Herns, Paris, 116
heteronormativity, 90, 134, 136, 138
hijabs, 11, 185, 186, 188, 189–190, 190, 191, 192, 192–193, 194, 195, 198, 199, 200, 202, 202n1, 203n7, 204n22, 204n24, 204n26, 205n37. *See also* headscarves
Hill, Jaclyn, 5, 9, 12n12, 65–67, 67, 69, 69–72, 72, 73, 74, 74–75, 75, 76, 76–77, 78, 79, 80, 81, 82n25
Hill, Jon, 76
HTI Collection, 105
Huda Beauty, 49, 185

identity, 1, 2, 3, 4, 8, 9, 10, 11, 17, 18, 26, 32, 42, 66–67, 68, 69, 70, 71, 72, 73, 74, 75, 76, 77, 78, 79, 80, 81, 83n29, 87–88, 89, 91, 92, 96, 97n4, 104, 110, 113, 114, 115, 120, 127, 128, 129, 133–134, 138, 139, 140n11, 141n23, 151, 154, 155, 178–179, 181, 186, 187, 191, 198, 202, 210, 211; layering, 198, 202; online identity, 26, 66–67, 68, 70, 73, 74, 75, 76, 79, 80, 81, 87, 91, 97n4; social identity, 20. *See also* gender
image (e.g., reputation, marketing image), 9, 10, 17, 18, 19, 20, 24, 28, 31, 44, 45, 46, 54n76, 62, 71, 78, 86, 87, 90, 94, 96, 97n8, 107, 108, 109, 120, 129, 134, 136, 137, 139, 187, 189, 193, 198, 199, 202
images (e.g., photos, designs), 20, 23, 46, 113, 116, 118, 119, 120, 134, 136, 146, 147, 148, 163, 175, 188, 189, 190, 193, 194, 195, 196, 199, 205n37, 205n40
India, 134, 140n16
individualism, 88, 96
Indonesia, 185, 188, 190, 202n3, 203n10
inequality, 29, 138, 201
influencers, 2, 3–7, 8, 9, 10, 11, 17–18, 19, 20, 20–21, 23–25, 26–27, 28, 29–30, 31, 32n1, 37, 49, 50, 65, 85–86, 87, 88, 89–90, 92, 96, 97n2, 98n21, 105, 149, 170, 174, 176, 185, 189, 192, 193, 202n5, 209, 210, 211. *See also* channel hosts; gurus
Instagram, 1, 5, 8, 28, 39, 42, 43, 44, 45–46, 49, 50, 85, 87, 89, 96, 105, 144, 146, 153, 162, 163, 174, 175, 176, 180, 185, 186, 188, 189, 190, 195, 203n10, 203n14, 203n21, 205n37–205n40, 209
interdiscursive performance, 71
intersectionality, 42, 199
Ipsy, 65
Islam, 185, 186, 187, 188, 189, 191, 193, 194, 195, 196, 198, 199, 200, 202, 203n7, 203n9, 204n22, 204n27, 204n32, 206
Islamophobia, 186, 191, 198, 199, 204n22
Italy, 133, 185

Jamie, Jake, 149
Japan, 8, 133, 140n16
Jay-Z, 203n12
Jeffree Star (brand), 6, 85, 86, 89, 90–96, 97n4. *See also* Star, Jeffree
Jeffree Star Cosmetics, 47, 78, 85, 86, 90, 91, 92
Jenner, Kylie, 50, 171
Johnson, Kandie, 5, 10, 103–104, 104–106, 106, 114, 117, 118–119, 120, 121n17
Jolie, Angelina, 104, 105, 118, 120
Judaism, 202n2
Juvia's Place, 26, 41

Kaepernick, Colin, 204n31
Kardashian, Kim, 162, 170, 171
Karim-Cooper, Farah, 108, 135
Kattan, Huda, 49, 185
Katya, 179
Kennedy, Sanders, 7
Kenobi, Obi-Wan, 170
Kenova, Angelica, 116
Khan, Sid, 189
Khatahtbeh, Amani al-, 195
Klaty, Ashley, 29
KodeeRants, 167–168, 181n6–182n7
Kriger, Yulia, 116

Kuckian, John, 7, 165, 176
Kuwait, 41, 188, 203n14

LaBeija, Crystal, 167–168
Lancôme, 37, 185, 192
Lee, Jung Eun, 76
Lee, Laura, 21–24, 25, 32n2, 33n8, 50
Levin, Rachel, 105
Lewinsky, Monica, 23
lifestyle, 7–8, 71, 79, 86, 91, 92, 130, 138, 144, 185, 186, 188, 191, 192, 194, 202, 203n12, 203n16, 204n24, 204n27, 204n32, 205n38, 210, 211
logo, 20, 169
Logo Channel, 171
L'Oréal, 170, 185, 192
loyalty, 74, 75, 77, 106, 193
Lukyanova, Valeria, 116
Lush, 50

M.A.C, 38
MAC Cosmetics, 87
Maguire, Emma, 105
Madonna, 180
Make Up For Ever, 38, 39, 40
Makeup Geek, 5, 19
MakeupArtistGorda66 (Marimar), 143, 145, 150, 150–152, 154
MakeupJunkieG (Georgia), 143, 145, 146–150, 154
Marbles, Jenna, 117, 120
Marie Claire, 174, 176, 177, 197, 198
marketing, 4–6, 8, 9, 10, 11, 17, 20, 37, 41, 42, 65, 76, 86, 87, 92, 93, 94, 96, 105, 108; self-marketing, 24, 32, 105
Marvel, 188
Marwick, Alice, 68, 70, 73, 79, 89, 98n21
masculinity, 109, 113, 120, 122n47, 129, 130, 132, 167, 179, 211
Mattel, 115, 164, 170, 171, 180
Mattel, Trixie, 181n4
Maybelline, 38, 105, 166, 169, 174
McKnight, Mindy, 105
microcelebrity, 9, 65, 66, 67, 68, 69, 70, 71, 73, 74, 75, 76, 78, 79, 81, 88–89, 90, 93, 96, 97n2. *See also* celebrity
Milton, John, 108, 113
Minj, Ginger, 179
Minnelli, Liza, 170
Mipster, 188, 203n12, 203n15
misogyny, 104, 107, 109, 112, 128, 132, 136, 187, 203n12
Modanisa, 192, 195
Modest Fashion, 11, 185–186, 186, 187, 188, 189, 190, 192, 193–194, 194, 195, 196, 198, 202n3, 203n15, 203n17, 204n22, 205n40
modesty, 186, 187, 190, 191
Montague, Lady Mary Wortley, 112
Morphe, 5, 69, 70, 75, 76, 77, 97n5
Mota, Bethany, 77, 105
MUA, Manny, 4–5, 6, 21, 163, 165, 173, 174, 179
Muhammad, Ibtihaj, 188, 202n4
Museum of Modern Art, 188, 203n13
MySpace, 47, 83n32, 174

Nabiilabee, 189
National Center for Transgender Equality, 138
Native Americans, 134
Netflix, 47, 99n68
New York Fashion Week, 45
Nicole, Stephanie, 4, 26, 30, 39, 47, 49
Nike, 192, 204n31
nostalgia, 74, 75, 120
NYX, 50

O'Connor, Flannery, 10, 161–162, 162–164, 164, 166, 171, 177, 178, 181
O'Reilly, Tim, 82n10
ocularcentricity, 145
oppression, 115, 128, 129–131, 132, 139, 186–187, 191, 201, 211

Paris Is Burning, 163, 182n7
participatory culture, 67, 69, 77, 81, 82n10, 144
participatory entitlement, 9, 10, 65, 67, 76–77, 78, 80, 81
Pat McGrath, 26
patriarchy, 10, 127, 138
Pearson, Tim, 170
performance, 21, 69, 71, 74, 86, 88, 90, 104, 106, 116, 117, 129, 133, 136, 140n11, 144, 148, 149, 155, 155n3, 180, 186, 188, 201, 202

personas, 8, 10, 26, 66, 67, 86, 90, 91, 94, 96, 97n5, 147
Phan, Michelle, 65–66, 67, 77–78, 81, 105
Pict, 110
Plain Jane, 26
political equality, 93
politics, 23, 25, 42, 90, 127, 145, 147
power relationships, 98n30, 115, 145
Press, Andrea, 68
The Princess, 181n4
producers, 82n10, 86, 87–89, 92–96, 145
prosumers, 89, 94–96
presumption, 89
public relations (PR), 19, 21, 46, 80
Puma, 45

Qatar, 41
The Queen , 168
Qur'an, 187, 195, 204n24

racism, 20–21, 27, 30, 42, 47, 48, 50, 83n32, 151, 152, 187, 191, 203n12
Rae, Issa, 50
Raja, 181n4
rants, 167–168, 172, 181n6–182n7
Raven, 171, 172, 174, 181n4
Reddit, 67, 69, 75, 76, 80
religion, 10, 108, 127, 162, 186, 187, 189, 195, 196, 197, 198, 200, 201, 202, 203n12, 203n15, 204n24–204n25, 204n27, 204n32, 205n45, 211
Revlon, 50
Rihanna, 9, 28, 35, 37, 38, 39, 41–42, 42, 43, 44–45, 46, 49, 185
River Island, 45
Rogers, Mary F., 114
RuPaul, 162–163, 171, 174, 181n1
RuPaul's Drag Race (RPDR), 163, 170

Saudi Arabia, 41, 191
scars, 119, 153–154
Schuman, Scott, 188
Schwandt, Nathan, 90, 97n5
self-branding, 10, 26, 68, 85, 86, 88, 89, 90, 92, 93, 94, 96, 97, 97n8, 144, 145
self-help, 189
selfies, 162, 163, 165, 170, 171, 172, 200, 201
Senft, Theresa M., 68, 82n12, 88
Sephora, 40
sexuality, 42, 68, 78, 83n29–83n30, 90, 98n36, 140n16, 162, 189, 195
sexualization, 132, 133
Shane and Friends, 98n36
Shape Tape, 28, 29, 34n40
Sherman, Bobby, 169
Simpson, Linda, 170
Singapore, 188
Sisters of Perpetual Indulgence, 172
16 Magazine, 169
slang, 34n44, 82n20, 83n33, 149, 154, 163, 165, 168, 171, 205n39
Smashbox, 50
Snapchat, 1, 5, 8, 17, 43, 44, 174, 209
Soare, Anastasia, 43
Soare, Claudia Norvina, 43
social comparison theory, 76
social media, 2, 7, 9, 19, 20, 21, 23–25, 41, 42, 43, 44, 45, 46, 48, 50, 67, 76, 80, 81, 82n5, 82n25, 85, 87–88, 90, 93, 96, 97n2, 97n13, 104, 105, 115, 162, 163, 165, 171, 174, 185, 189, 190, 193, 201, 202, 202n6, 204n27, 209, 210
social media influencers (SMIs). *See* influencers
socialization, 68, 133
Sokkarie, Rayyan, 199, 200
Southern Gothic, 161
spectatorship, 88
sponsorships, 17, 18, 19, 20, 25, 50, 66, 78, 104, 191
Springfield, Dusty, 169
Stance, 45
Star, Jeffree, 4, 5, 6, 7, 9–10, 12n10, 20, 21, 22, 27, 34n29, 47, 48, 65–67, 67, 69, 78, 79, 80, 80–81, 81, 83n30–83n32, 85–88, 89–96, 97n4–97n5, 97n8, 105, 163, 165, 167, 173, 174, 180. *See also* Jeffree Star (brand); Jeffree Star Cosmetics
star, 38, 44, 47, 50, 85–90, 93, 94, 96, 97n2, 164, 169, 176, 180, 181n1, 185. *See also* celebrity
staring, 143–144, 149
Starrr, Patrick, 5, 176
Stell, Marlena, 19–20, 20, 27
stigma, 128, 131, 135
stigmatization, 139, 187, 201, 202

strategic intimacy, 68, 70–71, 73
Streamy Awards, 169
subcultures, 51, 65, 66, 67, 69
subscribers, 1–2, 6, 17, 19, 21, 22–23, 25, 27, 30, 31, 47, 65, 67, 69–70, 71, 74, 75, 78, 85, 89, 93, 96, 135, 209
Sugg, Zoe Elizabeth, 105, 120
Swetnam, Joseph, 109
Swift, Jonathan, 10, 110, 112, 113, 116

Tang, Nyma, 4, 40, 43
Tarlo, Emma, 191
Tarte, 28, 29, 48, 50
tattoos, 43, 163, 174, 188, 203n14
Taylor, Elizabeth, 118, 119
terrorism, 198–199, 200, 201
Tertullian, 103, 107, 108
Toffoletti, Kim, 114
Too Faced, 4, 12n10, 13, 50
Torkia, Dina (Tokio), 188, 189, 190–191, 194, 195, 203n16, 203n20–203n21, 204n25–204n26, 204n33
tours, 69, 70–71, 73, 74, 75, 78–79, 79; beauty rooms, 69, 70, 79; closet, 69, 70–71, 73, 74, 75, 78, 79
trademark, 20, 44
transformation, 2, 6, 44, 87, 89, 92, 94, 96, 103–104, 105, 108, 114, 115, 116, 118, 135, 137, 148, 149, 167, 180, 186, 187, 193, 199, 202
transgender. *See* gender
transphobia, 135, 138
Trump, Donald, 104, 192
trust, 18, 19, 23, 26, 27, 30, 65, 78, 105, 127, 135, 151, 193, 196
Turkey, 188, 191, 202n3
tutorials, vii, 1–2, 3–4, 7, 8, 8–9, 10, 10–11, 12n10, 17, 18, 20, 24–25, 26, 27, 29, 30, 31, 32, 32n1, 65, 69, 71, 72, 74, 75, 85, 86, 88, 103–104, 105, 106, 107, 115, 116, 117, 118, 136, 137, 143–144, 145, 150, 153, 155, 161–163, 164, 165–166, 166, 168, 169, 170, 171, 172–173, 174, 176, 177, 178–179, 179, 180, 181, 188, 189, 192, 193, 194, 196, 200, 205n39, 209, 210, 211
Twitter, 1, 17, 22, 29, 50, 85, 87, 98n21, 105, 144, 176, 181, 181n6, 194

United Arab Emirates, 185; Dubai, 185, 188
United Kingdom, 37, 41, 68, 149; Birmingham, 199; England, 108, 124; London, 185, 199, 205n40
United Roots, 26

validation, 2, 7, 154
Vasquez, Renny, 171
veganism, 38, 85
Velour, Sasha, 170, 181n4
VH-1, 171
videos, 3, 4–5, 6, 6–7, 8, 9, 18, 19, 20, 20–25, 26–27, 27–28, 28, 29, 30, 30–32, 33n8, 34n29, 34n40, 38, 39, 40–41, 43, 44, 46–47, 51n7, 65, 66–67, 69, 70, 71, 72, 73, 74, 75, 77, 78, 79, 82n16, 83n31–83n32, 85, 88, 90, 91–93, 94–96, 97n5, 103, 104, 105–106, 114, 116, 117, 118–119, 136, 137, 143, 144, 145, 146, 147–149, 150, 150–151, 152, 153, 168, 170, 172, 173, 176, 180, 181n6, 183n28, 188, 190, 192, 193, 194, 195, 202n6, 203n12, 203n15, 203n17, 203n21, 204n22, 204n26, 205n38, 210, 211; apology, 21, 21–25, 33n8, 34n29, 48, 50; full face, 69, 78, 79, 118, 150, 167; lifestyle, 7–8, 71, 192, 211; makeup, 4, 7, 66, 193, 195, 196; product reviews, 4, 5, 7, 18, 19, 27–29, 39, 40, 45, 51, 65, 71, 75, 79, 86
videographers, 74
violence, 25, 122n47, 136, 137, 138, 166, 181
visibility, 1, 24, 68, 96, 163, 166, 169, 174, 178, 185, 186, 201, 204n31
Vivacious, 170, 171, 177
vloggers, 1, 2, 4, 5, 6, 7, 8, 9, 11, 12n10, 32, 32n1, 37, 47, 65–67, 67–68, 69, 70, 73, 74, 77, 78, 79, 81, 82n23, 83n29, 104, 105, 105–106, 106, 116, 117, 118, 120, 167, 168, 170, 177, 182n20, 202n6, 209, 210, 210–211
vlogs, 3, 5, 7, 13, 63, 76, 165, 167, 168, 170, 209, 210, 211
Vogue, 194
voiceover, 143
Von D, Kat, 43, 44

Watkins, Brandi, 76
Watt, Ian, 107
Weall, Isabelle, 143, 153
Web 2.0, 44, 82n10
Wolf, Naomi, 128
Wollstonecraft, Mary, 127–128

YouTube, vii, 2, 3, 4, 5–8, 9, 10, 11, 12n10, 17–20, 20–21, 22, 23, 24–25, 26–27, 27–28, 29, 31, 32n1, 34n29, 34n31, 34n32, 37, 38, 39, 40–41, 43, 44, 46–47, 47, 48, 50–51, 65–67, 67, 68, 69, 69–70, 71, 72, 75, 76, 77–78, 78, 79, 80, 81, 85–86, 87–91, 93, 94, 96, 97n5, 97n8, 97n13, 98n36, 103, 104, 105–106, 115, 116, 117, 119, 136–137, 141, 143–146, 147, 148, 150, 151, 152, 153, 154–155, 163, 164–165, 165, 168, 169, 172, 174, 179, 180, 181n6–182n7, 182n20, 186, 188, 189, 190, 194, 200, 203n15, 203n21, 204n22, 204n26, 204n33, 205n40, 209–211

Zamora, Gabriel, 21, 21–23, 24, 25
Zoella, 77–78, 105, 117

About the Contributors

Elizabeth Johnston Ambrose holds a PhD in eighteenth-century British literature—women's writing and is a professor in the English and Philosophy Department at Monroe Community College in Rochester, New York. She is a recipient of the SUNY Chancellor's Award for Excellence in Teaching (2017) and received the SUNY Traveling Lecturer Award (2017), which took her to St. Petersburg, Russia. In addition to her academic interests, she facilitates writing workshops for survivors of breast cancer and sexual assault and is cofounder of Straw Mat Writers, an award-winning writers group in Rochester. Her writing has been nominated for three Pushcart Prizes and a Best of the Net award and has appeared in many collections and journals, including *The Atlantic*, *McSweeney's Internet Tendency*, *Rogue Agent*, *The Belladonna*, *Emrys*, *Room*, *Women Studies Quarterly*, and *Feminist Formations*, among others. She is also the coeditor of two poetry collections and her first poetry chapbook, *Wild Things*, is forthcoming.

Anna Barritt is a PhD student in rhetoric and writing studies at the University of Oklahoma, where she teaches college writing and serves as assistant director of first-year composition. In addition to her work on social class and digital identity formation, her research interests include twentieth-century rhetorical theory, disability rhetorics, and cultural rhetorics.

Laken Brooks is originally from Lansing, North Carolina. She currently is pursuing her PhD in English at the University of Florida, where she studies accessibility, multimodal literature, digital humanities, and gender studies. Brooks has written about gender history for the National Park Service, the National Trust for Historic Preservation, *Lambda Literary*, *Frontiers*, *Gender Forum*, and other publications.

Clare Douglass Little earned her PhD in English literature from the University of North Carolina in Chapel Hill and is an associate professor of humanities and communication at Embry-Riddle Aeronautical University. She is the reviews editor for the journal *Studies in Popular Culture* and has published works on topics ranging from nineteenth-century crime fiction to pedagogy. She has always been interested in visual "texts," from the early Victorian illustrations she focused on in her early research to the visual representation of self and identity expressed through makeup and the online makeup tutorial, as featured in this work and her more recent scholarship.

Alexandra Hauke studied English and American studies as well as Hispanic studies at the University of Vienna and at the University of Maryland at College Park. She is currently a lecturer in American studies at the University of Passau, Germany, where her research and teaching focus on North American literatures, indigenous studies, detective fiction, American folk horror, ecofeminism, digital cultures, and American popular culture. She has written on law and legal cultures in Native American detective fiction, American ecofeminist gothic fiction, blackness in horror film, and hipster cultures, and has coedited collections on Native American survivance as well as twenty-first-century Canadian literatures and politics.

Katherine Anderson Howell is the editor of *Fandom as Classroom Practice: A Teaching Guide* (2018). An independent scholar, she makes her living as an esthetician. Her scholarly work has appeared in *Pennsylvania English* and is forthcoming in collections about race and fandom and independent scholarship. She is a Pushcart Prize nominee, with poems published in places as varied as *The Stillwater Review*, *Misfit Magazine*, and *Beltway Poetry Quarterly*, among others.

Michael V. Perez often mistook his mother's makeup drawer for a tool box when he was young. A failed drag queen and professional dancer, he started writing rather late, earned an MFA from the University of Houston, and has been published in *Sontag and the Camp Aesthetic*, *Queer Adaptations*, and, most recently, in *Essays on Billie Holiday*, an anthology he also coedited with Jessica McKee. His poetry has appeared in *GLASS Poetry Journal*, the *Journal of Florida Studies*, *Crab Orchard Review*, *BLOOM*, and *Route 7 Review*, among others. An assistant professor of humanities at Embry-Riddle Aeronautical University in Daytona Beach, Florida, his favorite product line has always been Clinique.

Fatma Sagir holds a PhD in Islamic studies from Freiburg University and is currently a post-doc researcher in cultural anthropology at Freiburg University with a focus on popular culture and Muslims. She is a teaching fellow at University College Freiburg and has a background in journalism. Her research focuses on young Muslims in digital culture with a focus on Muslim women influencers and Muslim fashion and lifestyle blogging. Other research interests include popular culture, fashion, social media, entertainment, and music.

April Wilson holds a master's degree in journalism and media communications from the University of Hertfordshire and plans to pursue academia in the future by completing her doctorate. She is particularly interested in the way in which the online world and community now shape our narratives and how we are perceived and perceive ourselves in this new digital world. She is also passionate about building an accessible academic community and thinks a key part of this is keeping the conversation and her research focused on the latest phenomena.

Florian Zitzelsberger studied English and German at the University of Passau, Germany, where he currently works as a research fellow in American studies and teaches literary and media studies. His research is prompted by an interest in American popular and queer culture and focuses on self-reflexivity and metareference across media, digital communication, ecocriticism, the American film musical, and queer theory. He has published several articles on contemporary film, covering hybridity in queer cinema, representations of gender and motherhood as well as theatrical remediation, alienation, and self-reflexivity (most prominently in the genre of the musical), which have, among others, appeared in *Humanities* and the *Iowa Journal of Cultural Studies*. Other publications include essays on environmentalist metafiction and queer narratology. His most recent work examines the intersections between metareferential forms, such as metalepsis, and queer signification, which constitutes the primary focus of his PhD project.

CPSIA information can be obtained
at www.ICGtesting.com
Printed in the USA
LVHW101252110223
739014LV00001B/9

9 781498 592451